Strategic Intelligence and National Security in South Asia

Strategic Intelligence
and
National Security in South Asia

Capt. (Retd.) S.L. Soni
Col. (Retd.) C.P. Bhargav

PRASHANT PUBLISHING HOUSE
DELHI-110094

Published by :
PRASHANT PUBLISHING HOUSE
C-34, 28 Foota Road, Gali-3,
West Karwal Nagar, Delhi-110094
Phone : 011-22963970, Mob. : 9810396373, 8826258746
e-mail.: prashantpublishinghouse@gmail.com

Strategic Intelligence and National Security in South Asia
Reserved
First Published 2019

ISBN : 978-93-88526-24-1

PRINTED IN INDIA
Published by Mr. R.K. Jha M/s Prashant Publishing House and Published at H.S. Offset House Press, Delhi.

Preface

The post-9/11 world has resulted in new and complex challenges for the Intelligence sector. Global threats and the function of Intelligence were relatively clear throughout the Cold War. There were two rival superpowers, familiar local leaders were the decision makers, enemies were conspicuous and existential threats to national security, both political and military (including nuclear), were largely transparent. Even terrorism was 'simpler' as it was predominantly local and organisations employing the tactic were well known, as were the countries supporting them.

Strategic analysis is perhaps the most important form of intelligence. It provides a framework within which other forms of intelligence collection and analysis take place, offers an overall assessment from the top down rather than from the bottom up, and helps to provide a basis for policy formulation, strategic planning, and resource allocation. Its weakness is its focus on macro-level issues rather than the more detailed levels of analysis.

Indeed, geography and political borders often aided traditional military intelligence analysis-it is a simple thing to develop threat scenarios if the potential enemy can only use certain terrain or sea lines of communication and then, only at certain times of the year-while simple factors of physics such as time and distance also provided opportunities for warning. Within the Internet, however, these limiting factors are absent, (although other limiting factors, such as geometry of network connectivity, might exist in a form useful to be incorporated into intelligence analysis), contributing to what can appear to be "instantaneous threats".

Although many of the intelligence methodologies and principles remain the same, new ways of thinking appropriate to the cyber-domain are essential. The lack of borders in cyber-space is a critical difference from the more familiar domains of intelligence. Indeed, geography and political borders often aided traditional military intelligence analysis-it is a simple thing to develop threat scenarios if the potential enemy can only use certain terrain or sea lines of communication and then, only at certain times of the year-while simple factors of physics such as time and distance also provided opportunities for warning. Within the Internet, however, these limiting factors are absent, (although other limiting factors, such as geometry of network connectivity, might exist in a form useful to be incorporated into intelligence analysis), contributing to what can appear to be "instantaneous threats".

Assessment of cyber-space threats requires not only a merger of old methodologies and new modes of thinking but also analysts willing and able to approach the art of threat assessment and warning from new perspectives. Only with a distinctive blend of the traditional and the new will it be possible to obtain real understanding of threats and vulnerabilities, to differentiate among types of intrusions and to forecast or anticipate specific incidents or clusters of incidents in ways that lengthen warning time. Enhancing the ability to identify perpetrators is also highly desirable: removing the cloak of anonymity would make perpetrators more concerned about the potential costs and risks of their actions and could have an important deterrent effect. In short, there are several fundamental questions at the heart of the intelligence process. They consist of variations on the who, what, when, where, why and how questions that are familiar parts of most research and analysis.

This is a reference book. All the matter is just compiled and edited in nature, taken from the various sources which are in public domain.

This book holds valuable information for those examining strategy-making, security and counterterrorism practitioners as well as researchers in addition to those interested in the politics of South Asia.

—Editor

Contents

1

Introduction

EVOLUTION OF THE NATIONAL SECURITY STRATEGY

Some of the concepts that we need to develop in order to use this economic view include direct and indirect costs (mentioned earlier), as well as marginal costs and investments. During the Gulf War, the US administration identified its objectives (among them, the liberation of Kuwait) and sought to achieve them with overwhelming force. Such limitations on the war's purpose created a postwar situation that left Saddam Hussein in power, still able to threaten both the region and the world.

Thus, during the course of the war, the United States had a clearly articulated goal of removing Iraqi forces from Kuwait. Its objectives did not include a regime change in Iraq, which did not seem necessary for accomplishing US aims in the region, even though the Iraqi leadership clearly constituted a centre of gravity. Indeed, Warden points out that "command is a true centre of gravity and worth attack in any circumstance in which it can be reached." Moreover, Gen H. Norman Schwarzkopf, commander of the coalition forces, makes the point that, although killing or removing Saddam was not an aim of the war, he "wouldn't have shed any tears" if the Iraqi dictator had been killed during the course of the war. However, the concept of limited war that prevailed at the time meant that, once the coalition had liberated Kuwait, it could not set its sights on Saddam.

At the time, risking military and civilian lives to remove the Iraqi regime seemed unnecessary. After all, we had established our objective and achieved it. Why risk destabilizing the region and setting ourselves up for a nation-building responsibility? The first Bush administration took what appeared to be the sensible approach. We would contain Iraq through the use of international sanctions, which would weaken Saddam and, hopefully, lead to his downfall or at least keep him in check. Unfortunately, we miscalculated. A rigorous economic examination of the situation might have resulted in a different outcome.

First, we erroneously believed that sanctions would weaken the regime's power over the Iraqi people. Sanctions have rarely affected a totalitarian regime enough to force its capitulation. North Korea has endured sanctions for 50 years, but its fundamental form of government remains unchanged. Sanctions against Cuba have yielded similar results. Such dictatorial regimes become stronger because the general populace- weakened by famine, lack of access to medical care, and other problems brought about by sanctions- can neither resist nor overthrow the oppressing government.

Coercive economic measures can have other perverse effects, such as the creation of smuggling activities and black markets. In fact Gen Wesley Clark, supreme allied commander Europe during the Balkans campaign, points out that "in the Balkans, for example, the economic sanctions implemented against Serbia during the early 1990s are widely credited with helping Serb President Slobodan Milosevic strengthen his control through the encouragement of black market and smuggling activities. At the same time these sanctions imposed burdens on neighboring countries like Bulgaria, Macedonia, and Romania, whose leaders were unanimous in opposing any extension of the sanctions regime."

Second, we mistakenly counted on sufficient consensus to ensure international compliance with the sanctions program. Evidently, the sanctions had some effect on Saddam's ability to maintain his weapons programs, but his constant search for sources yielded some fruit- specifically, the revelation that the Ukraine supplied antiaircraft systems to Iraq. Although such systems are not weapons of mass destruction, it seems that, given enough time and money, the determined dictator was able to find sources for such materiel.

The third miscalculation assumed the effective monitoring of developments within Iraq. But Saddam's government, willing to lie at every turn, easily manipulated the inspection plan. Germany also circumvented the utility of sanctions after World War I by using many of the same tactics.

Rogue States and Preemptive Action

As noted previously, the media focused on the apparent sanctioning of preemptive action by President Bush's national security strategy. Such action certainly seems an attractive strategic option in some cases to ensure national security. The rise of nonstate actors (i.e., terrorist organizations) means that unless our containment efforts with "rogue states" are effective, the release of weapons of mass destruction into the wrong hands could happen quite easily.

The efficacy of containment operations is extremely difficult to predict; therefore, once we decide to take action (preemptive or otherwise) we should have a strong bias toward regime change as a necessary condition for success. If a regime's actions are so provocative that they require armed intervention by the United States, we should give strong preference to removing that regime as part of the intervention.

Clearly, every case does not call for regime change, but it seems to be a good "default" position. The British did not force a regime change after the Falklands War, but neither did they see a need to continue sanctions in order to contain Argentina in the future. A discussion of the costs of the Gulf War later in this chapter will explain how an economic view can lead to this proposition. What defines provocative actions? The *National Security Strategy* spells out five attributes that rogue states tend to share. Specifically, they

- brutalize their own people and squander their national resources for personal gain of the rulers;
- display no regard for international law, threaten their neighbours, and callously violate international treaties to which they are a party;
- are determined to acquire weapons of mass destruction, along with other advanced military technology, to use as threats or offensively to achieve their aggressive designs;
- sponsor terrorism around the globe; and
- reject basic human values and hate the United States and everything for which it stands.

These actions give a clearer understanding of which countries may provoke the United States to action. However, it is extremely unlikely that the war on terrorism would lead us to armed intervention in every state that shares many, if not all, of the above attributes.

If we are to make efficient decisions about where to intervene, we must be able to assess the costs and benefits of such actions. Which countries pose the greatest threats and are likely to require intervention? Those countries that have access to valuable natural resources are the most probable candidates since they are likely to have the ability to finance their operations and make an impact beyond their borders. Countries with significant natural resources may also threaten modern economies (especially within a region) by withholding access to those raw materials. We also should assess potential threats on economic as well as moral and foreign-policy grounds. Nevertheless, totalitarian regimes whose countries lack natural resources are not likely to produce smoothly functioning economic systems that generate substantial wealth; therefore, most of these rogue states will not have the means to pose a substantial threat to the United States. We may choose to engage these countries on moral grounds (e.g., to prevent genocide) or to help friends in the region, but a direct security threat to the United States is less likely in these cases. On the other hand, countries that do have access to valuable natural resources such as oil can use them to sponsor mayhem around the globe.

Costs versus Investments

As we implement this new security strategy, we must take the long view of the consequences of our actions. For example, one argument for terminating the Gulf War of 1991 prematurely was that we did not want to destabilize Iraq and be forced into bearing the cost (in terms of both money and personnel) of a lengthy nation-building effort. This concern, however, turned out to be a false economy. Instead of conducting a nation-building campaign that could lead to a self-sufficient country, we had to maintain large numbers of troops in the region to contain Iraqi actions. The United States needs to clarify its analysis of the debate over containment versus nation building.

Containment actions result in costs, whereas nation-building expenditures are more akin to investments that pay dividends in the future. But we need not go on a massive nation-building campaign throughout the world. We should simply clarify our analysis of the costs of nation building versus sanctions, especially regarding containment operations. This dilemma demonstrates the differences between costs and investments. Costs tend to maintain the status quo, but investments provide increased returns and economies of scale in the future.

SOUTH ASIA'S MANIFOLD CHALLENGE

The concept of "the international community", if it is to have practical meaning and encapsulate the notion of "solidarity without borders" instead of being an empty slogan, must come to terms with the multitude and gravity of the challenges confronting the peoples and nations of South Asia (Bangladesh, Bhutan, India, Maldives, Nepal, Pakistan and Sri Lanka). The scale of the problems faced in the region and the numbers of people involved are so huge that success or failure in South Asia pose defining challenges to the core mandates of the United Nations as the global arena for problem-solving. South Asia by itself accounts for one-fifth of "We the peoples of the United Nations". Developments in South Asia cut across the major faultlines of the UN system with respect to the challenges of economic development, environmental protection, food and water security, democratic governance and human rights, nuclear war and peace, inter-state and internal conflicts, and new security issues such as AIDS (acquired immune deficiency syndrome) and international terrorism. What happens in South Asia will surely shape the contours of the global community in the decades ahead.

Two of the central purposes of the United Nations as expressed in the UN Charter – to maintain international peace and security and to promote social and economic advancement – make it imperative for the organization to address these issues in South Asia. The United Nations University (UNU), in collaboration with the UN agencies in Japan, organized an international conference in May 2002 on "The United Nations and South Asia". UNU in Tokyo is particularly well suited as a forum for discussing these issues as the major UN agencies are located in its headquarters building in Tokyo, "UN House". The South Asian embassies in Japan offered their support for the conference and collaborated in its organization. The conference was well timed in that 2002 marked the fiftieth anniversary of the establishment of diplomatic relations with Japan by India, Pakistan and Sri Lanka. But it was ill timed in that on that date India and Pakistan were in the middle of the biggest and most tense mobilization of their full military mights along the full length of their border. Yet, by presenting a forum for communication between different actors within the various sectors, the conference helped to alleviate the substantial lack of interaction and thus contributed to improved efforts at addressing the problems in South Asia.

The chapters in this volume are revised versions of the papers presented at that conference. Their emphasis is on discussing issues of particular relevance to the region and exploring the potential for improvement in both domestic and international efforts at alleviating the problems of South Asia. If and where appropriate, the role that the United Nations can play in this respect is also underscored.

One of the more interesting features of this volume is the divergence of cultures and writing styles of the scholars and the practitioners (officials, politicians, generals). Academics are addicted to notes, whereas practitioners are allergic to them. Many academics have to be reined in so that their contributions form chapters in a book instead of mini-tomes in themselves, whereas some practitioners have to be coaxed into extending their brief vignettes to a length and intellectual weight suitable for publication by a university press. Two of the UNU's five mandated tasks are to serve as a bridge between the normally isolated worlds of scholarship and policy and to serve as a platform for dialogue. This volume is testimony to the need for dialogue not only between participants from the different nations and societies of a deeply divided region of the world, but also between the different professional cultures in the modern world.

Former prime minister of India, I. K. Gujral, expresses the hope that the recent international interest in South Asia is not temporary and based solely on the threat of terrorism and nuclearization, but rather reflects a realization that the world community cannot be safe or happy unless it involves the billion-plus people of South Asia in the critical decisions regarding peace, security and development. According to Gujral, the most serious current challenge facing South Asia is terrorism. But the fight against terrorism cannot be won by force alone. It is of course necessary to fight the jihadi culture. But, even without jihad, there would still be manifestations of terrorism in all South Asian countries in the form of insurgency movements. Therefore there is an urgent need to address the root causes of terrorism, such as lack of good governance, low levels of human development, and new threats such as drug trafficking and the spread of AIDS. Although the main responsibility for the problems and their resolution lies with the South Asian countries, the region has not been brought into the global developmental mainstream by the international community. The international community needs a peaceful, cooperative and dynamic South Asia; it is in its interest to facilitate this.

Gujral sees great potential for development in South Asia in the fields of science and technology, as well as in traditional industries such as chemicals, pharmaceuticals, heavy industries, steel and electronics. For this potential to be realized, however, regional cooperation is necessary. India, as the leading power, can afford to be accommodative to promote such cooperation. Sartaj Aziz, while calling for a comprehensive programme to reduce poverty in South Asia, also asks for UN action to reduce tension between the region's two nuclear powers. There is an urgent need to accelerate the pace of economic and social progress in the region and to meet the challenges of globalization. The United Nations must assume and discharge its responsibility to focus on the inequalities of the globalization process and regain a leadership role in providing a level playing field.

Nor can the international community continue to overlook the security problems in the region. International assistance is needed to fight terrorism and extremism in the region as well as to stabilize Afghanistan. At the same time, Aziz calls for the United Nations to curb "liberal imperialism", that is, the notion that the so-called "postmodern" world can use force, pre-emptive attack or even deception to violate international boundaries with impunity.

Peace and Security

An immediate concern of the international community is the region's impact on international peace and security. South Asia poses many potential threats to regional and global peace and security: it has two nuclear powers engaged in a major territorial dispute; there are several dominant insurgency conflicts here; terrorism is pronounced; and the refugee situation has the potential to be deeply destabilizing. There are also significant cross-regional linkages with respect to relations with China (one of the five permanent members of the UN Security Council), Central Asia (and Russia beyond), the Middle East and South-East Asia. How can domestic and international efforts at resolving conflicts in the region be improved?

Inter-state Conflict

Since the end of the Cold War, the global pattern of conflict has shifted from inter-state to intra-state conflicts (many of which have transnational regional links), yet one of the remaining potential inter-state conflicts is found in South Asia.

The situation is aggravated by the fact that the two potential belligerents are armed with nuclear-armed weapons. Whereas the stability of the nuclear deterrence between the superpowers during the Cold War was itself somewhat suspect, the relationship between Pakistan and India is qualitatively different and even more volatile. The two countries share a long border, which allows little time to decide whether to "use or lose" nuclear weapons in response to a perceived threat.

Furthermore, Pakistan and India are involved in a territorial dispute over Kashmir. This dispute has already resulted in two wars between the countries and the possibility of armed conflict has not yet been eliminated. Neither country has second-strike retaliatory capability, which makes both of them more vulnerable to a pre-emptive strike than was the case between the superpowers during the Cold War. South Asia's relationship with and ties to neighbouring countries also have implications for the involvement of the international community in the region. A complicating element is India's disputed border with China, a third nuclear power with tangible interests in the region. Resurgence of Islamic fundamentalism in the region is also a cause for concern for regional stability. The disruptive nature of this potential conflict is exacerbated by domestic political volatility in all South Asian countries. It is imperative for the United Nations to contribute to a de-escalation of this conflict in order to maintain international peace and security. Stephen Cohen cautions that, in light of the failure of past predictions, it is impossible to predict future use of nuclear weapons by India and Pakistan with any confidence. It is likely that the future will look much like the current situation – a stable relationship between China and India and a rocky one between India and Pakistan, but with innate common sense or external mediation preventing an outbreak of nuclear conflict. However, Cohen also acknowledges the large number of political and military variables that might affect possible outcomes with regard to the nuclear future of South Asia, only some of which can be influenced or controlled by outside powers. He offers two suggestions: the international community should assist in managing crises; and security planners in the region should avoid overconfidence in deterrence and keep their arsenals low so as to reduce the scale of the catastrophe if there should be a regional war.

Echoing many of the same themes, Christophe Carle emphasizes that the future security of South Asia depends on the relationship between Pakistan and India; the other security threats of the region pale in comparison. He points to the elements of instability in the subcontinent's nuclear deterrence. Contiguity undermines the development of effective and reliable command and control systems and, with ballistic missiles, decision-making time may be reduced to 5–10 minutes. The nuclearization of South Asia and the inherent volatility of the nuclear equation in the region mean that external actors, particularly the United States, have become increasingly important. Thus South Asian (in)security has been internationalized.

BUILDING SECURITY AND CONFIDENCE WITH CHINA

Except for the brief period of confrontation between 19591992 and the diplomatic freeze that followed for next few years the relations between China and India had never been conflictual in nature. But because of the complicated colonial legacies - which were further compounded by the Cold War dynamics and by the border war of 1962 - mutual distrust and threat perceptions have continued to undermine all efforts towards building confidence. One may ask why confidence and security building measures (CSBMs) between India and China are so critical to the evolution of their multifaceted and multilayered *rapprochement*? The one line answer would be that these CSBMs present a perfect barometer for any crystal gazing into the future of these two Asian giants. However, this answer remains far too simplistic to explain the complexity of Go-Indian ties. And it is in this context of complications that this essay tries to examine and highlight Sino-Indian CSBMs in terms of their being the first significant step forward untying the knots in the bilateral relations and mutual perceptions.

Firstly, to deal with the theoretical elements of Sine-Indian CSBMs, it has been unjustifiably fashionable to view Sino-Indian CSBMs essentially in the framework of western ready-made models. If anything, the CSBMs in the Asian context have far preceded all western models and, therefore, are neither borrowed from nor identical to those leading to the Final Act of the Helsinki process of the Conference on Security and Cooperation in Europe (CSCE) that was concluded in 1975. Beginning from the Joint Defence Council of 1948 that effected the division of assets and armed forces between India and Pakistan to the Sino-Indian *Panchsheel* Agreement of 1954, and later the Indo-Pak Simla agreement of 1971, various formal and informal agreements had already effected these CSBMs like "non-use", or the "selective use" of armed force and created various other mechanisms. Therefore these CSBMs had been institutionalised in Asia far earlier. Besides, these were also far more broad based than the Western CSBMs, including those that were later incorporated the Document of the Conference on Disarmament in Europe held in 1986 at Stockholm (Sweden).

Coming to the salient features of what can be described as the Asian CSBMs that distinguish the Sino-Indian CSBMs from most of their comparable Western models, one sees the near absence of a subjective feeling in the Asian context of an imminent threat which is so central to all those Western conceptions of CSBMs. In Asia's rather lose polycentric situation, nations had never been so clearly divided as are the communist and liberal democratic traditions that characterise the bipolar division of the West. Similarly, the second basic condition of equality of the military strength between the potential parties to the conflict, again seems very much a Eurocentric feature of CSBMs and is generally missing in the Asian situation. China, India and Pakistan can themselves be cited as ideal examples of this asymmetry of power. Nevertheless, CSBMs have continued to evolve amongst these three countries. Thirdly, the inter-state boundaries which form the basic element of European CSBMs are itself a major problem and therefore the very objective towards which most Asian CSBMs seek to provide solutions, Also, Asian CSBMs are generally backed by ever widening network of measures like state sponsored people-to-people contacts which are aimed at expanding mutual trust and understanding between the entire social elite on both sides.

Nor should we regard the Asian CSBMs in general and the Sino-Indian CSBMs in particular as the byproduct of the post-Cold War peace dividend although the global factors, have surely been much more influential in moulding the European CSBMs than those between Asian countries. This is because unlike Europe, (a) the conflicts in Asia were never seen to be vital to the national interests of both the super powers: and, (b) the middle ranking powers like China and India have become increasingly independent from the regimented bipolar world order of the Cold War years. To give two most apt examples, contrary to Cold War trends, India had initiated its CSBMs during the mid-1970s and India's Foreign Minister, Atal Behari Vajpai, paid his first visit to Beijing at the lime when China was launching its war against Vietnam and the Soviet forces were about to enter Afghanistan yet, despite India's closeness to Moscow, the new Cold War of the early 1980s did not disturb the smooth evolution of Sine-Indian *rapprochement* Similarly, following the June 1989 Tiananmen Square incident, while most of world powers had imposed sanctions thus completely isolating China, the relations between China and India not only continued to be smooth but experienced a greater momentum: the period from the second half through 1989 and 1990 saw 10 high-level visits between the two countries that included visits to New Delhi by Vice Premier Wu Xueqian in October 1989 and by Foreign Minister Qian Qichen in March 1990. The credit for this goes to (a) this unique Asian way of trial and error which, therefore, lends some sort of originality of these Sino-Indian CSBMs, and (b) to the political leadership of both the countries who were able to take and stand by such bold initiatives.

If anything, it is their expanding interactions at various levels that has been the greatest single factor behind the evolution of Sino-Indian CSBMs. Starting from their exchange of Ambassadors in 1976, these expanding official and business interactions can be divided into three major phases. The first phase (1976-1988), was characterised by both *China and India looking at* each *other* simply gauging the potential for expanding mutual goodwill and trust. Second phase (1988-1996), which witnessed five formal summits interspersed by hectic initiatives and agreements towards evolving and consolidating CSBMs. Then having established this strong network of CSBMs the recent four agreements signed during President Jiang Zemin's visit to New Delhi in November 1996, Sino-Indian *rapprochement* has now entered into its third and final phase where the two are expected to take concrete decisions on more difficult issues like the boundary question.

A quick glance through this evolution from freeze to fervour shows how, though no breakthrough has yet been achieved on the crucial boundary question quite a substantial progress has been made considering the complicated and knotty ground realities. The historic f 988 visit to Beijing by Prime Minister Rajiv Gandhi had worked as a catalyst in facilitating a U-turn in Sino- Indian relations. Especially, considering Indian sensitivities vis-a-vis China, this visit itself was an extremely bold initiative. But more than this, in the Joint Communiqué at the end of this visit India agreed, for the first time, to dropping its earlier policy stance of asking for settlement of the border as a precondition for any improvement in relations in other fields. Secondly, India not only agreed to describe Tibet as an integral part of (not just an autonomous region) of China but also expressed "concern over anti-Chinese activities by some Tibetan elements in India" -a proviso which was criticised by some as a clear sell-out of the Tibetan interests. India's over-reaction towards Tibetan protesters during the visit by Premier Li Peng in 1991 was another demonstration of India's resolve in not letting Tibet become a problem in the way of Sino-Indian *rapprochement.* All this meant that, Rajiv Gandhi's visit had finally abandoned India's discredited forwards policy and, at least during the interim, accepted China's long-standing demand for the maintenance of tranquillity on the line of actual control (LoAC).

There were also some legal hurdles to this visit. The historic November 1962 resolution of Indian Parliament had bound successive Indian leaders from making any move towards improving Sino-Indian ties until they had obtained every inch of India's sacred land claimed or taken by the Chinese. But this December 1988 visit by Rajiv Gandhi to Beijing became possible because of another major resolution that was passed by the All India Congress Working Committee on November 5, 1988 urging the government to seek a settlement through "peaceful negotiations" based on "mutual interest" and "acceptable to the peoples of both countries" even if it took time. Apart from minor objections, no main national political parties raised any hue and cry against these "concession" by Rajiv Gandhi. This was because (a) the Congress Party, at this time, had an overwhelming majority in Indian Parliament and (b) the earlier major, initiative towards building peace with China had been taken during the Janata Party government in February 1979. Moreover, eight rounds of border talks (initiated during Foreign Minister, Huang Hua's visit to New Delhi in 1981) had already created some sort of favourable backdrop.

Apart from these interactions at the political level, Rajiv Gandhi's visit also opened avenues for direct military interactions. Because of the 1962 war, any interaction between the military personnel or on defence related matters remained a taboo until the early 1990s. The first exchange in this direction was made by the senior serving officials of the National Defence College (New Delhi) and the National Defence University (Beijing) respectively visiting each other in 1990 and 1992.The two have also since been considering undertaking an arrangement for an institutional exchange wherein at least one officer could attend the others training courses. The military-to-military dialogue was taken to a higher level by India's Defence Minister, Sharad Pawar's visit to China in July 1992. This opened the way and was followed by Vice Chief of China's People's Liberation Army, Lt. General Xu Huizi, visiting India in December 1993 followed by a visit by their Defence Minister, Chi Haotian's visit to India during September 7-13, 1994. From the Indian side, Chief of Army Staff, General B.C. Joshi and Chief of Naval Staff, Admiral V.S. Shekhawat paid reciprocal visits to various defence facilities in China during July 1994 and March 1996 respectively. This increasing interaction and transparency between the two military establishments has surely contributed to the building up of mutual confidence.

Once again, just like the lack of interactions and other historical legacies had coloured their visions during the earlier years, increasing information and confidence has led to revision and rectification of various policies on both sides. One good example of this spectrum of biases in perceptions can be seen in the way various China watchers interpreted the incident when in May 1992 China detonated a 150 megaton nuclear device just hours after President R. Venkatraman arrived in Beijing. While some called it an act of intimidation, others described it as an expression of China's solidarity with India in their strategic defiance of Washington. However, with persistent efforts from both sides, a relatively more objective understanding of each other has started to emerge during the 1990s. Observing the tenor of policy pronouncements from both sides there appears to be an obvious shift of emphasis away from the assertion of huge territorial claims or high moral principles increasingly towards "mutual concessions" and "accommodation "from the Chinese side and on historical, legal, geographical realities from the Indian side with both now calling for a "fair, reasonable, and mutually acceptable" compromise solution to their boundary question.

Also both sides today have far greater mutual understanding on various issues ranging from global problematic like the US nuclear non-proliferation to regional and bilateral contentions like Kashmir, Tibet, and border. As a result, while owing to their ideological systems and methods of operation the two had appeared to be dramatical opposites during the 1950s over the years the two sides have begun to appreciate and emphasise on their similarities and evolved common approach on certain issues like nuclear disarmament, trade and human rights. On the nuclear question, for example, while China has sought to keep its own nuclear build-up completely insulated from the ongoing disarmament debates between Moscow and Washington: yet, Beijing has also generally kept a low profile on India's nuclear and missile programme and, in fact, assisted India by supplying heavy water at a crucial stage in January 1995. Nevertheless, there still exist differences of approach on various issues and inspite of substaintial improvement, India has continued to be deeply concerned about China's supplies of nuclear components, materials and knowhow to other countries in India's neighbourhood. This is especially true of China's indulgence with Pakistan. Yet, in the end, all this has never discouraged India from making efforts at improving ties with both Beijing and Islamabad.

From the Indian side, these efforts for *rapprochement* had all started as early as late 1960s. Later, starting from Sardar Swaran Singh's (then Foreign Minister) offer in August 1970 "to settle all matters...peacefully through bilateral negotiations," India not only became the first one to take many major initiatives but also became the first one to declare and actually resume its Ambassadorial level diplomatic relations with Beijing. Besides, India also made many other goodwill gestures towards China like installing telex links in each others embassies, supporting China's candidacy for the Manila-based Asian Development Bank, inviting China to a regional UNESCO conference in New Delhi, and Prime Minister Mrs. Indira Gandhi herself making a personal gesture by visiting and signing the book of condolences in the Chinese embassy in New Delhi as mark of respect for the late Premier Zhou Enlai. The first feelers from the Chinese side came in May 1960 and April 1961 from then Vice Premier Deng

Xiaoping who revived Zhou Enlai's 1960 proposal for a package deal on the boundary question. Here, Deng proposed Chinese recognition of the McMahon Line in the eastern sector in return for Indian acceptance of the status quo along the LoAC in the western sector. In fact, according to Mrs. Gandhi's foreign policy Advisor, G. Parthasarthy, Mrs. Gandhi had even agreed to accept the Chinese package deal only that, with the Chinese assent, the formal announcement had been postponed until after December 1985 general elections. Soon the assassination of Mrs. Gandhi in October 1984 and later the Sumdorong Chu valley incident in July 1966 completely rocked this spirit of accommodation and delayed major initiatives by f9w more years.

A clear shift in China's South Asia policy, however, began to occur from late 1960s when Beijing gradually gave up its earlier post-1962 tactics of providing moral and material support to India's smaller neighbours which was aimed at: (a) tying New Delhi down to the South Asian region and, (b) trying to offset India's preeminence even in this smaller region. In 1969, for example, China not only refused to supply weapons to Nepal and gave only muted response to India's peacekeeping in Sri Lanka, it even told General Ershad of Bangladesh to expect no more Chinese support on their river water dispute with New Delhi. This has since resulted in improving India's relations with both Bangladesh and Nepal. Putting an end to its dilly-dallying of late 1980s, the Rao-Li joint statement of December 1991 clearly told China's closest ally Pakistan that Beijing now regards Kashmir as a bilateral issue between India and Pakistan. Since then China's position on Kashmir has also undergone a marked change on at least two basic counts: (a) by describing it as a bilateral issue between India and Pakistan that should be dealt not under UN resolutions of 1954 but the 1972 Simla Agreement, and (b) by broadly agreeing to underline the fear from "Islamic fundamentalism". In the second case, the Joint Statement did not directly mention either India's Kashmir or China's Xinjiang yet, as both these provinces share common borders with Pakistan, the statement has clear implications for Islamabad. But nothing perhaps stands comparison to the first Magna Carta on Sine-Indian CSBMs that came two years later and was a part of the next Rat-Li Joint Statement from Beijing.

By any standards, this nine-point "Agreement on Maintenance of Peace and Tranquillity along the Line of Actual Control (henceforth MPTA), signed between two Prime Ministers Narasimha Rao and Li Peng at Beijing's Great Hall of the People on September 7, 1993 has been the corner-stone of Sine-Indian CSBMs. Though already in vogue since the Rajiv Gandhi visit to Beijing in 1988, it was this agreement that formally institutionalised the process of Sine-Indian CSBMs.19 Picking up strings from India's first CSBM agreement of April 1954, the MPTA reiterates its faith in *Panchsheel* and asserts that these Five Principles of Peaceful Coexistence should form the basis of all inter-state relations. But unlike in the earlier Sino-Indian *Panchsheel* agreement where India unilaterally made major concessions, the MPTA clearly represents equality of two nations and lays out various CSBMs that should further buttress Sino-Indian rapprcchement. This business-like spirit is crystal clear throughout its concise text that details on number of specific points. The second CSBMs agreement was signed during President Jiang Zemin's visit to New Delhi in November 1998. This is a 12 Article document that partly fulfils the agenda of their first CSBM agreement of 1993 and it further seeks to extend the CBMs to more specific and sensitive areas in the military field. Going by its first Article that reads "Neither side shall use its military capability against the other side", it virtually stands out as a No War Pact and both sides have also projected it in that light. The agreement begins with (Article II) recognising that both have "different perceptions" on certain segments of border for which the two have agreed "to speed up the process of clarification" and under Article X both sides agree 40 exchange maps indicating their respective perceptions... as soon as possible." It is this businesslike approach to these sensitive questions that gives hope for the future as it depicts !heir growing mutual confidence on the current pace of their *rapprochement.*

As regards evolving CBMs in the military field, the agreement makes a serious attempt at effecting reductions in their military manpower and equipment deployed in the border areas. There had been major confusion as China does not consider their deployments in Tibet as being open for mutual reductions where India believes that Chinese forces on the Tibetan plateau have clear one-to-ten advantage against Indian forces. Accordingly, Article III provides that keeping with "the principle of mutual and equal security" all future ceilings are expected to be based on "perimeters such as the nature of terrain, road communications and other infrastructure and time taken to induct/deinduct troops and armaments." Article IV clearly categonses certain type of offensive weapons withdrawal of which will be given priority These include combat tanks, infantry combat vehicles, guns (including howitzers) with 75 mm or bigger calibre, mortars with 120 mm or bigger calibre, surface-to-surface missiles, surface-to- air missiles and to start with the two sides will "exchange data on the military forces and armament" that are to be reduced. It also exhorts the two sides to 'avoid holding large scale military exercises involving more than one Division (15,000 troops) in close proximity to the LoAc" and to inform the other side on "type, level, planned duration and areas of exercise" in case it involves more than a Brigade (5,000 troops) and about deinduction "within five days of completion." The other side is free to seek any number of clarifications as it deems necessary. Taking a major step forward, the two agree that no combat aircraft which "include fighter, bomber, reconnaissance, military trainer, armed helicopter and other armed aircraft" shall be allowed to fly "within ten kilometers" of the LoAC "except by prior permission" from the other side (Article V).

Similarly, Article VI prohibits any use of "hazardous chemicals, conduct blast operations or hunt with guns or explosives within two kilometers" of the LoAC unless it is "part of developmental activities" in which case the other side shall be informed "through diplomatic channels or by convening a border personnel meeting, preferably five days in advance." Then to "strengthen exchanges and cooperation between their military personnel and establishments" Article VII provides that the two sides shall (a) increase "meetings between their border representatives at designated places, (b) expand "telecommunication links" between these border points, and (c) establish "step-by-step medium and high-level contacts between the border authorities" of the two sides. Should any land or air intrusions take place "because of unavoidable circumstances like natural disasters" the other side is expected under Article VIII to "extend all possible assistance to them" and the two shall exchange information and have consultations to work out "modalities of return of the concerned personnel." And finally, as won as the Sino-Indian Joint Working Group on Boundary Question starts "mutual consultations" (Article Xl) for "detailed implementation measures", each side shall have (Article IX) "the right to seek clarification" regarding the "manner in which the other side is observing the agreement" or on any "doubtful situation" in the border region. Finally, under Article XII though all Hindi, Chinese and English versions are "equally authentic", but "in case of divergence, the English text shall prevail." This agreement has since been ratified by both sides and instrument of ratification were exchanged at the JWG's tenth meeting in New Delhi in August 1997.

These two agreements apart from being a major take-off point for many fresh initiatives, have also provided a major boost to existing "mechanisms" for their border related CSBMs. The Joint Working Group on Boundary Question has been one most effective and generic forum for implementing Sino-Indian CSBMs. To begin with, the JWG has institutionalised regular meetings of military commanders from both sides at the following four points: Bumla and Dichu in the eastern sector, Lipulekh near Pithoragarh (U.P.) in the middle sector and Spanggur near Chushul in the western sector. These meetings are organised and conducted by these area commanders from the two sides to establish facts on the ground and can also be held more than once in case of any exigencies. Besides, commanders on both sides are now provided with "hotline" links to ensure consultations in case of any intrusions or other emergencies. Advance notices of proposed military manoeuvres on one side is provided to the other and mechanisms for handling possible intrusions on either side are put in place. The high point of these JWG meetings occurred during its eighth meeting during August 1995 at New Delhi where the two sides agreed to actually dismantle four border posts in the Wangdong tract where troops had been deployed at an alarming proximity to each other. Apart from their land-based troops, the two air forces have also been building ties and officers of the People's Liberation Army-Air Force (PLAAF) have already visited India's Air Force bases in 1995. Similarly, the two navies have also been working together allaying each others doubts about Chinese naval presence in Myanmar or India's maritime capabilities at its Fortress Andaman. India has offered to China's envoy to visit Indian naval base at Port Blair in Andaman and Nicobar. At a certain stage there were even reports of China and India preparing for joint military and naval exercises which, however, was denied by the Chinese side.

Then there are various other bold initiatives that come about from outside the framework of JWG. Within less than two months of the MPTA, for example, a Chinese ship "Zheng He" made a port visit to Bombay, which was the first of its kind in last 35 years. Before this only INS Mysore had visited Shanghai in 1958. Also, working on the basis of Chiunese *guanxi* (personal contacts) principle, exchanges between other opinion makers and members of strategic research institutions (like Institute for Defence Studies & Analyses, United Services Institution of India, Centre for Policy Research, and Rajiv Gandhi Foundation from India and China institute for Contemporary International Relations, China Association for Friendly International Contact, Fudan University etc. from China) have also been increasingly formalised. Similarly, *Xinhua, People's Dai and Beijing Review* have their accredited correspondents in India and India's *Press Trust of India* has a resident reporter in Beijing. The agreements on exchange of scholars (between the Indian Council for Social Science Research and Chinese Academy of Social Sciences signed at New

Delhi in January 1992) and their Agreement on Radio and Television Cooperation (signed in Beijing on September 7, 1993) have broadly contributed to expanding mutual awareness. The Festival of China was staged in India in 1992 and Festival of India was held in China in April 1994. In fact, the Communist Party of China now has direct links with the Indian National Congress, the Bharatiya Janata Party and the Communist Party of India (Marxists). The two had also tried opening up direct flights between New Delhi and Beijing and now have telecom lines between various cities of the two countries. Contact have also evolved between various NGOs like trade unions and woman organisations, stimulating a great deal of interest and confidence.

In the de-ideologised post-Cold War world, trade has come to be perhaps the most durable CSBM which raises stakes in mutual security and peace amongst states, Though compared to their size and total foreign trade, the volume of Sino-Indian bilateral trade remains still very small yet, more than what is visible in terms of statistics, their border trade has substantially increased the traffic of goods and people in their border regions thus consolidating their border related CSBMs.

Garbyang (in Uttar Pradesh) was the first border port to be opened in February 1991 followed by Gunji (in Uttar Pradesh) in 1992 and later Shipki La (in Himachal Pradesh) in 1994. A fourth border point agreed upon in principle is yet to be opened. India has suggested an eastern route originating in Sikkim on which China has been evasive as it means recognising Sikkim's accession to India.

As an alternative, a route from Kalimpong in Dajeeling District in West Bengal, passing through Sikkim to Yatung in Chumbi Valley, is likely to be agreed upon. Amongst its other intangibles, in 1994, India became China's largest trading partner in South Asia overtaking China's long-standing close friend and ally Pakistan, This obtains for India a greater leverage and psychological advantage vis-a-vis Sine-Pakistan ties. And finally, talking of statistics, according to a recent study by US based Centre for Global Trade Development that monitors trade patterns of 220 countries, has predicted that trade between China and India may cross $ 25 billion by the year 2000. According to the study, this is possible because at their current rate of growth India's total annual exports are expected to reach $ 90 billion and that of China (plus Hong Kong $225 billion after 1997) to $425 billion per annum. The Sino-Indian Joint Business Council has, however, put the figure at a much moderate level of $ 5 billion by 2000.

2

India's National Security and Defence Response

India has been subjected to wars in every decade of its Post – Independence existence and increased armed insurgencies, proxy wars and terrorism of the Islamic fundamentalist variety. India has been so subjected to aggression because in the last fifty years, it exhibited the propensity to be pacifist or defensive in nature.

It shied away from the use of power despite its size and resources. The resultant effect was that India's adversaries perceived India as a "Soft State" incapable of strong military responses even when its national security interests were threatened and trampled upon both externally and internally.

INDIA'S INTERNAL SECURITY REFORMS UNION GOVERNMENT CHOICES IN SECURITY REFORM

Given India's limited resources, New Delhi's increasing re-allocation of its overall security resources towards internal and border security, and 'continental' defence against near neighbours like Pakistan tends to detract from military modernisation and development of force projection capability. One way of illustrating this is to show that the share of defence spending on the 'blue water navy', the classic tool of force projection, has remained in percentage terms fairly constant over the last few decades, shifting only from 13 per cent of the defence budget in 1994 to 14.5 per cent today.

This percentage share is low for a power seeking a force projection capability. For example, it compares with a percentage share for the US Navy of 26 per cent. Against this, concentration on close-in coastal defence and security has risen dramatically following 26/11.

Another way of measuring the costs of internal security is to look at the rising cost of police and paramilitary forces in relation to military forces. State police numbers have been rising at well above the rate of the population increase, from 1.37 million in 1997 to 1.75 million in 2007 (available positions – there are about 1.5 million police in situ.) This rise reflects the position of the Union Government that India is under-policed. As well as this rise in police numbers, the Union Government's burden of expenditure on homeland security has also risen significantly. Since 9/11, the percentage share of homeland security (not including the Coast Guard or state police) in relation to defence spending has risen from 11.76 per cent in 2000-01 to 18.5 per cent in 2009-10 (budget estimate). The Union Government now supports police forces costing Rs 12,817 crore (US$2.27 billion), up from Rs 5,677 crore (US$ 1.2 billion) in 1999-2000 – or a rise of 126 per cent in nominal terms.

The data suggest that there has been a proportional shift within India's security spending between power accretion spending and internal security spending. This is not to say that conventional defence spending has not been rising handsomely, but rather that internal security has become an urgent focus of the Union Government.

Internationally, however, this proportional shift has been overshadowed by the far greater global interest on India's rise as a military power. Although there has been a shift in emphasis in favour of internal and border security spending, the focus of that shift is still in favour of 'hard' (or some might say 'repressive') use of power and against other instruments for achieving better governance outcomes. In this equation, the various paramilitary forces, the armed constabulary (numbering nearly half the state police), the Coast Guard and the various intelligence agencies might be considered as 'hard' power.

'Soft' elements, on their part, might be said to consist of the police working to protect the community from crime, the legal structure, various measures to ensure governance, justice and accountability, and approaches that seek to alleviate the lot of those with grievances, such as economic support for tribal and Muslim populations or granting greater autonomy to separatist regions. Diplomatic, economic and aid efforts designed to create a more robust regional grouping in South Asia also fall within this 'soft' category.

This chapter focuses only on India's security choices in relation to its internal security mechanisms rather than its diplomatic, trade and aid activities in the South Asian region or the needs of national defence against attack by another country.

But it is worth noting that, although regional security building is an extremely difficult area of activity for India as the regional 'giant', it is a crucial activity in terms of India's wider security, not least in achieving cooperative regional outcomes against transnational terrorism and crime. Nor do we deal with the various attempts of the government to meet the needs of disaffected minorities such as tribals, Muslims or those in other areas, seeking separation or greater autonomy.

Equally, these are absolutely vital areas of activity for balanced approaches to counter-terrorism and counter-insurgency. Due to the magnitude of these topics, however, they cannot be covered in this chapter.

Given the reality of India's federal structure, it will be natural to expect the Union Government to be most active in areas of its jurisdiction such as defence, federally funded paramilitary forces, the national intelligence agencies, central police and centrally administered laws. State and local level activities will tend to get a lesser emphasis, at least from the Union Government. Thus, many of the activities at the 'soft' end of the spectrum, such as policing reform and 'community policing', will not fall directly within the jurisdiction of the Union Government.

As for state governments, while some may have an incentive to improve these aspects of security in their jurisdictions, others will be less active in the pursuit of reform. A state political class that has the police under its influence, for example, will be far less willing to conduct meaningful police reforms than one that is not. And it is because of this that many states have resisted efforts to reform the police, including the efforts of the Supreme Court and various police reform commissions.

It is a central tenet of this chapter that the Union Government should develop ways of providing additional focus on so-called 'lower order' issues of security, such as anti-corruption measures, the rights of individuals and modernisation of the police and judiciary, even though they fall predominantly within state government jurisdictions. Without leadership from the centre in these areas, the current drive for greater internal security – especially as it has been developed since the attacks of 26/11 – is unlikely to prove sustainable. Although the Union government is clearly restrained in the level of its activity in respect of these areas by the Constitution, there are a number of ways it can become more active and activist and these areas.

INDIA'S SECURITY CHOICES

As we consider India's rise to power, there are two main scenarios that come to mind. According to the first and most commonly held, India's current trajectory will continue in a 'straight line'. Exponents of this view hold that India's underlying growth rate of 7-9 per cent and growing military capability mean that by 2030 it will join China and Japan as one of Asia's three great powers.

By 2030, India will have the world's largest population. It will have the world's third largest economy in purchasing power parity terms (PPP) after China and the US. It is likely to remain democratic and will have enormous 'soft' power potential, resulting from its large English speaking population, vociferous free press, innovative IT industries, vibrant civil society and widely influential Bollywood film industry. Its navy will be able to range at will over the Indian Ocean and beyond. It will have a fleet of nuclear submarines and an independent nuclear deterrent capable of deterring even China. It will be a major power in space, with the capacity to 'neutralise' enemy satellites.

According to the second and more pessimistic analysis, this new superpower will be expected to rise out of one of the most-troubled sub-regions of the globe – South Asia. South Asia will continue to have more people living in poverty than any other region in the world for the foreseeable future. It will be awash with economic and political refugees. Its great rivers and ground water will be under severe stress. Its regional association, the South Asian Association for Regional Cooperation (SAARC), will still be struggling to provide a viable forum, according to which all in the region can 'rise on the same tide' through enhanced trade, security, travel and cultural exchange. Pakistan, India's neighbour of 166 million and a long-term adversary, will have added another 85 million mouths to feed and jobs to find. It will be subjected to extreme environmental stress. Hundreds of thousands of its young men will have been educated in madrassas that provide inadequate modern education and extremely narrow interpretations of Islam. Bangladesh – another neighbour which has already despatched an estimated 10 million illegal immigrants to India – may well be struggling to accommodate the estimated 10-15 millions of its population currently living on and farming low lying areas, subject to ever-increasing inundation resulting from climate change.

Trapped within this region (or so this pessimistic scenario goes), India will confront its own demons. It will be ever more dependent on costly imported energy. Its mega cities will be struggling to provide sufficient fresh water, accommodation and sanitation. Riots over distribution of drinking water – as witnessed in 2009 in Mumbai – will be frequent events. Antiquated infrastructure and restrictive labour laws will constrain labour-intensive manufacturing that could provide jobs for the massive rural population seeking a better life. Corruption will continue to be a major burden on governance, as democratisation spreads to new classes who are hungry for its benefits but impatient with its norms. Maoists will continue to recruit those in the poorest states suffering from corruption and poor governance. Maoist-generated unrest will jeopardise India's extractive industries, which happen to lie within the regions most seriously affected. Criminality will continue to flourish under a creaking legal system that provides near impunity to the wealthy and powerful and no rapid legal punishment for the guilty. Criminals, corruption and terrorism together will continue to erode the security of citizens and tarnish India's investment reputation.

In many states, the massive police service, which today totals 1.5 million for India as a whole (not including paramilitary forces and un-filled police positions), will remain an ineffective, repressive, colonial-era relic, incapable of investigating crime, providing security to communities, supporting human rights or lifting intelligence from the grassroots to the strategic level. India's 150 million Muslims – 75 per cent of whom belong to underprivileged groups and occupations – will still not have the benefits of the Constitution provided for Dalits and tribals. As the community sinks further in comparative terms, its members will provide more people willing to engage in violent, home-grown Jihad, assisted from across the border in Pakistan.

According to this sombre view of the future, these difficulties in India's polity will continue to resonate across borders in South Asia, just as the domestic difficulties of India's large neighbours will resonate in India. They will be transmitted by a brand of democratic politics, which seeks to blame the neighbour for local ills, by refugees and economic migrants, by sharpening religious misunderstanding as the region's traditional syncretic values erode in a world of globalisation and by ever-deepening cross-border environmental problems, particularly relating to the sharing of the diminishing river waters upon which hundreds of millions depend.

Thus, South Asia will continue to be caught in a vicious circle of local and national troubles that wash back and forward across borders like so much political 'flotsam and jetsam'.

These two scenarios are at the outer extremes of what is likely to occur. Reality will likely be somewhat closer to the middle. But it will nevertheless veer towards one end or the other of the spectrum. Governments of the region will make choices that will have a role in shaping reality. This is particularly true of Indian governments – India being the giant of the region and having greater capability of influencing outcomes.

This chapter is especially concerned with Indian choices around the problem of security. The concept of security can range from the traditional, realist idea of security as constituting freedom from threats to the existence of the nation state, to the concept of 'comprehensive' or 'human' security. The latter involves a focus on the security of individuals within the state and surrounding countries, rather than on the existential security of an individual state. It includes all aspects of the welfare of individuals, including their human rights, gender rights, environmental rights, health, nutrition, education, employment, security from violence (whether from state or non-state actors), and so on.

In this chapter, we will be concerned with security from existential threats to the nation (as an important basis for the security of individuals within the nation) along with threats of physical violence and property threats to governments and individuals. Such threats can come from other nations, state actors such as security personnel and police, corrupt politicians and officials, terrorists, criminals and insurgents.

We will not be considering directly some of the broader aspects of human security, encompassed by issues such as lack of water or food or work, environmental problems, or pandemic diseases – serious though they may be. But we do consider such factors indirectly because of their role in triggering violence, terrorism, insurgency and social dislocation.

This relationship between deprivation and security is present throughout India, but is most noticeable as it applies to the tribal, Maoist-affected belt that covers east-central India. Here, environmental degradation, poor governance, poverty, human rights abuses and corruption have each played major roles in triggering the discontent that lies at the heart of the Maoist revolt.

Our primary concern is to demonstrate that there is a 'seamless web' between security of communities at the grassroots and security of nations and sub-regions (in this case India and South Asia). Such a line of analysis requires linking mechanisms between lower and higher order security issues. It needs to be explained, for example, why an attack on a police contingent in Chhattisgarh can be relevant to India's higher order security and even to its rise as a power. It is this linking process, we argue, which means that it is as important for governments successfully to address lower order security issues as it is to tackle higher order issues.

This approach to security is by no means unique or new: many recent Indian commentaries have covered similar ground. This chapter does, however, bring the added perspective of an Australian security analyst. Australia, as a Westminster-style democracy with a federal structure similar to India's, has experienced similar difficulties with establishing its internal security architecture. Australia's experience with internal security and terrorism is, however, obviously of a much less intensive nature than India's. And as a small, resource-rich nation, it also has many more available resources with which to deal with the problem.

POST-26/11 SECURITY REFORMS

In common with many countries, India's internal security architecture has evolved in an ad hoc way. The National Security Guard (NSG) was founded in 1986 in the aftermath of the 1984 Operation Blue Star. The Multi-Agency Centre (MAC), an intelligence 'fusion centre' within the Intelligence Bureau (IB), was first mooted in the aftermath of the intelligence failure associated with Kargil in 1999 and re-furbished in the aftermath of the 26/11 attacks. Due to this ad hoc process and because of India's federal structure, the current security architecture is characterised, in the words of Home Minister Chidambaram, by the fact that "there is no single authority to which these organisations report and there is no single or unified command which can issue directions to these agencies and bodies." It is also plagued by 'turfdom', fragmentation and careerism.

According to its status as a Westminster-style democracy, the apex of India's security architecture is the Prime Minister and the Cabinet and various offices attached to them. The Cabinet Committee on Security (CCS) consists of ex-officio ministers (the Prime Minister, Minister of Home Affairs, Minister of Defence, Minister of External Affairs and Minister of Finance). It is supported by a National Security Council (NSC), with representatives from the above ministries and the Deputy Chairman of the Planning Commission and National Security Adviser (NSA-who answers to the Prime Minister). The NSC, in turn, is serviced by a secretariat of officials. The NSA is responsible for the Joint Intelligence Committee (which brings together the heads of various intelligence agencies), the Aviation Research Centre (ARC) and the National Technical Research Office (NTRO). The Cabinet Secretariat is responsible for the external intelligence agency, the Research and Analysis Wing (RAW). The Ministry of Finance hosts the Financial Intelligence Unit (FIU). The Ministry of Defence hosts the Defence Intelligence Agency (DIA) and the respective arms of the defence forces host their own intelligence agencies. The Ministry of Home Affairs (MHA) hosts the major domestic security intelligence agency, the Intelligence Bureau (IB), which in turn hosts the MAC. The MHA also hosts the various central government police and paramilitary services, such as the Indian Police Service (IPS), central paramilitary forces (which in turn hosts the NSG), various border paramilitary forces such as the Border Security Force (BSF), the Central Reserve Police Force (CRPF – used to support states in crisis), the Central Bureau of Investigation (CBI), and recently formed National Investigation Agency (NIA).

The major connectivity in terms of intelligence between the Centre and states comes about through the state offices of the IB, through the fact that the Centre can insert its various agencies into the states at the request of the states, through the newly created Subsidiary Multi-Agency Centres (SMACS) and through the connectivity between the SMACS and state police Special Branches. Under the Constitution, except in the case of President's Rule, intelligence relating to national security or investigations relating to the central government's jurisdiction (such as fraud in a central government agency or those relating to the newly created NIA), these relationships all exist according to the invitations and goodwill of the states. Thus if a state does not wish to call in the central government agencies, it need not do so.

As with other federal structures, such as Australia and the US, the artificial bifurcation of intelligence between state and central authorities constitutes a major impediment to the flow of intelligence between the grassroots and the central agencies. This natural tendency of federations is greatly exacerbated in India because of the vast size of the country. Further, intelligence agencies everywhere are extremely poor at sharing intelligence, and India is no exception. They are restricted in doing so by different 'intelligence cultures', the existence of multiple agencies essentially doing the same thing ('stove-piping'), lack of trust and the natural desire to protect sensitive sources. Unfortunately, the police are particularly prone not to share intelligence for all the above reasons and because of a police culture that can often be sceptical of the intelligence function.

The hallmark of sound intelligence in the age of terrorism is the ability to fuse the intelligence gathered at the grassroots with that gathered and analysed at intermediate, national and international levels – what has become known in the US as 'connecting the dots'. Intrinsically, this demands that police and the intelligence agencies work closely together at all levels and develop the capability to share intelligence. It requires that intelligence be 'sucked up' from operations to the analytical and strategic levels. In turn, it requires a sound relationship between the police and the communities they are policing. It also involves trust, compatible data sharing arrangements and adequate security for information and intelligence. Ideally, it requires that all this happens in as near as possible to real time, which in turn implies sound data sharing and analytical systems. But however sophisticated the systems, the sharing of intelligence always Under Section 356 of the Constitution, the central government may dismiss a state government and govern the state directly if the state is deemed to exhibit a failure of the constitutional machinery. If, after six months, no workable majority has emerged, fresh elections must be held.

Since he took over the Ministry of Home Affairs portfolio in December 2008 in the aftermath of the 26/11 attacks, Mr Chidambaram has already conducted a series of reforms and has outlined further major reforms. Reforms, either anticipated or accomplished, include the following (compiled from press reporting and from Chidambaram's speech in December 2009):

Re-vitalisation of the Intelligence Agencies and Counter-Terrorism Mechanisms

- The Multi-Agency Centre (MAC), within the Intelligence Bureau (IB), has been re-furbished and strengthened. The IB has been given an additional Rs 147 crore for the purpose. So-called 'Subsidiary Multi-Agency Centres' (SMACs) have now also been established in the states.
- The MAC and SMACs are to be linked by a dedicated, secure network. In all, 30 locations (including the MAC, the SMACs and a number of police Special Branches) are to be linked by this network.
- • A new, over-arching counter-terrorism organisation is to be created by end 2010, to be called the National Counter-Terrorism Centre (NCTC)
- To incorporate the MAC, NIA, NTRO, JIC, NCRB and National Security Guard (NSG)
- To have an operations division (presumably to include the NSG)
- And thus to minimise the current bifurcation between agencies currently controlled by the NSA and the Ministry of Home Affairs.
- To enable a more rapid response to major terror attacks than was achieved on 26/11, NSG hubs have been established in Hyderabad, Bengaluru, Chennai and Kolkata and two additional regional response groups have been located in Hyderabad and Kolkata. Each hub is staffed by 250 people.
- The Border Security Force (BSF) has been significantly upgraded and re-equipped and 29 additional battalions are to be raised. The Central Reserve Police Force (CRPF) and other central paramilitary forces have also been significantly upgraded.
- In the next 12-18 months, 21 existing, standalone databases will be networked through NATGRID. According to Chidambaram, NATGRID will provide "quick, seamless and secure access to desired information for intelligence/enforcement agencies".
- In a recent development, the National Security Adviser has resigned, possibly opening the way for an integrated security architecture, one more fully reflecting the objectives laid out by Chidambaram.

Strengthening of Coastal and Border Defences

- Coordination has been strengthened between the Coast Guard, Navy and coastal police.

- 64 coastal police stations have been operationalised.
- 56 interceptor boats have been purchased (of 204 scheduled).
- A vessel tracking and monitoring system is being considered.
- Intensified patrolling is in place.
- ID cards are to be issued to fishermen and possibly also coastal residents.
- Following the exposure of serious gaps in the visa system by the Headley case, the Mission Mode Project (MMP) will be implemented. This will provide for online visa and foreigners' registration and tracking with the objective of creating a secure and integrated service delivery framework for facilitating legitimate travellers and strengthening security. It is estimated to cost Rs 1,011 crore and will be implemented over a period of four-and-a-half years.

Policing and Legal Reform

- The National Investigations Agency (NIA) has been established and is now staffed by a small number of investigators and analysts
- The remit of the NIA is to investigate terrorism crimes under the Unlawful Activities (Prevention) Act and other crimes, such as drug-related crimes, counterfeiting, and major organised crime and money laundering, that have international or multi-state implications.
- The Union government has assisted with funds for the recruitment of 400,000 additional state police
- It has promulgated guidelines for non-corrupt recruitment and developed an electronic system to ensure 'hands free' and non-corrupt recruitment. This system has already been implemented for central recruitment.
- The Union government is to assist with connectivity between police stations and the establishment of a system for police called Crime and Criminal Tracking Network System (CCTNS) "to facilitate collection, storage, retrieval, analysis, transfer and sharing of data and information at the police station and between the police station and the state headquarters and the central police organisations".
- The Home Minister has admonished states to implement 'community policing'.
- He has also requested that "to organise and analyse information derived from the community, the state police Special Branches should be restructured as a specialised and self-sufficient cadre of the State police in terms of personnel, funds and equipment." To this end, on January 7, 2009, the central government circulated a proposal to restructure the

Special Branch in the State police forces. The implementation of the proposal will mark the beginning of a long-haul effort to restructure the intelligence-gathering machinery at the district and state levels.

- The Union Government will assist state police to establish 24x7 command and control posts and quick response teams (QRTs), properly equipped and trained.
- States are admonished to establish (where they don't have them) antiterrorism units (ATUs) to pre-empt and investigate terrorist attacks.

Analysis

The collective changes outlined above, if fully implemented, would amount to an internal security 'revolution' in India. The idea of a NCTC, to bring a number of important agencies under one umbrella, act as a 'fusion centre' for terrorist related intelligence, minimise 'stove-piping', and provide operational coordination, closely reflects changes introduced in the US following 9/11, especially the establishment of the umbrella NCTC there, under the auspices of the Director of National Intelligence (DNI). This mimicry of the US architecture in part arises from the early assistance provided by the Federal Bureau of Investigation (FBI) in the aftermath of 26/11 and a subsequent series of visits to the US by senior Indian politicians and officials, including the Home Minister and Prime Minister.

But do the changes go far enough? Do they 'press the right buttons', and are they likely to be successful in providing better governance throughout the Indian Union – a prime consideration of this chapter in its approach to counter-terrorism and counter-insurgency?

In all such architecture relating to federations like India, Australia, Canada and the US, there are five major heuristic 'gaps to be bridged':

- between overseas and domestic intelligence;
- between military and non-military intelligence;
- between central and state intelligence;
- between the intelligence agencies and police intelligence; and
- between intelligence and the operational counter-terrorism role (response), which is in turn divided into:
- investigations;
- operational coordination in event of an attack; and
- consequence management.

These five major 'gaps' are heuristic in the sense that each and every inter-agency relationship also needs to be bridged. But they represent the major conceptual divides and provide a useful point of departure for the analysis.

We will now briefly critique the proposed Indian architecture in light of each of these five main areas.

INDIAN COUNTERMEASURES POST MUMBAI ATTACKS

Immediately after the Mumbai attacks several measures were taken by the Indian administration amidst much public debate- mostly criticism as to how vulnerable Indian cities are to terrorist attacks. These measures were:

- Creation of NSG hubs in the major metropolitan cities
- Diplomatic pressure on Pakistan for the arrest and trial of Lashkar-e-Taiba's top leadership
- Creation of a new National Investigation Agency (NIA)
- Amendment of Unlawful Activities (Prevention) Act
- Increased budget allocation for Homeland Security Agencies
- Coastal Security Scheme
- Creation of a Police Commando Force in Mumbai
- Arrest of key Lashkar-e-Taiba operatives

Within a week of the attacks Indian Prime Minister Manmohan Singh announced the setting up of NSG hubs in different parts of the country. The first phase included setting up of hubs in Mumbai, Kolkata, Chennai and Hyderabad. All four of the hubs have been established and the last one was inaugurated in the winter of 2011. The regional NSG hubs were set up with the intent of reducing response time in case of a terrorist attack. In a country like India, which faces terrorist threat not just from external terrorist groups like Lashkar-e-Taiba but from homegrown terrorist and insurgent groups, even though it is necessary to have these regional hubs for quick deployment and response, security experts also feel that increase in the number of personnel or hubs is not going to solve the problem. Former National Security Advisor M.K. Narayanan said at a conference that the idea of setting up of NSG hubs was 'archaic' and a 'major mistake'. "I am concerned about the current emphasis on increasing the size and numbers of the NSG. I also have reservations about the establishment of four regional hubs. The NSG is an elite special force intended to meet a specific situation and not intended to confront the normal law and order situation… Its strength does not lie in its numbers, its uniqueness lies in the fact that it consists of the bravest of brave personnel, of great virtue and ability, specially trained for undertaking the most difficult tasks... increasing numbers, to my mind, is bound to dilute both quality and capability of the force"

The National Security Guard which was established in 1986 was modelled after the German GSG-9 and raised as an elite anti-hijacking, anti-terror and bomb disposal force. In the years before as well as after the attacks in Mumbai, they have mostly been used for VIP security. In 2012 the NSG for the first time in many years pulled out its 900 commandos from VIP security details and put them to train for and perform counter-terrorism and anti-hijacking operations. The boost that the NSG got after the Mumbai attacks was a step in the right direction but no Mumbai like attack after 2008, the force seems to now be caught up in a fight for budget allocations, equipment acquisition and improving their capability in terms of personnel and training.

As the interrogations of the lone surviving terrorist, Ajmal Amir Kasab, proceeded and reports of Pakistani state support as well as Lashkar-e-Taiba's involvement surfaced, Indian officials blamed Pakistan for providing sanctuary and letting terrorist activities emanate from their soil. Indian administration since then has been trying to pressure Pakistan through diplomatic channels as well as through the international community to crack down on Lashkar-e-Taiba and bring the masterminds of the Mumbai attacks to book. In early January 2009, India sent evidence to Pakistan which linked the Mumbai attacks to Pakistani terrorists including data from the satellite phones which were used by the 10 gunmen to keep in touch with their handlers as well as what was described as 'Kasab's confession.' The evidence dossier was also sent to countries whose citizens were the victims of the attack such as the United States, as India tried to corner Pakistan diplomatically into bringing the perpetrators to justice.

In a time frame of three years since, 15 such dossiers have been provided to the Pakistani administration by the Indian government and officials of both countries have met on 13 different occasions. And even though Pakistan has acknowledged that the plan to attack Mumbai was hatched on Pakistani soil, India feels Pakistan has done little to cooperate and hasn't taken any real hard steps to crack down on terrorist activity. It has been almost 5 years since the first dossier was provided and on the 5th anniversary of the attacks, Indian officials still press for a speedy and just trial of the masterminds.

Another major initiative taken by the government was the setting up of a federal National Investigative Agency by passing the National Investigative Agency Act and making relevant amendments to the already existing Unlawful Activities (Prevention) Act. Both these measures were taken within a month of the Mumbai attacks and were passed by both Houses of the Parliament almost at the same time.

At present the NIA is functioning as the Central Counter Terrorism Law Enforcement Agency in India and has dealt with 72 cases till date. Even though there was a dire need for a Federal Investigative Agency, the haste in which this Act has been conceived has left unresolved many issues about the NIA's constitutional validity, functioning, and scope.

The constitutional basis for the creation of the NIA remains a matter of debate. The areas of policing and public order lie within the exclusive legislative competence of the States and not with the Centre (Central government). States would be extremely chary of accepting or cooperating with any agency that encroached on that power. Furthermore, the NIA Act has been drafted in a way that it focuses only on investigation but not on prevention. In order for the NIA to be effective in preventing federal crime, it needs to be able to warehouse, process and coordinate the flow of critical information.

The Amendments to the Unlawful Activities (Prevention) Act which were brought about almost parallel to the NIA Act also felt significant but were vague in character and meaning. The amendments define 'an act of terrorism' but for the Act to have any real prevention or enforcement powers the definition needs to be more specific in sketching out the difference between civilians and combatants as well as between political and personal motives.

Further the Act lacks any kind of provision for a review mechanism. It grants immunity from prosecution or other legal proceedings to the central and state governments, and their employees.

One of the more progressive steps which seems promising and likely to have a real effect on India's counter-terrorism policies is higher budget allocation for the Ministry of Home Affairs which is responsible for internal security, border management, para military forces etc. The allocation for India's homeland security agencies was increased by 25 percent in the budget 2009-2010. The allocation of budget for the Ministry has since increased yearly. The budget in recent years also included the Coastal Security Schemes which were initiated in 2005, well before the Mumbai attacks in 2008, and completed its first phase in 2011.

The Coastal Security Schemes were initiated with the aim of improving surveillance and patrolling along the Indian coast with the strengthening of the Marine Police Force. Under Phase-1 of the scheme 73 Coastal Police Stations, 58 Out Posts and 30 Barracks were approved with 204 boats and vehicles. Phase-2 was approved in 2010 and is set to be completed by 2015. 131 Coastal Police Stations, 180 boats/vessels, 60 jetties and 373 vehicles have been approved under Phase-2.

The issue of maritime security and the lack of it surfaced and gained much attention after the Mumbai attacks. The fact that 10 men could easily enter Indian waters and gain entry into India's financial capital armed with explosives, made the Indian government a target of the civil society's outrage and frustration.

Candle light vigils and heated public debates forced the administration to review the matter of coastal security and accelerate the implementation of the Coastal Security Scheme. But even though the Home Department and police are regularly claiming to have enhanced the coastal security system, the projects launched for this still remain on paper. Many coastal states failed to reach the target number of coastal police stations under Phase-1 and yet more have been sanctioned under Phase-2. States are also struggling with the maintenance and repair of equipment and vehicles. The intelligence community in Mumbai has got around 250 intelligence inputs this year with some referring to the possibility of terrorists using the sea to carry out attacks. Despite this, coastal police stations have not been built and the boats have been under repair for nearly two years. Yet another example of an ineffective countermeasure is the creation of an elite commando force under the Mumbai Police Department. The commando force called Force One was created for swift action in an event of Mumbai style attack and again it failed to even stand up on its feet. Till 2012, three years after its formation, the force was struggling to get the funds allocated to it by the State government and was struggling to cope with shortage of equipment such as special rifles, bulletproof vests, pistols and even ammunition for training and practice.

The most successful of all countermeasures though has been the arrest of key Lashkar-e-Taiba operatives. In 2013, Indian security officials arrested Abdul Karim Tunda- an expert bomb maker for the terrorist outfit. In 2012 approximately 61 operatives were killed in encounters with Indian security forces including Lashkar Division and District Commanders. Around 48 were arrested and 8 sleeper cells were neutralized. The arrests included key recruiter for Lashkar from India and Nepal Mohammad Omar Madni and Chief Coordinator for Jammu and Kashmir Manzoor.

Looking at the numbers, it certainly seems like the intelligence community is successful in gathering critical information as well as preventing further attacks but in my opinion they still have a long way to go. In 2013 itself, there has been a record of 254 infiltration bids made by terrorists along the India-Pakistan border. In 133 cases, the terrorists were made to 'return' to Pakistan territory, while they successfully crossed over in 84 cases. The operatives that crossed over in these 84 cases could well be planning another Mumbai. As seen in most of the counter measures analyzed above, they were carried out in haste without much deliberation or debate after the attacks in Mumbai. The poorly formed and impulsive decisions were then tangled in bureaucratic processes, slow paper work and murky politics. A senior journalist, Praveen Swami, commenting on the police reforms after the Mumbai attacks wrote in an article, 'The Indian Fine Art of Faking Security'- "India's post-

26/11 police reforms painted stripes on a donkey — and passed it off as a tiger." But the alarming as well as disconcerting fact is that it is not just the police reforms which are being passed off as a tiger but India's counter-terrorism policies as a whole seems to be a striped donkey which when under attack will shed its stripes and show its true colors. Indian authorities continue to boast and reiterate the fact that they have launched many counter measures post Mumbai and they have been successful because there has not been another Mumbai like attack after 2008. Although that it is true, it is hardly a metric that can be used to measure success for counterterrorism policies. Most of these measures were taken to show to the world as well as to pacify the public sentiment that 'we are doing something.' Instead, for a review of the success or failure of these measures some basic questions should be addressed: Is the dependence on certain factors that terrorists or anti-terrorists can exploit as vulnerabilities increasing or decreasing? How seamlessly do terrorist organizations and networks interact? How seamlessly do new government anti-terrorist organizational structures and networks interact? Is the international operating environment becoming more or less inviting or restrictive for terrorists or for those combating them? Is it easier or harder today for terrorists to inflict the damage they seek to do?

INDIA'S NATIONAL SECURITY STRATEGY

National interests lead to the drawing up of national security objectives and the formulation of national security policies. India's national security objectives have been adequately stated in the MEA Annual Report of 1998-99, reproduced above. The only aspect that really needs to be added is to strive to weaken the China-Pakistan collusive nexus in nuclear and missile technology and military hardware. It should be India's objective to marginalise Pakistan's military power by 2010-15 and eliminate its interference in India's internal affairs. India's national security policies must be so formulated that India is in a position to provide leadership to other countries in the Southern Asian region so as to be able to exercise a reasonable degree of influence over their policies and actions to further its own security interests. India's security lies in establishing a confrontation free external environment. For this, India must be prepared to use all elements and instruments of national power to influence the actions of countries that follow policies and initiate measures inimical to India's national interests. Such policies would require matching strategies backed by necessary resources being devoted to diplomatic, military, intelligence and other efforts to achieve the desired objectives.

India's strategic frontiers extend to Tibet in the north, the Central Asian region, including Afghanistan, in the northwest, include the Saudi Peninsula in the west, extend to Mauritius and Diego Garcia in the Indian Ocean and the ASEAN countries in the east, including the Malacca Straits. India's national security strategy must reflect India's strategic interests in these regions. In the prevailing uncertain geo-strategic environment and unstable world order, with the primacy of the nation-state being gradually eroded, no country can afford to "go it alone" in organising its national security. Even the US, the world's only remaining superpower, has formulated a well-crafted strategy of alliances to further its wide-ranging security interests. In this age of globalisation and trade blocks, the trend is inexorably towards collective security. India too needs to form strategic partnerships with countries sharing a mutuality of interests to countervail its adversaries. India's abhorrence for military alliances and its efforts towards pursuing a fiercely independent foreign policy have been well founded. However, India has found it difficult to single-handedly eliminate or even reduce the external threats and foreign-sponsored internal security challenges. India needs to establish strategic linkages with the US, Russia (as it will once again rise from the quagmire it is in at present to become a major power), Israel, Iran, Myanmar, Vietnam, Taiwan, Japan and South Korea to counter-balance China's growing power and influence.

One of the major reasons for the continuing violation of India's borders and the destabilisation of India through proxy wars is the prevalent perception of India as a soft state that is if not unmindful at least not adequately concerned about its external and internal security. This perception is founded on India's failure to exploit the advantages gained during the 1947-48, 1965 and 1971 conflicts with Pakistan and on its purely reactive handling of Pakistan's proxy war over the decade of the 1990s. India's continuously reducing defence expenditure throughout the period 1985-1999, even as the threats to its security increased manifold due to Pakistan's nuclearisation in 1987 and its proxy war against India from 1989-90 onwards, also sent a message of being relatively unconcerned. Inimical neighbours have always exploited such weaknesses to their advantage and so has been the case with India. Quite clearly, India now has no option but to adopt pro-active strategies to deal firmly with the threats confronting its security.

While India's nuclear doctrine of no first use and a credible minimum deterrent has been clearly stated, the strategies to be followed to give effect to this doctrine have not been spelt out except in passing in the recommendations of the National Security Advisory Board (NSAB) while formulating a draft Nuclear Doctrine. In fact, till the time of writing, the issue is yet to be debated in Parliament. The first inescapable ingredient of India's nuclear strategy would be overt signs of weaponisation - mere declaratory statements are not enough. If India's "nuclear capability is to become a source of power and influence during crises rather than only a strategic deterrent to total war... (a) public stance on the actual nuclear capability, the range and accuracy of delivery systems, the kilotonnage of warheads... the authorisation (procedures) for launch, and the custody of codes and interlocks for authorising a launch..." will be necessary. Having consciously abjured a first use doctrine, India's retaliatory strike strategy has to be based on destroying the adversary's large industrial and population centres if deterrence is to be successfully maintained. Only if the adversary's political and military leadership is convinced that the cost of a first strike would prove to be unbearably high, will it be deterred from doing the unthinkable. If India's retaliatory response strategy lacks credibility and the adversary is convinced that he can bank on an ambivalent Indian response, he may be tempted to risk a first strike. Deterrence is ultimately a mind game and turns on credibility.

Some other aspects that would enhance the credibility of India's nuclear deterrence include the establishment of a viable command and control system with well publicised procedures for nuclear decision-making, a clearly enunciated chain of succession, at least the partial transfer of the custody of nuclear warheads to the armed forces units designated to launch them and a well-conceived targeting philosophy. However, real credibility will stem from a demonstrated delivery system capability and an established programme for building the required number of missiles. While India's delivery systems are adequate to retaliate against nuclear threats from Pakistan, India is yet to develop a 5,000 km class missile to retaliate against a Chinese threat and other threats that may manifest themselves in future. In fact, unless the N-5 agree quickly to adopt a time bound nuclear disarmament programme, only a remote possibility at present, India has no option but to develop an inter-continental ballistic missile (ICBM). Some commentators have written about such a programme named Surya but there has been no official confirmation. The status of the advanced technology vehicle (ATV) project for a nuclear powered submarine is also not clear. Unless India demonstrates the will to develop the required delivery systems and commits sufficient funds and efforts to their development, India's nuclear deterrence will continue to lack credibility.

In view of the doubts expressed by leading Indian nuclear scientists like Dr. P. K. Iyengar regarding the viability of the thermonuclear test carried out in May 199842 and the need for more tests if weapons in the megaton class or even 200 kiloton (kt) fusion warheads are to be developed, India will have to develop a suitable strategy to find a way around the CTBT to enable further testing without inviting a fresh round of sanctions and international opprobrium. In case India's nuclear warhead capability remains confined to 15 to 30 kt fission warheads, it will lead to the sub-optimal utilisation of India's meagre fissile material stockpile. With negotiations for the FMCT staring it in the face and the likelihood of an early agreement being reached, India would be hard put to stockpile adequate fissile stockpile for the total number of warheads that its retaliatory strategy and targeting philosophy may require. These are the tough issues confronting the development of a potent nuclear strategy. While there are no easy answers, a determined diplomatic stance and a tough negotiating position with some hard bargaining can achieve the desired results. The world is gradually getting used to the idea that a "cap, reduce, eliminate" policy is no longer feasible and that India's nuclear weapons, born primarily out of the need to safeguard national security, cannot now be rolled back.

Simultaneously with developing a credible nuclear deterrent, India must continue to pursue its nuclear disarmament efforts. The best nuclear strategy would undoubtedly be the total elimination of nuclear weapons from the face of the earth. However, this is one aspect in the affairs of mankind where progress will continue to be excruciatingly slow. This will have to be vectored into India's nuclear calculations. India must also seek to discuss and agree upon mutual nuclear risk reduction measures (NRRMs), particularly with China and Pakistan. Since neither China nor Pakistan is willing to negotiate a mutual no-first-use treaty with India, it would be in the interest of all the protagonists to ensure that sufficient safety checks are mutually in place to reduce the risk of knee-jerk responses in situations of panic and accidental nuclear war. The holding of discussions for NRRMs need not be linked to the lack of progress on other issues of concern such as a halt to Pakistan's sponsorship of terrorism in India. The possibility of the unleashing of nuclear weapons, even if unintended, is too horrific to make its reduction contingent upon other political and diplomatic considerations, no matter how deeply vexatious the issues concerned might be. The first aim of a well-rounded nuclear strategy should be to ensure that deterrence does not fail, whether by design or by default, and that the nuclear genie remains tightly bottled up - as it has been since August 1945.

It is apparent that India's world view has changed since Pokhran-II to one that is more assertive and more willing to reach out to safeguard national security, even if the new thinking is not very clearly and lucidly articulated officially. Indian defence analysts are becoming increasingly more forthright in spelling out specific policies and actions to reduce and gradually eliminate the manifold threats and challenges to national security. Bharat Karnad strongly advocates that Vietnam should be propped up as a nuclear counter to China to ensure the same level of discomfiture to China as China's collusion with Pakistan is causing to India. He rationalises that India would not be violating any international treaties in offering nuclear know-how to Vietnam and the international opprobrium that is bound to result would be justified in terms of India's larger security interests. He recommends that India must exploit the growing anti-Pakistan sentiments in Pakistan Occupied Kashmir (POK) and the Northern Areas of Gilgit and Baltistan and that India should sponsor and support an Azad Kashmir Liberation Front and provide its members "diplomatic, political and moral support" exactly like Pakistan claims to do to Kashmiri militants.

Bharat Karnad is also of the view that India's special operations capability needs to be increased to about a division worth of Special Forces troops to sustain covert special operations inside POK on a long-term basis to counter Pakistan's proxy war through pro-active trans-LoC operations. Appearing as a defence analyst on a TV programme, Lieutenant General Satish Nambiar (Retd.), Director, United Service Institution of India, New Delhi, recommended that trans-LoC operations be launched by the Indian army to raise the cost for Pakistan to sponsor foreign mercenary terrorists for operations in J&K. Mulayam Singh Yadav, a former Defence Minister and a member of Parliament, has publicly demanded "hot pursuit" operations across the LoC to stop Pakistan's trans-LoC terrorism. Ever since Lashkar-e-Toiba's brutal massacres in J&K on the night of August 1, 2000, in which 100 innocent people were killed, there has been a spate of editorials and opinion pieces in leading Indian dailies demanding hot pursuit and other trans-LoC operations. Leading Indian analysts like Brahma Chellaney have questioned whether a strong, stable and prosperous Pakistan is in India's interest.

It is emerging quite clearly that the limit of tolerance of the Indian people has been crossed and there will be greater demands on the government in future to adopt pro-active trans-LoC measures to put an end to Pakistan's proxy war against India. "... India will have to exploit Pakistan's weaknesses with a strategic blueprint that incorporates military, political and unorthodox elements. The main aim should be to start hitting Pakistan wherever it will hurt and whenever it least expects such counteraction." Since it is necessary to raise the ante on the LoC, India will have to be prepared for a larger conventional conflict with Pakistan that may not remain confined to the LoC and may spill over to the international border. Hence, India's strategy must be to further develop its conventional superiority to fight and win a limited war with Pakistan in a nuclear environment. Victory in such a limited war should be measured not through inflicting a comprehensive military defeat on Pakistan, as that in any case is not possible below the nuclear threshold, but by destroying a substantial portion of Pakistan's war waging potential so as to marginalise the Pakistan army as the force majeure in Pakistan's polity. It should be clear to all perceptive observers that the real problem between India and Pakistan is not the Kashmir issue or any other issue but the Pakistan army that drives Pakistan's foreign policy and is the progenitor of Pakistan's proxy war strategy to "bleed India through a thousand cuts". The early marginalisation of the Pakistan army should be a major national priority.

With China India faces a "capabilities-intentions" dilemma. While China has systematically resolved its long-standing, complex and seemingly intractable territorial and boundary disputes with Russia, Vietnam and the Central Asian Republics through protracted negotiations in a spirit of mutual accommodation and there is peace on these borders, it has shown remarkable intransigence in following the same approach with India.

China continues to profess its willingness to resolve its territorial and boundary dispute with India through peaceful negotiations. Despite the Border Peace and Tranquillity Agreement signed in 1993 and the Confidence Building Measures in the military field mutually negotiated in 1996, there has been little change in the ground situation. China either fails to or does not deliberately wish to accept that the best confidence building measure would be to first delineate on the map and ground the Line of Actual Control (LAC).

As long as the LAC is not clearly demarcated, border clashes can occur between the two opposing armies at any time in the disputed areas and these can lead to another border conflict. Though there is a fair possibility of such a conflict between the two nuclear-armed adversaries being fought below the nuclear threshold, it could rapidly escalate to nuclear exchanges that may not remain limited to battlefield targets. China is known to be engaged in modernising its armed forces and acquiring offensive conventional capabilities, including the creation of rapid reaction forces based on strategic airlift. It is also engaged in developing information warfare capabilities. Since China has successfully resolved its territorial disputes and boundary problems with most other neighbours, the new capabilities would be available to be used against India.

The only deduction that can reasonably be drawn is that China wishes to put its territorial dispute with India on the back burner for the time being, while it consolidates its economic and military power and is engaged in resolving the Taiwan dispute and in settling its claims to various islands in the South China Sea. Michael D. Swaine and Ashley J. Tellis have written that the basic logic underlying China's "indefinite postponement" approach has been to "steadfastly avoid conceding any Chinese claims with respect to the dispute, while simultaneously seeking to prevent the dispute from vitiating the pacific environment that China needs to complete its internal transformation successfully." Swaine and Tellis list several advantages of this approach:

- It positions China as a conciliatory state seeking to resolve all outstanding disputes peacefully.
- It does not increase the demands on China's military's forces at a time when the PLA is relatively weak and when the Chinese economy needs all the breathing room it can get.
- It prevents balancing coalitions from arising against China in the event Beijing pursued more coercive strategies.
- And, it delays the resolution of these disputes at least until the balance of power changes substantially in favour of China. At that time, both simple usurpation and coercive bargaining might become more attractive, although it is unclear today whether the Chinese leadership would conclude that the benefits of such actions easily exceed the costs.

China may choose to settle the territorial dispute with India at a time of its own choosing when it is militarily far more powerful. It may opt to do this either through coercive diplomacy or even by seeking a military solution. It is in India's interest to strive towards an early resolution of the territorial dispute with China so that India has only one major military adversary to worry about.

India would also be able to re-deploy at least some of the 10 to 12 mountain divisions and perhaps four to six squadrons of the Indian Air Force from the Tibetan border in the east and the northeast to the western border to gain a decisive military edge against Pakistan. India may even be able to "downsize" a few army divisions and utilise the savings that will accrue for the long-overdue qualitative upgradation of the army. Perhaps these are the real reasons that compel China to drag its feet in resolving its territorial and boundary dispute with India so that it can support Pakistan, its friend and ally, to continue to destabilise India through its proxy war without fear of major military retaliation.

India's strategy should be to develop adequately powerful leverages to make it incumbent on China to act quickly to resolve the territorial dispute between the two countries. Developing the strategic linkages mentioned above could do this. There would be immense advantages in commencing the sale of modern military hardware to Vietnam, including some quantities of Prithvi missiles with launchers under government-to-government soft loans.

The Defence Research and Development Organisation (DRDO) could provide technical know-how to Vietnam's nascent armament industry. If it becomes necessary, India should also be ready to play the Tibet card, something it has consciously avoided doing for almost half a century since China launched its brutal suppression of the human rights of the Tibetan people. The Chinese people's latent yearning for democracy could also be discreetly encouraged. The large number of multinational companies (MNCs) that are unhappy with their business ventures in China could be persuaded to invest in India instead through attractive offers. This would make both business as well as strategic sense.

Attempts to ensure a stable and peaceful external security environment would be meaningful only if internal security was first ensured. Throughout the last two decades of the 20th century, India's handling of militancy has lacked a firm and well-coordinated approach. India's reactive strategy of fighting Pakistan's proxy war through security forces' operations limited within its own territory has not produced the desired results. In addition to the trans-LoC pro-active measures mentioned above, India's internal security strategy needs to follow a three-pronged approach. Firstly, all security forces' operations in the states affected by armed militancy should be conducted in a comprehensively coordinated manner with well-streamlined procedures for the acquisition and sharing of intelligence. Secondly, there is an inescapable need to organise a national level para-military counter-insurgency force with the army's ethos and standards of training and, at least initially, army leadership. Such a force could be based on an existing police force like the CRPF that could be designated as the Central Government's primary counter-insurgency strike force. Its charter will have to be modified accordingly to relieve it of other law and order duties. Or, a new elite force could be raised from scratch for the purpose. The haphazard raising of additional police force battalions, guided more by turf battles rather than hard-nosed national security considerations, must stop.

It is also imperative that the army's involvement in counter-insurgency operations must be reduced gradually from the peak level of approximately 120,000 (six divisions equivalent) in 1998[49] as it is by now well recognised that the prolonged employment of the army for such tasks hampers its training and operational preparedness for conventional military operations. Ideally, internal security problems should be handled by the Ministry of Home Affairs without seeking the army's help.

However, in proxy war situations involving well-trained foreign mercenary terrorists equipped with sophisticated weapons, it may become necessary to deploy the army. Such deployment should be for short-duration surgical operations only and even then, the army's specialised counter-insurgency strike forces like the Rashtriya Rifles (RR) should be employed and not regular infantry battalions. If the present level of Pakistan-sponsored militancy is not rapidly reduced to more manageable levels by trans-LoC pro-active operations, it will be necessary to increase the number of RR battalions to between 75 to 80 to reduce the involvement of regular infantry battalions. Finally, armed militancy can never be eliminated only through security forces' operations. Ultimately it is a battle of hearts and minds and only a political solution can eliminate the root causes of militancy and assuage the feelings of hurt of the alienated people. The government must initiate a political dialogue with all parties concerned to find a lasting solution to the complex problems confronting the nation in J&K and the northeastern states while simultaneously expediting developmental activities. Good governance is also an important ingredient of a successful internal security strategy.

Effective border management strategies go hand in hand with well-conceived internal security strategies. The infiltration of well-armed mercenary terrorists from Pakistan, mass migrations from Bangladesh into lower Assam, narcotics and small arms trafficking across India's vast land borders and long coastline, the smuggling of consumer goods and fake Indian currency from Nepal, the operations of ULFA militants from safe hideouts in Bhutan and the sanctuaries available to the insurgent groups of the northeastern states in Myanmar and Bangladesh, have all added to India's border security challenges. While the BSF should be responsible for manning all settled borders, the responsibility for unsettled and disputed borders, such as the LoC in J&K and the LAC on the Indo-Tibetan border, should be that of the army. The principle of 'single point control' must be followed if the borders are to be effectively managed. Divided responsibilities never result in effective control. While full operational control on the LoC is already with the army, it is not the case on the LAC with China. On the LAC, the ITBP, which is under the Ministry of Home Affairs (MHA), is responsible for the Ladakh, Himachal Pradesh and the Uttar Pradesh segments while the army is deployed in Sikkim. The Assam Rifles, another MHA force but under the army's operational control, manages the LAC in Arunachal Pradesh. On the other hand, on the Tibetan side, Border Guards divisions of the Chinese army under a single commander manage the entire LAC. The BSF must be withdrawn from its internal security commitments and reverted to border management that is its primary role. Ad hoc measures in utilising police forces for operational tasks for which they are not trained, invariably leads to the lack of a cohesive response to critical situations affecting national security and further complicates the resolution of existing problems.

Achieving self-reliance in critical weapons technologies is another important ingredient of India's national security strategy. Stringent technology control regimes have been applied by the western powers as a consequence to India's independent line on nuclear weapons even though India has behaved extremely responsibly as a nuclear power and has refrained from proliferating nuclear weapons and ballistic missile technologies, unlike China that is a signatory to the NPT and the MTCR. Though such technology denial regimes have only slowed down India's quest for self-reliance and not stopped it altogether, the present dependence on imports for major defence equipment needs to be reduced quickly and eliminated by 2020-25. The efforts already underway in indigenous weapons research and development need to be further stepped up. At the same time, India should establish closer strategic ties with countries like France and Israel that may be willing to enter into joint weapons development agreements with India. The leverages provided by India's weapons procurement programmes should be exploited to gain access to cutting edge defence technologies. Defence cooperation programmes need to be made more meaningful to establish strategic linkages with countries of consequence. The full importance of military diplomacy and its vast potential in furthering national security is yet to be realised in India. Other important national security strategies that need to be instituted include those for maritime and energy security, food, water and environmental security and for security against organised crime and cyber terrorism.

INDIAN SECURITY CHALLENGES

Six of India's neighbours rank in the top 25 dysfunctional states in the world, as tabulated by the Failed States Index of the Fund for Peace. India is uniquely positioned to be a driver of interstate cooperation in South Asia, which is a 'predominantly Indocentric region' because, in terms of religion or culture, or both, 'India has something in common with [each of] its immediate neighbours but the neighbouring states of India do not share similarities of such magnitude or depth among themselves.'

Yet India has been unsuccessful in generating such cooperation. Despite the great strides it has made in economic growth, it remains mired in the security dilemmas of its own region. As Vikram Sood suggests, 'Globally, India is being recognised as a rising economic power but not in the region where economic development has become hostage to security issues.' Varun Sahni describes India's regional status as one of 'contested dominance'. The two types of regional security challenges for India. The first is a set of what might otherwise be classified as domestic law-andorder problems were it not for the involvement of India's neighbours. The second relates to bilateral disputes between India and its neighbours over resources, particularly land and water. Territorial disputes (prominently, Kashmir and Siachen with

Pakistan, and Arunachal Pradesh and Aksai Chin with China) fall within this category.

Subnational Ethnic Movements

Indian populations in border regions tend to share common ethnic bonds with populations in adjacent countries. This is true, for example, of Tamils and Sri Lanka, Muslims in Kashmir, Punjabis with their cousins in Pakistan, Indian populations bordering the Tarai region of Nepal, and even Keralites and their ties to Gulf countries. The broad territorial division of ethnic groups within India and the strength of regional ethnic identities ensure that Indian policy towards the countries in question is often attentive to the preferences of domestic actors in these regions, as with Sri Lanka, where at one time the Indian government acquiesced in the brutal armed tactics of the Liberation Tigers of Tamil Eelam (LTTE). Similarly, there is 'widespread sympathy' in Indian border regions for the campaign for autonomy in the Tarai region of Nepal, for which 'most [Indian] politicians and bureaucrats do not hesitate to express moral support'. And Pakistan was widely believed to have supported Sikh separatist movements within India's state of Punjab during the 1980s.

Secessionist Movements and Insurgencies

Because of India's vast size and heterogeneous society and polity, it has been home to many (often armed) movements aiming for sovereign status separate from the union. Some of these secessionist movements have allowed neighbouring countries interested in destabilising India to interfere in its internal affairs. The separatist assertion of regional identities has sharply accentuated the importance attached by Delhi to the territorial integrity of the Indian Union ever since independence. Indeed, this theme first arose during the early months of independence, when Delhi made every effort (including the use of force) to integrate the 536 princely states of India into the Union. It was echoed in the military action taken by India to wrest control of Goa from the Portuguese in 1961; in India's integration of Sikkim into the Union in 1975; and ultimately in the lack of official support given to the LTTE, seen first and foremost as a secessionist movement. It is also reflected in India's longstanding policy of rejecting involvement in its neighbourhood by nations outside South Asia. Concern over territorial unity thus runs deep in Indian foreign policy.

New Ethnic Groups

The cross-border movement of large populations from neighbouring countries has resulted in the creation of new (or newly large) ethnic groups in India, thus complicating policy towards the originating countries. Two examples stand out—the migration of Tibetans escaping Chinese persecution, and the steady inflow of immigrants (legal and illegal) from Bangladesh—with implications for Delhi's relationship with both countries. In the case of China, India has walked a tightrope between official recognition of Tibet as an integral part of China and granting asylum to the Dalai Lama and his followers on Indian territory. Tibetan migrants have integrated relatively well into Indian society. By contrast, the domestic response to Bangladeshi immigrants has been much less forgiving, possibly as a result of their purely economic motivation for migration, leading to riots in Assam against migrant Bengalis as far back as the 1960s and 1970s. This has produced a negative impact on Indo-Bangladeshi relations, with India in 1984 initiating construction of a still unfinished 4,000-kilometre concrete barrier along the Indo-Bangladeshi border.

Religious Conflict

Religion has a significant impact on social stratification and political mobilisation in India. The religious composition of Indian society influences social and economic policy, particularly with regard to minority rights. The frequent occurrence of violence between religious groups—predominantly between Hindus and Muslims—in various parts of the country, sometimes on a startling scale, has led to instances of radicalisation, for example through the Students' Islamic Movement of India (SIMI). Religiously inspired terrorism has also been attributed to Hindu activists following serial bomb attacks in the predominantly Muslim town of Malegaon in 2006. While the Bharatiya Janata Party (BJP) generally proved responsible when in power (1998–2004), its connections with radical Hindu organisations hostile to Islam and Christianity have at times stoked tension, which early on benefited the party politically, as in the case of the demolition of the Babri mosque in 1992 and the Gujarat riots of 2002.

In the former case the BJP's connections with these organisations tended to polarise public opinion further, while in both cases cadres from these organisations were involved in events on the ground. The BJP's current lack of traction is largely attributable to an ageing leadership and ideological fatigue, as well as a failure to build on limited breakthroughs into southern India. But it is likely to persist as a potentially volatile faction in Indian politics, and one that could complicate relations with Muslim countries.

Bilateral Issues: China

Increasingly, China is more worrying than Pakistan for India, whatever the provocations launched against India from within the latter's territory. While India has experienced significant economic success over the past 20 years, China initiated its economic reforms well before India did, and has consistently outstripped India's impressive growth by 2–3 percentage points every year since then. The result is that China's economy has expanded to nearly three times the size of India's, enabling Beijing to invest significantly in its military sector. Thus, while China and India are often grouped together as 'emerging' countries, China is well on the way to establishing itself as the principal global competitor of the US, while India, for all its recent economic achievements, lags well behind.

India's relationship with China has been a tense once since the mid-1950s, reaching its nadir with their border war of 1962, in which India suffered a humiliating defeat. The Sino-Indian border disputes continue to be a thorn in the side of bilateral relations. And mutual needling by the two capitals abounds (although it mostly does not involve Pakistan). The matter of Tibet looms over the bilateral relationship. After a tense decade in Lhasa following China's takeover in 1950, India gave asylum to the fleeing Dalai Lama in 1959, since when the Tibetan refugee population in India has grown steadily. Tibet is a hot-button issue for China, a nation at least as worried about territorial integrity as India. Beijing watches the Dalai Lama's activities in India keenly—and its anxieties about a seemingly powerless Dalai Lama living there may not be as irrational as they seem, in the light of history. In 1910 the 13th Dalai Lama, the immediate predecessor of the current incumbent, fled a Chinese Qing dynasty invasion of Tibet, establishing residence in India. Three years later, he reclaimed his throne and authority in Tibet triumphantly, the distant Qing regime having collapsed. India and China, while cooperating in a variety of multilateral processes ranging from trade negotiations to discussions on climate change, are increasingly competitors in a global race for wealth, energy and influence as emerging (or, in China's case, now emerged) powers.

Whether in commodity-rich Africa or the oil and gas fields of Central Asia, India and China are increasingly rubbing up against each other. To complicate matters, both nations espouse parallel nationalistic mythologies of civilizational greatness that breed a sense of entitlement to Great Power status and a tendency to be irritated by the pretensions of others. Indian analysts fear a Chinese strategy of encirclement in Asia. This refers to China's numerous investments in building up port facilities in the Indian Ocean, seen by some strategists as a 'string of pearls' strategy to constrain India's freedom of manoeuvre. China's booming exports and hunger for international markets have also led it to develop substantial trading relationships with India's neighbours.

China's penetration of India's neighbourhood presents a finely calibrated challenge to Indian foreign policy, seen by some as deriving from the following calculus: 'Restricting India to the Asian subcontinent remains Chinese policy. The tactics are simple: keep borders with India tranquil but do not solve the [border] dispute, trade with India but arm Pakistan and wean away Nepal, Bangladesh, and Myanmar.'

Bilateral issues: Pakistan

The last 60 years have witnessed two major wars (in 1965 and 1971) between India and Pakistan, and two major acts of aggression by Pakistan (in 1948 over Kashmir and 1999 in Kargil), in addition to numerous smallscale incidents across their borders. During the Cold War, Pakistan was the ally of choice for both the United States and China in South Asia, while India inclined towards, and eventually allied itself with, the Soviet Union. Pakistan received billions of dollars' worth of military aid and equipment over the years from its major patrons, much of which was employed in conflicts with India and to sponsor insurgency in Indian-occupied Kashmir. Pakistan's alliance with China, which has endured since the 1950s, is a much greater source of worry to India than Pakistan's erratic friendship of convenience with the US, particularly in respect of China's transfer of nuclear weapons technology and missile systems to Pakistan.

In recent years both China and the US have established a more balanced approach to the Indo-Pakistani rivalry, notably at the time of the Kargil war of 1999. Pakistan's nuclear tests of 1998, following those of India in the same year and establishing at least notional nuclear parity, promoted strategic stability of sorts in the volatile relationship. But peace initiatives involving Indian prime ministers Vajpayee (1998–2004) and Singh (since 2004) and their Pakistani counterparts have failed to yield meaningful results. The deadly terrorist attacks in Mumbai in November 2008 created fresh challenges in Indo-Pakistani relations.

However, international pressure eventually forced Islamabad to acknowledge Pakistani connections with the perpetrators, and after a long freeze bilateral high-level contacts resumed, albeit amid much mutual distrust, in 2009. Prime Minister Singh has been roundly criticised by many at home for his handling of the Mumbai attacks and his post-Mumbai overtures towards Pakistan. However, others have praised the resumption of dialogue with Pakistan. Siddharth Varadarajan suggested: 'Over time, India has realised the best way to deal with the threat of terror is by strengthening its internal capabilities while utilising engagement as a lever for influencing Pakistan's behaviour over the long run.' C. Raja Mohan, while supporting Dr Singh's overtures, nevertheless worries about Pakistan as a reliable interlocutor: 'Put simply, is Pakistan a country or a grievance? States negotiate with others on the basis of an enlightened self-interest and are open to give and take. But revanchists consumed by real and imagined grievances find it hard to split the difference in a negotiation.' Further significant terrorist attacks credibly linked to Pakistan would probably force targeted retaliation, and could produce wider escalation if not carefully managed, including by Washington and Beijing.

Bilateral Issues: Sri Lanka, Bangladesh, Nepal

India's relationships with other nations in its region are far from settled. India's hegemonic status—or at least its perceived aspiration to this status—creates threat perceptions among its smaller neighbours. They see India's varying military (and other) interventions with and in neighbouring countries in terms of 'the outward projection and demonstration of military might'. In the case of the Sri Lankan conflict, India's justifications for military intervention during the 1980s were based on the security imperatives associated with the influx of Tamil refugees, the purported risk to commerce, and the danger of external Great Powers involving themselves in the conflict; but India's peacekeeping action proved counterproductive, alienating the Tamil community, the LTTE and the Sri Lankan government. Similarly, India's action in 1971 in East Pakistan to relieve West Pakistan's military oppression, while justified in humanitarian terms and on the basis of massive refugee flows to India, was widely viewed internationally and in the region as primarily an attempt to dismember an archrival.

Moreover, contrary to India's expectations, the assistance it rendered to Bangladesh did not win it an ally but rather produced a neighbour that has often proved prickly and resentful. While some in India saw the hand of Maoists in Nepal behind the early success of India's own Naxalite movement, any such claim today is far-fetched. However high-handed India's past approach to Nepal has been, and however hostile Maoists in Nepal may have been towards India, the Naxalite movement in India is homegrown and driven by local factors.

Bilateral Issues: Afghanistan

Aside from smaller nations such as Bhutan and the Maldives, perhaps the one country in the region where India's involvement has not played against it to date is Afghanistan. Indians tend to see Delhi's Afghan policy as altruistic. But this assessment glosses over a simple calculus—the need to prevent Kabul from tilting excessively towards Pakistan and allowing itself to be subsumed by Islamabad into its security space. Delhi worries that when the US-led NATO forces begin to pull out, as the Netherlands and Canada have pledged to do in 2010 and 2011 respectively, Kabul could submit to the combined influence of Pakistan (supported by China) and the Taleban, leaving India as the loser in a geostrategic tug-of-war. As of mid-2010 Delhi's worries are not ill-founded: desperate for an exit strategy of its own, Washington appears to be encouraging a negotiated solution to the conflict that could only strengthen Pakistan's hand locally. India is rumoured to have opened up channels of its own with the Taleban, despite maintaining that there is no distinction between 'good' and 'bad' Taleban.

A western withdrawal from Afghanistan would leave numerous Indian assets there highly vulnerable. Even under present circumstances, with NATO troops thick on the ground, the Indian embassy in Kabul was attacked twice in 15 months in 2008–2009. Delhi's remaining option if NATO and President Karzai compromise with the Taleban, that of seeking (perhaps with Moscow, conceivably also with Tehran) to revive the Afghani Northern Alliance, would doubtless prove a disappointing and expensive consolation prize.

INDIAN INTELLIGENCE: THE FIDDLING HAS TO STOP...

The evolution of the Indian intelligence community since 1947 has been on the basis of periodic reviews of our enquiries into perceived intelligence failures. After the Sino-Indian war of 1962, a review of the performance of the IB led to the creation of the Directorate-General of Security (DGS). After the Indo-Pakistan war of 1965 and the Mizo revolt of 1966, a review of the performance of the IB led to the decision to divest the IB of the responsibility for the collection of external intelligence and to create the Research & Analysis Wing (R&AW) by bifurcating the IB for this purpose. The DGS, which was previously under the charge of the Director, Intelligence Bureau (DIB), was transferred to the charge of Secretary (R), as the head of the R&AW is known.

A crisis-driven review is retrospective in nature. It looks into the past—what went wrong, why, and how can its recurrence be prevented? A need-driven review is prospective in nature. A review of the performance of the intelligence community before and during the 1999 Kargil conflict by a Special Task Force, headed by Shri G.C.Saxena, former head of the R&AW, led to the creation of the Defence Intelligence Agency as a nodal point for the analysis of all military intelligence, whether collected by the civilian or military intelligence agencies. The idea was that it would work under the supervision of the proposed Chief of the Defence Staff. Since the re-commendation by another Task Force for the creation of this post has not yet been implemented, one understands that the DIA now functions under the Chief of the Integrated Defence Staff.

The review by the Task Force headed by Shri Saxena also led to the creation of the National Technical Research Organisation (NTRO), to focus on the collection of technical intelligence (TECHINT). The Task Force was of the view that the NTRO should handle all future investments in manpower and equipment and future collection efforts and that the existing capabilities of the IB, the R&AW, the DGS and the military intelligence agencies should not be affected, since their existing capabilities played an important role in counter-terrorism. The Task Force was also of the view that the new agency should focus on cyber intelligence and cyber counter-intelligence for which at that time (in 2000), there was no significant capability in the existing intelligence agencies.

One understands that this recommendation was modified during implementation. Instead of letting the R&AW and the DGS maintain their existing capabilities, there was a bifurcation of these capabilities in order to transfer some of them to the NTRO. Instead of undertaking a crash programme for the development of a capability for cyber intelligence and cyber counter-intelligence, it started performing some of the tasks, which were already being performed by the R&AW and the DGS. The obvious result: an emaciated DGS and a weakening of our capabilities for the collection of TECHINT regarding China and terrorism. Instead of creating capabilities, which did not exist before 2000, there was a highly disputed partition of the existing intelligence assets.

In the past, the highest priority was to the collection of intelligence about State actors, particularly about State adversaries. Now, enhanced priority is given to the collection of intelligence about non-State adversaries such as terrorist organizations.

These were crisis-driven reviews undertaken after perceived intelligence failures in order to identify deficiencies and act to remove them. Since 1947, India has never had a need-driven review of our intelligence assets and capabilities. A crisis-driven review is retrospective in nature. It looks into the past—what went wrong, why, and how can its recurrence be prevented? A need-driven review is prospective in nature. It looks into the likely needs of the future and creates assets and capabilities to be able to meet those needs as and when they arise.

In other countries such as the US, one has crisis-driven reviews as well as need-driven reviews. A need-driven review is undertaken every time a new President or Prime Minister takes office. Unless one has a clear idea of the likely future intelligence needs in the short, medium and long-terms, one cannot build up human and other resources, which would be in a position to meet those needs. It is high time we have a need-based review of our intelligence assets and capabilities and make such reviews a regular feature whenever a new Prime Minister takes over. Reviews of performance and capabilities should not wait for disasters and crises before they are undertaken.

Intelligence priorities have undergone considerable changes during the last decade. In the past, the highest priority was to the collection of intelligence about State actors, particularly about State adversaries. Now, enhanced priority is given to the collection of intelligence about non-State adversaries such as terrorist organizations, trans-national crime mafias, narcotics smugglers, money-launderers etc. Intelligence agencies all over the world have been facing difficulty in upgrading their capabilities for the collection of intelligence about non-State adversaries.

The ability to collect intelligence—whether about a State or a non-State adversary—depends on one's ability to penetrate. It is easier to penetrate a State than a non-State actor. The conventional tradecraft and techniques of intelligence collection, which served us well for penetrating a State actor, are not adequate for the penetration of a non-State actor. The state of our intelligence agencies and the way they have evolved over the years have not paid attention to the requirements of this transition. As the non-State actors become more and more unconventional in their reflexes and responses, the intelligence agencies responsible for monitoring and countering them cannot continue to be conventional in their reflexes and responses.

The IB has evolved into a hotch-potch agency handling collection of intelligence relating to law and order and internal security, performance of physical security and immigration control tasks, counter-intelligence and networking with the police and intelligence set-ups of different States. We have to set up a new agency focusing on the collection of intelligence about non-State actors through human and technical penetration.

The R&AW too has evolved into a hotch-potch agency handling collection of external intelligence relating to State as well as non-State adversaries and networking with foreign intelligence agencies. At a time when terrorism has become global in dimension and reach, the R&AW's counter-terrorism capabilities are hardly global. At a time when the global terrorists are fast mastering the use of the Internet, mobile telephones and other scientific gadgets, the R&AW is yet to acquire a similar mastery of net-centric counter-terrorism and the use of advances in science and technology in counter-terrorism.

The dangers of conventional wars with State adversaries have not disappeared. The Indian State is better prepared and better endowed today than it was in the past to counter State adversaries, but its ability to counter non-State adversaries and their unconventional wars is inadequate as seen from the spread of ideological terrorism across the tribal belt in Central India and the unextinguished prairie fire of jihadi terrorism across India as a whole. We have had successes in our fight against pan-Islamic jihadi terrorism with trans-national linkages, but the successes have not yet been significant enough to dent their strength and motivation.

The threats to our internal security from non-State actors will keep us preoccupied in the short and medium terms. These threats have acquired new dimensions in the form of threats to maritime trade and coastal establishments, energy security and critical infrastructure and terrorism involving the likely use of weapons of mass destruction material. If the intelligence agencies have to play their due role in effectively preventing these threats from materializing, they have to develop new tradecrafts and new techniques for the penetration of non-State actors through human and technical moles for the collection of intelligence. This is a specialized and full-time task which neither the IB nor the R&AW, as they are constituted today, would be able to perform adequately.

We have to set up a new agency focusing on the collection of intelligence about non-State actors through human and technical penetration. It should have the powers to operate everywhere–inside India or in the neighbouring countries or elsewhere–from where threats to our internal security from non-State actors could arise. It has to have a mix of civilian and military experts, and scientific and technical personnel. Since collection of cyber intelligence to facilitate net-centric counter-terrorism would be one of its essential tasks, it should also tap the private IT sector for assistance and co-operation.

So long as our disputes and differences with Pakistan and China remain, we have to maintain a strong intelligence capability–human as well as technical–with regard to likely threats from them. How should be maintain and further develop the existing capabilities with regard to State adversaries, while creating new capabilities with regard to non-State actors? That should be the question before our national security managers. The R&AW and the military intelligence Directorates-General would continue to be the driving force for this purpose. The time has come to have a second look at the present policy of the R&AW claiming a monopoly in the field of external intelligence and discouraging any enhanced role for the military-intelligence Directorates-General in this regard. The days of the intelligence Empire have to go. The intelligence empire has to be replaced by the intelligence community working jointly in the national interest.

Our capability with regard to Pakistan is good, but not good enough as one saw in 1999. Our capability with regard to China is better than it was in 1962, but is not as good as China's capability with regard to India. In promoting a policy of renewed friendship and détente with India, China has not downsized the India-centric capabilities, which it had built up in the days of its confrontation with India. On the contrary, it has continued to strengthen them. India, on the other hand, has allowed the good vibrations with regard to the improving relations with China to induce once again a feeling of complacency and somnolence. Nothing illustrates this more dramatically than the way we have allowed, since 2000, a gradual attrition of the China-dedicated capabilities of the DGS. Counter-intelligence continues to be a weak point in our intelligence set-up. The regularity with which penetrations take place in sensitive departments and intelligence agencies is a disturbing testimony to this. A review and revamping of our counter-intelligence capabilities is an urgent need of the hour. In India, there is hardly any understanding outside the intelligence community of the way the intelligence agencies ought to function and the way they actually function. The intelligence agencies prefer it that way.

Concepts regarding intelligence management have been changing rapidly across the world just as concepts regarding national security management, defence management, economic management and business management have been changing. These concepts relate to factors such as open vs secret intelligence, operations vs analysis, secrecy in operational matters vs transparency in administrative matters, accountability to the parliament and the public vs safeguarding the needs of operational secrecy.

Unfortunately, the winds of change sweeping across the intelligence communities of other countries have left us untouched so far. Indian intelligence agencies continue to lead the life of a frog in the well. Many questions, which should have been posed years ago, still remain to be posed: Should it be made clear to the intelligence agencies and their officers that their performance would be judged by the quantum and value of the secret intelligence provided by them and that they need not report open information? Should the annual audit reports of the accounts of the intelligence agencies by the officers of the Comptroller and Auditor-General of India with their objections and actions taken thereon be made available to the Estimates and Public Accounts Committees of the Parliament? Should there be a dedicated intelligence oversight committee of the parliament to look into aspects such as the quality of the human resources in our intelligence community, the methods of their recruitment and training, promotion policies, the value of the produce from the consumers' point of view and its cost effectiveness? How can we meet the need for a constant weeding-out of unsuitable officers ? We should show the courage and readiness to pose these questions and find answers suited to our needs instead of aping the rest of the world.

In India, there is hardly any understanding outside the intelligence community of the way the intelligence agencies ought to function and the way they actually function. The intelligence agencies prefer it that way. The agencies try to create an impression as if intelligence is a highly esoteric profession, which non-professionals would not be able to understand. They should, therefore, keep out of it. This attitude has to change.

What our policy-makers have been doing till now is not revamping our intelligence capabilities, but fiddling with them. The fiddling has to stop and genuine revamping has to start.

SYNOPSIS OF RESEARCH AND ANALYSIS WING

The Research and Analysis Wing (R&AW) is India's primary external intelligence agency. It was formed in September 1968, after it became apparent that the newly independent Republic of India lacked a credible external intelligence gathering agency after after the Indo-China War of 1962 and the Indo-Pakistani War of 1965. Its primary function is the collection of external intelligence, counter-terrorism, sabotage, counter-sabotage and covert external operations; in addition, it is responsible for obtaining and analysing information about foreign governments, corporations and individuals, in order to assess and advise Indian foreign policymakers. Until the creation of RAW, the Intelligence Bureau [IB] handled both internal and external intelligence.

Formation & History

Following an intelligence failure during the 1965 Sino-Indian Border War, then Prime Minister Jawaharlal Nehru order a dedicated foreign intelligence agency to be established, which became the Research and Analysis Wing. Prior to its inception, intelligence collection was primarily the responsibility of the Intelligence Bureau, an incorporated vestige of the Colonial Raj. In 1933, sensing the political turmoil which eventually led to the Second World War, the Intelligence Bureau's responsibilities were increased to include the collection of border intelligence along Unified India. In 1947, after independence, Sanjeevi Pillaii took over as the first Indian Director of the IB. Having been depleted of trained manpower by the exit of the British, Pillaii attempted to run the bureau on MI5 lines. Following the Indo-Pakistani War of 1965, in which the Army was alerted to cross-border infiltration by civilian intelligence, the Indian Chief of Army Staff General Jayantha Nath Chaudhury called for a more cohesive intelligence-gathering.

Around the end of 1966, the concept of a separate foreign intelligence agency began to assume concrete shape. In 1968, after Indira Gandhi had taken over, it was decided that a full-fledged second security service was required. R. N. Kao, then deputy director of the Intelligence Bureau, submitted a blueprint for the new agency and was appointed as the Chief of India's first foreign intelligence agency. The R&AW was given the responsibility of strategic external intelligence, human as also technical, as well as concurrent responsibility together with the Directorate-General of Military Intelligence for tactical trans-border military intelligence up to a certain depth across the LOC and the international border.

The RAW was started as a wing of the main Intelligence Bureau with roughly 250 employees and an annual budget of Rs 2 crore (approximately $450,000) four decades ago. In the early seventies, its annual budget had risen to Rs. 30 crores while its personnel numbered several thousand. The Joint Intelligence Committee (JIC), under the Cabinet Secretariat, is responsible for co-ordinating and analysing intelligence activities between the RAW, the Intelligence Bureau and the Defense Intelligence Agency (DIA). In practice, however, the effectiveness of the JIC has been varied. With the establishment of the National Security Council in 1999, the role of the JIC has been merged with the NSC. The RAW's legal status is unusual, in that it is not an "Agency", but a "Wing" of the Cabinet Secretariat. Hence, R&AW is not answerable to the Parliament of India on any issue, which keeps it out of reach of the *Right to Information Act*.

In 1971, R.N. Kao, director-founder of the RAW, had persuaded the Government to set up the Aviation Research Centre (ARC). The ARC's mandate was aerial reconnaissance and replaced the Indian Air Force's former reconnaissance aircraft and by the mid-70s. R&AW, through the ARC, had high quality aerial pictures of the installations along the Chinese and Pakistani borders. In 2008-09, the Governmen of India was rumoured to have added another intelligence agency dedicated to collection of technical intelligence. The National Technical Facilities Organisation (NTFO), also known as National Technical Research Organisation (NTRO), is believed to be functioning under R&AW, although it remains autonomous to some measure. It is believed to be dealing with technological espionage, and research on imagery and communications using various platforms.

Objectives

The objectives of the R&AW at present are:

- To monitor political and military developments in adjacent countries, including China and Pakistan, which have a direct or indirect bearing upon India's national security and upon the formulation of its foreign policy; Technical and Technological espionage under the auspices of the National Technical Facilities Organisation (NTFO).

- To make the control and limitation of the supply of military hardware to Pakistan, mostly from European countries, the USA and China, a priority.
- To gather intelligence on leadership, capabilities and organization of various insurgency groups operating in adjacent states that pose a national security or integrity threat, and to thwart these using covert operations, assassinations, sabotage, indirect political coercion and exo-agent and interagent collusion where possible.
- To further geopolitical goals, encourage a strategic balance and evince a deterrence of external collusion with domestic insurgency groups by establishing working relationships with secessionist agencies abroad.
- To provide security for India's nuclear program.

Organization

The structure of the RAW is a matter of speculation, but brief overviews of the same are present in the public domain. Attached to the HQ of RAW at Lodhi Road, New Delhi are different regional headquarters, which have direct links to overseas stations and are headed by a controlling officer who keeps records of different projects assigned to field officers who are posted abroad. Intelligence is usually collected from a variety of sources by field officers and deputy field officers; it is either pre-processed (vetted) by a senior field officer or by a desk officer. The desk officer then passes the information to the Joint Secretary and then on to the Additional Secretary and from there it is disseminated to the concerned end user. The Director RAW is a member of the JIC Steering Committee and is authorized to brief the Prime Minister should the need arise.

The chief of the RAW is designated Secretary (Research) in the Cabinet Secretariat, which is part of the Prime Minister's Office (PMO). Most of the position's occupants have been experts on either Pakistan or China. The head of the Research & Analysis Wing (RAW), the external intelligence agency, enjoys greater autonomy of functioning than their counterparts in the UK and US and has the same privileged direct access to the Prime Minister as their UK counterparts. The control of the Cabinet Secretary over the RAW is limited to administrative and financial matters, with very little say in operational and policy matters. They also have the benefit of training in either US or the UK, and more recently in Israel. The Secretary (R) reports on an administrative basis to the Cabinet Secretary, who reports to the Prime Minister (PM). However, on a daily basis the Secretary (R) reports to the National Security Advisor.

An Additional Director is responsible for the Office of Special Operations and intelligence collected from different countries processed by large number of Joint Secretaries. Reporting to the Secretary (R) are: Two Special Secretaries and one Special Director of the ARC, the Aviation Research Centre; Four Additional Secretaries, responsible for different geographical regions; A large number (above 40) Joint Secretaries, who are the functional heads of various desks. Another important branch under the operational control of the RAW is the Directorate General of Security (DGS). This agency has oversight over organizations like the Special Frontier Force (SFF), the Special Services Bureau (SSB) &c. Liaison with the military is maintained through the Military Intelligence Advisory Group and the Military Advisor to the Director RAW.

Recruitment

Initially, the R&AW relied primarily on trained intelligence officers who were recruited directly. These belonged to the external wing of the Intelligence Bureau. In times of great expansion, many candidates were taken from the military, police and other services. Later, the agency began directly recruiting graduates from universities. Today, R&AW has its own service cadre, the Research and Analysis Service (RAS) to absorb talent. Recruitment is mostly by deputation from the Armed Forces or Civil Service Officers. The Civil and Defense Service Officers permanently resign their cadre and join the Research and Analysis Service (RAS). However, according to recent reports, officers can return to their parent cadre after serving a specific period in the agency if they wish to. Some officers of the RAW are members of a specialized service, the Research and Analysis Service (RAS), but several officers also serve on deputation from other services. The RAW has sub-organizations like the Aviation Research Center (ARC), the Radio Research Center (RRC) or the Electronics and Technical Service (ETS), which have considerable capacity for technical intelligence gathering.

Operations

Numerous missions were assigned to RAW upon its creation. These included monitoring political and military developments in neighboring countries that affects Indian national security. Consequently, considerable attention is paid by RAW to Pakistan and China, countries that are traditional rivals of India. RAW has evolved from its origins as a part of the Intelligence Bureau to develop into India's predominant intelligence organization.

Pakistan has 'accused' the Research and Analysis Wing of sponsoring sabotage in Punjab, where RAW is alleged to have supported the Seraiki movement, providing financial support to promote its activities in Pakistan and organizing an International Seraiki Conference in Delhi in November-December 1993. RAW has an extensive network of agents and anti-government elements within Pakistan, including dissident elements from various sectarian and ethnic groups of Sindh and Punjab. Published reports in Pakistan allege that as many as 35,000 RAW agents entered Pakistan between 1983-93, with 12,000 working in Sindh, 10,000 in Punjab, 8,000 in North West Frontier Province and 5000 in Balochistan. The RAW also provided training and arms to the Bangladeshi freedom fighters known as the 'Mukti Bahini' in the Indo-Pak War of 1971. The RAW's aid was instrumental in the creation and liberation of Bangladesh in 1971.

During the course of its investigation the Jain Commission received testimony on the official Indian support to the various Sri Lankan Tamil armed groups in Tamil Nadu. From 1981, RAW and the Intelligence Bureau established a network of as many as 30 training bases for these groups in India. Centers were also established at the high-security military installation of Chakrata, near Dehra Dun, and in the Ramakrishna Puram area of New Delhi. This clandestine support to the Liberation Tigers of Tamil Eelam (LTTE), some of whom were on the payroll of RAW, was later suspended.

Starting in late 1986 the Research and Analysis Wing focused surveillance on the LTTE which was expanding ties with Tamil Nadu separatist groups. Rajiv Gandhi sought to establish good relations with the LTTE, even after the Indian Peace Keeping Force [IPKF] experience in Sri Lanka. But the Indian intelligence community failed to accurately assess the character of the LTTE and its orientation towards India and its political leaders. The LTTE assassination of Rajiv Gandhi was apparently motivated by fears of a possible re-induction of the Indian Peace Keeping Force (IPKF) in Sri Lanka and a crackdown on the LTTE network in Tamil Nadu. The RAW was heavily criticized in 1999, following the Pakistani incursions at Kargil. Critics accused RAW of failing to provide intelligence that could have prevented the ensuing ten-week conflict that brought India and Pakistan to the brink of full-scale war. While the army has been critical of the lack of information they received, RAW has pointed the finger at the politicians, claiming they had provided all the necessary information. Most Indian officials believe that in order to prevent another such occurrence, communication needs to be increased between the intelligence agencies, which would require structural reform.

Amalgamation of Sikkim: Bordered by Tibet, Nepal, Bhutan and West Bengal in the Eastern Himalayas, Sikkim was ruled by a Maharaja. The Indian Government had recognized the title of Chogyal (Dharma Raja) for the Maharaja of Sikkim. In 1972, the RAW was authorized to install a pro-Indian democratic government there, concomitant of which, in less than three years, Sikkim became the 22nd State of the Indian Union, on April 26, 1975.

Operation Kaktus: In November 1988, the People's Liberation Organisation of Tamil Eelam (PLOTE), composed of about 200 Tamil secessionist rebels, invaded Maldives. At the request of the president of Maldives, Maumoon Abdul, the Indian Armed Forces, with assistance from R&AW, launched a military campaign to throw the mercenaries out of Maldives. On the night of November 3, 1988, the Indian Air Force airlifted the 6th parachute battalion of the Parachute Regiment from Agra and flew them over 2,000 km to Maldives. The Indian paratroopers landed at Hulule and restored the Government rule at Malýÿ within hours. The operation, labelled Operation Kakus, also involved the Indian Navy. Swift operation by the military and precise intelligence by RAW quelled the insurgency.

Operation 'Chanakya': This was the R&AW operation in the Kashmir region to infiltrate various ISI-backed Kashmiri separatist groups and restore peace in the Kashmir valley. R&AW operatives infiltrated the area, collected military intelligence, and provided evidence about ISI's involvement in training and funding Kashmiri separatist groups. The R&AW was successful at: i) unearthing the links between the ISI and the separatist groups; and ii) in infiltrating and neutralizing the militancy in the Kashmir valley. The RAW is also credited for creating a split in the Hizb-ul-Mujahideen. Operation 'Chanakya' also marked the creation of pro-Indian groups in Kashmir like the Ikhwan-ul-Muslimeen, Muslim Mujahideen etc. These counter-insurgencies consist of ex-militants and relatives of those slain in the conflict. Ikhwan-ul-Muslimeen leader Kokka Parrey was later himself assassinated by separatists.

The Northern Alliance in Afghanistan: After the rise of Pakistan and American-backed Taliban in Afghanistan during the Soviet war, India decided to side with the Northern Alliance and the Soviet Union. By 1996, the R&AW had built a military hospital at the Farkhor Air Base and used the airport to repair and operate the Northern Alliance's aerial support. The relationship was further cemented in the 2001 Afgan war. India supplied the Northern Alliance high altitude warfare equipment worth around $810 million, and the R&AW was also able to determine the extent of the Kunduz airlift.

Operation Leech: Surrounded by the Arakans and dense forest, Burma/Myanmar had always been a worrisome point for Indian intelligence. As the major player in the area, India sought to promote democracy and install friendly puppet governments in the region. To these ends, it is alleged that the RAW cultivated Burmese rebel groups and pro-democracy coalitions, in particular the Kachin Independence Army (KIA). India allowed the KIA to carry limited trade in jade and precious stones using Indian territory as a conduit and later supplied them weapons. It is further alleged that the KIA chief Maran Brang Seng met RAW officials in Delhi twice. However, after it became apparent that the KIA became the main source of training and weapons for northeastern rebel groups, the RAW initiated a campaing of assassination of KIA leaders that included six top leaders, including the military wing chief of National Unity Party of the Arakans (NUPA), Khaing Raza, and the arrest and termination of several other Arakanese guerillas.

Special Operations in Punjab: In the mid 1980's, the R&AW set up two covert groups, Counterintelligence Team-X(CIT-X) and Counterintelligence Team-J(CIT-J), the first directed at Pakistan and the second at Khalistani groups. Rabinder Singh, an R&AW double agent who defected to the United States in 2004, helped run CIT-J in its early years. Both these covert groups used the services of cross-border traffickers to ferry weapons and funds across the border, much as their ISI counterparts were doing. According to former R&AW official and noted security analyst B. Raman, the Indian counter-campaign yielded results. "The role of our cover action capability in putting an end to the ISI's interference in Punjab", he wrote in 2002, "by making such interference prohibitively costly is little known and understood." The 'War on Terror': Although RAW's contribution to the War on Terror is highly classified, the organization gained some attention in the Western media after claims that it was assisting the United States by providing intelligence on Al-Qaeda and Taliban targets for the war on terrorism in Afghanistan. Maps and photographs of terrorist training camps in Afghanistan and Pakistan, along with other evidence implicating Osama bin Laden in terrorist attacks, were given to US intelligence officials. R&AW's role in the War on Terror may increase as US intelligence has indicated that it sees R&AW as a more reliable ally than Pakistani intelligence. It has further come to light that a timely tip-off by R&AW helped foil a third assassination plot against Pakistan's former President, General Pervez Musharraf.

Controversies

The main controversies which have plagued the R&AW in recent years are over bureaucratization of the system, favoritism in promotions, ego clashes and inter-departmental rivalry. R&AW also suffers from ethnic and representative imbalances in the officer level. In 2006, Indian magazine Outlook reported that although India has a Muslim minority numbering around 160 million, not a single high level muslim officer existed in R&AW. Noted security analyst and former Additional Secretary B.Raman has criticised the agency for its asymmetric growth and has sought to summarize its abilities in the following: "while being strong in its capability for covert action it is weak in its capability for intelligence collection, analysis and assessment. Strong in low and medium-grade intelligence, relatively weak in high-grade intelligence. Strong in technical intelligence, weak in human intelligence. Strong in collation, weak in analysis. Strong in investigation, weak in prevention. Strong in crisis management, weak in crisis prevention."

In September 2007, R&AW was involved in a controversy due to a high profile Central Bureau of Investigation Task Force raid at the residence of Major General (retired) V K Singh, a retired Joint Secretary of R&AW who has recently written a book on R&AW where it was alleged that political interference and corruption in the intelligence agency has made it vulnerable to defections. A case under the Official Secrets Act has also been filed against V K Singh. Another controversy erupted for the agency when a senior technical officer was arrested by the CBI on graft charges, on February 4, 2009. The scientist, a Director level employee, worked in the division that granted export licenses to companies dealing in sensitive items, including defence-related equipment. He was accused of demanding and accepting a bribe of Rs.1 lakh from a Chennai based manufacturer for obtaining an export license.

In June 2004, the spy scandal involving former Joint Secretary and head of R&AW's South East Asia department Rabinder Singh's defection to the United States seriously tarnished the image of the organization as an effective agency. The RAW had already become suspicious about his movements and he was put under physical and telephone surveillance following the mistrust. He was confronted by Counter Intelligence officials on 19 April 2004, Despite all precautions, Rabinder Singh managed to defect with 'sensitive files' he had allegedly removed from R&AW's headquarters in south New Delhi. The embarrassing fiasco and major national security failure was attributed to weak surveillance, shoddy investigation and lack of coordination between the Counter-Intelligence and Security (CIS), the IB and the R&AW. Recently in an affidavit submitted to the court, R&AW deposed that Singh has been traced to and put under surveillance in New Jersey.

In 2007, a spy scandal involving a Bangladeshi DGFI agent and known by the name of Diwan Chand Mallik was brought to light when he was known to have known posessed some important documents damaging to national security. A case of forgery was filed at the Lodhi Colony police station against the individual on the basis of a complaint by a senior R&AW official, however he was failed to be taken into custody.

3

Intelligence for Cyberspace Security Challenges

Although many of the intelligence methodologies and principles remain the same, new ways of thinking appropriate to the cyber-domain are essential. The lack of borders in cyber-space is a critical difference from the more familiar domains of intelligence. Indeed, geography and political borders often aided traditional military intelligence analysis-it is a simple thing to develop threat scenarios if the potential enemy can only use certain terrain or sea lines of communication and then, only at certain times of the year-while simple factors of physics such as time and distance also provided opportunities for warning. Within the Internet, however, these limiting factors are absent, (although other limiting factors, such as geometry of network connectivity, might exist in a form useful to be incorporated into intelligence analysis), contributing to what can appear to be "instantaneous threats".

Assessment of cyber-space threats requires not only a merger of old methodologies and new modes of thinking but also analysts willing and able to approach the art of threat assessment and warning from new perspectives. Only with a distinctive blend of the traditional and the new will it be possible to obtain real understanding of threats and vulnerabilities, to differentiate among types of intrusions and to forecast or anticipate specific incidents or clusters of incidents in ways that lengthen warning time. Enhancing the ability to identify perpetrators is also highly desirable: removing the cloak of anonymity would make perpetrators more concerned about the potential costs and risks of their actions and could have an important deterrent effect. In short, there are several fundamental questions at the heart of the intelligence process. They consist of variations on the who, what, when, where, why and how questions that are familiar parts of most research and analysis.

HISTORY OF CYBER SECURITY

The history of successful counterattacks in the world of cyber security is a short one. There are an increasing number of papers and publications which make proposals, but concerns over legal issues as well as technical challenges have kept the list of successes small. In Sept. 1998, the Pentagon is reported to have counterattacked some activists who were doing a Denial of Service attack of the Department of Defense's websites, responding to their requests with an applet which ran on the attackers' machines and forced them to reboot. In 1999, a California ISP Conxion wrote a script which caused DoS packets sent to the World Trade Organization's website to be sent back to the attackers. Of course, such an attack would not have worked if the attackers had used what's known as "IP address spoofing", which would have made the packets appear that they came from a different computer from where they did.

In 2001, several defences were created in response to the Code Red II worm. One, called CRclean, if it received a probe from the worm, would make use of a back door which the worm placed on the infected machine to load a neutralizing agent and halt the spread of the worm. But it would also install itself on that machine.

Another, called CodeGreen, would actually scan the internet for computers with the IIS vulnerability that allowed CodeRed, then download the patch and place it on the machine, and clean up the back doors. It is clear that there are serious legal and ethical issues with both of these worms, even the former, which is still a worm even though it only reacts to attacks. In 2003, the Welchia worm was released onto the Internet. Welchia would remove the Blaster worm and patch the vulnerability that Blaster used to spread. However, Welchia also caused severe network congestion.

In late 2004, Lycos Europe got fed up with spammers and launched a popular campaign called "Make Love Not Spam" which attracted over 100,000 users. Users could install a screen saver on their desktop which would send requests to websites which were known to advertise via spam. This effort was sucessful in causing some of the sites to change locations. (http://www.makelovenotspam.com) Lycos reportedly got around the illegality of DDoS attacks by claiming to only take 95% of the target sites' bandwidth, though, David Dittrich finds this reasoning dubious at best. Lycos ended this campaign in December 2004.

Some companies such as Symbiot Security are currently developing counter attack tools and devices, but there is a lot of skepticism about deployment of devices because of liability concerns.

Cyber security Incident Response

Counter-attacks are part of the overall process of cyber security incident response. This consists of five stages:

1. Intrusion detection.
2. Identifying the attacker.
3. Defending against the attack.
4. Designing and deploying a counter attack.
5. Post-conflict investigation and support.

Intrusion Detection: Intrusion detection first identifies if there is an intrusion or intrusion attempt in the network or machine connected to network. Monitoring can be done on the network or on end-hosts. Firewalls and virus scanners also contribute. There are various techniques, such as anomaly detection, and policy-based approaches. Identifying the Attacker: This very important step towards counter-attack, basically knowing who your enemy is and where is he located. Identifying the attacker can be difficult, since an attacker may use one compromised host to attack another. Also, with today's network architecture it can be quite difficult to locate the real attacker. Packets can be sent with spoofed source addresses, and tracing them through multiple hops and different autonomous systems can be a complicated process. Finding out the specific server and location can be critical in determining what the counter attack would be.

Defending against the Attack: Before an attack, software patches are used to fix vulnerabillities. More interesting are defences once an attack against a real vulnerability has happened. Diversions can be set forth to surprise an attacker. Or once the attack has been detected, countermeasures can be put in place to stop further damage.

Also, diversion tactics like Honey Pots can be used to keep the rest of the network safe. The information from these diversions (or information gained during the delays caused by these tactics) can be harnessed to engineer a specific counter attack. Designing and deploying a counter attack: Counterattacks take a surprising variety of forms. Designing a counter attack should take into account the following factors: the method of attack; the support of the network infrastructure (*i.e.* are ISPs performing egress filtering); collateral damage; and costs. Post Counter attack investigation and support: In order to aid the post counter attack investigation a counter attack should have inbuilt mechanism to log its trail and its operation history. Ideally, it will also provide a means of discovering the hacker's techniques and identity. The more risk hackers have of being discovered, the less likely they are to go hacking.

Anti-worms

A worm spreads itself by sending out packets which look for certain responses from computers. It will analyse those responses to deduce if it thinks the replying machine has the vulnerability that it exploits. These packets represent a worm's 'signature.' The machine the worm is targeting can detect the signature of the worm and thus know its mode of propagation. An anti-worm is generated, which exploits the same vulnerabilities as the original worm or uses the back doors opened by the original worm. The antiworm would either fix the attacking host, neutralize the worm, or bring it down gracefully, potentially informing the owner. It may also install itself for further propagation.

In addition to the stated goal, an antiworm adheres to following guidelines to minimize collateral damage:

- It is bug-free and does leave other vulnerabilities that could be exploited further.
- It can be uninstalled gracefully when owner asks for it.
- It makes minimal changes to host that it operates on.
- It should not be able to be used for propagating malicious content.

The countermeasure, or 'Neutralizing Agent' used, can take several forms. For example, it could patch the vulnerability and remove the botnet or worm. Less invasive changes include blocking the port over which the worm sends messages, or using a mutex and rebooting the machine to lock the botnet from being able to execute.

Also, one would have to remove any backdoors left by the worm.

In addition, deployment strategy of the antiworm will determine its effectiveness and collateral damage it may cause.

- *Active Deployment*: The antiworm is itself a worm; it propagates across the network by scanning and seeking exploited vulnerabilities. This is the fastest way to remove the original worm from the network, but this also causes the most collateral damage by affecting the network traffic a lot.
- *Passive Deployment*: The anti-worm waits on a host till another host attacks it, and then the antiworm cures only the attacking host. Collateral damage is bare minimum, but the anti-worm is left behind on the new host.
- *Controlled Deployment*: The anti-worm propagation is control via some statistic of number of infected/vulnerable host to number host it cured. This can be very effective and efficient.

- *IDS base Deployment*: The anti-worm uses the intrusion detection sensors which monitor traffic and may deploy an anti-worm against an attacker. As with passive deployment, collateral damage is limited to computers actively launching attacks, but this is less invasive because it does not leave a worm, it just neutralizes the machine.

Spam

Spam is unsolicited e-mail. A virus is a programme which, when executed, installs malware such as root-kits, key-stroke loggers, etc. These programmes are then used to send sensitive information to the attacker without the user's consent.

Both spam and viruses spread through e-mail and require human interaction to activate them.

Email servers as well as the hosts can detect spam with the help of spam detectors like Symantec's TurnTide. Once the spam is identified one counter attack is achieved by automatic flooding of the Sender Server with bounced e-mails and mail notification to server's administrator. (Even if sender addresses are spoofed, one may be able to identify the last mail server that forwarded a message.)

Botnet

An attacker establishes a botnet by first spreading a virus or worm that takes over the vulnerable hosts. Each worm or virus then calls Home to tell that it has successfully captured the Host. It also establishes a command channel such that the Attacker through the home can control the host. Botnets can be used for DDOS attacks, phishing etc.

Counter Attack

- Counter attack involves identifying the attacker by monitoring the compromised Host and intercepting its communication to the Home machine. The Home machine is probably the attacker's base or intermediate node for communication between the host and the attacker base machines. Once that machine is identified, you hack back into that machine bring it down. For hacking back, you can use same techniques as used by the hackers to take control of the attacking machine.
- Taking down the Home machine only removes the attacker for a short duration, the network of compromised hosts still exists. A more effective counter attack would be to takeover or monitor the command channel for communication between the Home and other compromised hosts. If possible, identify other compromised hosts and fix them or take them down as preventive measure.

CAPABILITIES OF CYBER INTELLIGENCE

Individual cyber intelligence capabilities have been applied for decades, some since the earliest days of IT system design. Beyond the inflection point of a unified, comprehensive approach, there have been significant advancements in the overall discipline. Given the importance of cyber intelligence in today's environment, business executives should join their IT colleagues in understanding how this discipline is evolving. Here's a look at four critical topics:

Cyber Security

Many cyber security efforts were geared to detecting and protecting against intrusions of the perimeter. As threats shifted to inside the trust zone (*e.g.*, employees who inadvertently enable security breaches), new tools and techniques were needed. Identity and access management solutions were siloed systems—with isolated entitlements, activity logging, and controls. Pattern detection of higher-order threats was extremely difficult because these solutions had limited access to the context of external events. Technology solutions were manually operated, which the business perceived as a nuisance and often circumvented. The chief security officer (CSO) or chief information security officer (CISO), if they existed at all, were typically technologists with deep domain knowledge, but without a seat in the boardroom.

Today, cyber security is increasingly framed as a combination of architecture, practices, and processes—with equal focus on internal and external threats. Highly integrated tool sets and investments in cyber analytics have helped connect dots and identify previously undetectable exposures. Automated identity management tools are incorporated into day-to-day tasks, including smart cards, biometrics, fingerprint, and handprint scanners. The CSO role has become commonplace, requiring a mix of technology and leadership skills and gaining a seat at the boardroom table.

Cyber Forensics

In the past, incident investigations would conclude once a root-cause analysis was completed. These self-contained analyses were rarely used to augment existing controls or update policies. At best, a script was created to improve response in case a breach recurred.

Cyber forensics now looks beyond the host to the network layer, determining the source (inside or outside the organization) of the malware. This determination is correlated with other internal and known external threats using cyber analytics, in an attempt to identify future vulnerabilities. Forensics results are part of a closed-loop cycle in cyber intelligence, improving directly affected and associated controls.

Cyber Analytics

In the past, cyber analytics was a reactive approach based on situational awareness and descriptive analysis. It provided an understanding of the value of business analytics, but without the models to apply the patterns.

These days, this discipline is an established tradecraft of analytics, reinforced by the realization that threats and opportunities are often hidden in plain sight. Cyber analytics is predictive, prescriptive, and a part of a closed-loop cycle of continuous refinement based on other cyber intelligence activities.

Cyber Logistics

Supplier security reviews were typically limited to deal signings and cursory annual audits. Notably in manufacturing, companies relied on several ever-changing sub-contractors and small hardware providers, each with its own risk profile, which created potential weaknesses upstream in the supply chain. Personnel checks occurred only during the hiring or contracting process, with clearance processing handled by largely unknown third parties.

Today, cyber logistics includes extensive analysis to identify, assess, and mitigate risks posed by vendors subject to foreign ownership, control or influence, or other significant concerns prior to a purchase or the awarding of a contract. It entails the continuous assessment of suppliers, including organization structures and corporate activity as well as ongoing confirmation of the integrity of goods. Cyber intelligence strategies include provisions for personnel security such as verifying the legitimacy of background investigation agencies, proactive foreign travel risk advisory, and automated reinvestigations of executives and privileged roles.

New Approach to IT Security

Intelligence expert Terry Roberts says cyber intelligence, a new approach to IT security, could make significant gains in the coming year. "The good thing is, this isn't really rocket science," says the chair of the Intelligence and National Security Alliance's Cyber Council.Pilot projects are underway to determine if methods employed by the 17 federal intelligence agencies could be adapted to safeguard non-classified but sensitive information in the private sector. To succeed, Roberts says, the government and private sector must collaborate and share information. "In a year or two, we could actually have the private-public partnership established, with the beginnings of an unclassified cyber-intelligence approach," Roberts says in an interview with Information Security Media Group (select one of the Podcast Options at right to listen).

Roberts edited the alliance's just-issued paper, Cyber Intelligence: Setting the Landscape for an Emerging Discipline, which discusses how the current cyberthreat landscape requires a new way to share intelligence in unclassified cyberspace.

"It's important to understand that when we use the word *intelligence* that we're really talking about knowledge, not just information, and we're not necessarily talking about something that has to be classified," Robert says. "When we're talking about intelligence as an approach for the cyber arena, it's really about pulling together all the information that we know, processing it, analysing it and providing unclassified, situational awareness and situations of warning to both government and industry."

In the interview, Roberts discusses the:

- Difficulties of industry to adapt the highly sophisticated approach the federal intelligence agencies employ to share cyber intelligence. "What we are not doing really is applying those intelligence techniques and tradecraft to the unclassified arena," she says. "Think about it this way: 90 percent of infrastructure in the cyber arena is owned by industry, and 90 percent of the information or data of cyber activity is in the unclassified arena. But we're not focusing on that realm in a comprehensive, consistent manner that we can provide unclassified cyber intelligence to all of industry."
- Multidisciplinary skills that cyber intelligence requires. "In the beginning nuclear age, you brought in people with the technical body of knowledge, then your brought people with a body of knowledge on that particular adversary, the culture, the leadership, and you brought it all together so you would have a 360 view," she says. "We haven't been doing that in the (private-sector) cyber realm.

"Actually, in cyber intelligence, you need analytics types of folks, you need people who understand the network environment, that operational background; you need people with technical background who understand the particulars of an attack vector or a fraud approach or sabotage approach that's being used. And, those folks together, need to be looking at the data, analysing it and coming up with so what, the impact of what they're seeing today and what that means for the future."

NATIONAL CYBER SECURITY POLICY

The NCSP essentially speaks of a framework for the protection of information in cyberspace by eliminating vulnerabilities. Major clauses include greater emphasis on research and development of indigenous security technology, and their effective testing and deployment. The policy also calls for enhanced public and private partnership vis-à-vis technical and operational cooperation, aimed at encouraging organizations to adopt individually tailored IT regulations and infrastructure, in conformity with international best practices. Development of human resources through training programs and other capacity-building measures is another crucial priority. The policy envisions creating a workforce of 500,000 cyber specialists in the next five years. Auxiliary services like the protection of private information in process, transit and storage; the creation of a well-defined legislative framework to deal with criminal investigations and prosecution; and the promotion of individual responsibility in dealing with cyber security also find a mention in the policy.

The policy has also facilitated the creation of a new agency called the National Critical Information Infrastructure Protection Centre (NCIIPC), charged with protecting assets in sensitive sectors such as defence, finance, energy, and telecommunications. The Indian Computer Emergency Response Team (CERT-In), which was previously tasked with security of national assets, now protects cyber assets in non-critical areas, and also acts as the nodal agency for all cyber security emergencies with round-the-clock functionality.

Despite being a positive step towards securing India's cyber assets, the NCSP is far from answering all nuances of the cyber threat, as they exist today.

The most critical factor is the lack of details, along with a feasible nationwide strategy to achieve the objectives set out in the policy. Unlike statutes, policies passed by the Indian legislature are neither binding nor enforceable, but merely provide guidelines for a standard operating procedure. In this regard, the NCSP does not maximize its potential for optimum benefit. The text of the policy is easy to comprehend, as it basically outlines the perceived requirement to amend the existing framework and make it better suited to countering the threat of cyber attacks today. Yet the NCSP fails to comment on any political, economic or legal measure it intends to implement to achieve this objective. The Indian government budgeted just $7.76 million for cyber security in 2013, compared with at least $751 million spent by the U.S. government on its cyberspace programs.

"Indian agencies don't have enough resources. Their budget should be at least 10 times bigger if they have to function properly," says Subimal Bhattacharjee, a cyber security expert and former India head of the U.S. information systems giant General Dynamics.

A crucial point missing entirely from the NCSP is the security concerns in the telecom industry. Today, telecommunications are fully integrated into cyberspace, since the advent of internet protocols on mobile devices, and this has been identified as one of the primary factors for the increase in the number of attacks. Russian cyber security solutions firm Kaspersky Lab placed India second on its 2013 list of those countries must vulnerable to attacks on mobile phones.

For its telecom industry, India incorporates equipment and infrastructure from global telecom companies, primarily Huawei Technologies Co.,Ltd., a leading Chinese telecommunications and networking equipment company, founded by Ren Zhengfei. It should be noted that Ren Zhengfei, an ex-major with the PLA, enjoys extensive ties with the Chinese military and the Communist Party, having been elected a member of the 12th National Congress of the Communist Party of China. For their part, the U.S. and U.K. have severely curbed Huawei's foray into their respective markets.

Another notable point on which the NCSP maintains an ambiguous silence are the deliberations presently underway on setting up a fully fledged Indian Cyber Command, under the aegis of the defence services, to engage in network-centric warfare. Should this actually happen, a question of jurisdiction will arise, one that could easily become a quagmire.

Even though the NCSP was released over a year ago, any benefits are yet to materialize. In the meantime, Indian companies and government organizations continue to defend themselves against unconventional warfare, which they do not understand in its entirety. Still, as the Dell Software Global Security Survey reports, companies in the Asia-Pacific have at least begun to prioritize their IT policies, to be in a better position to counter threats.

CERT-In's recent survey labels the *.in* domain as the most frequently attacked, which is alarming as this address is primarily used by government agencies and a few major private companies. Full statistics of the survey can be found here. Meanwhile, the Indian government seems to have realized the urgency of the need to develop cyber security training. In January 2013, the University Grants Commission directed technical universities and institutions to add Cyber Security and Information Security as subjects for higher studies. Premier institutes like the Institute for Information Security and Indian School of Ethical Hacking now offer these technical courses, as do a few major private universities in India. The key to cyber security in India lies in the effective operationalization of the NCSP. Workshops, seminars and courses aimed at informing the general public about the issue of cyber security, coupled with feasible public-private partnerships will work to offset the threat to India's online assets in the long run.

INDIA'S ICT INFRASTRUCTURE

The growth of IT sector in India has been fuelled by equally impressive growth in telecommunication infrastructure. The world is moving towards converged networks being referred as 'Next Generation Networks (NGN)'. In the coming decade the NGN is likely to replace the legacy networks. This upcoming national information infrastructure would be marriage of IT and telecommunication infrastructure with various regulatory and security challenges that need careful scrutiny.

Regulatory issues concerning regulators around the world:

The deployment of NGN throws up many regulatory challenges. License conditions and regulations need to be revisited with a light touch regulatory approach with participation of all stakeholders to ensure smooth transition.

In case of legacy networks the business model, network and competition were already in place before establishment of formal regulatory framework. NGN permits us a window of opportunity to review regulatory framework by proactive consultation process and spirit of accommodation amongst all stakeholders. Regulators in many developing countries including India (TRAI, 2008) have begun process of firming up broad principles for NGN deployment ahead of actual transition.

Telecom sector in India is on a growth profile, and time is ripe to examine regulatory and licensing approaches for NGN deployment. New competitive networks are just being established and consumer's take-up of IP services and Broadband is at a nascent stage.

The recommendation on the security of NGN by expert committee on NGN vide para 3.4.2.2 (TRAI,2008) states:

"NGN-eCO acknowledged that security is of paramount importance to any network. Therefore, TEC may be asked to work on various aspects of security for the country keeping in view the global trends".

Imperatives for India's response to Cyber Threats

If one looks at the challenges India faces in the backdrop of the task of steering our ICT infrastructure on a sustainable and safe trajectory various factors emerge which suggest a synergetic approach. The ICT infrastructure should support diverse social objectives of empowering our rural masses, E–Governance, E-Commerce and disaster warning/relief. The details of India's initiative to secure her cyber infrastructure as available through open source is in stark contrast to the initiatives taken by the USA in the aftermath of attacks in September 2001. While it is true that each country should initiate measures as suitable for its needs and at a pace that is viable in its context, India with her aspiration to be IT superpower in the coming decade can ill afford to lag behind. Various lead agencies in USA to protect her critical Infrastructure as described in 'The national strategy to secure cyber space' document (DHS, 2008).

The Homeland Security Act of 2002 in USA provides the basis for Department of Homeland Security (DHS) responsibilities in the protection of the Nation's Critical Infrastructure and Key Resources (CI/KR). The act assigns DHS the responsibility to develop a comprehensive national plan for securing CI/KR and for recommending "measures necessary to protect the key resources and critical infrastructure of the United States in coordination with other agencies of the Federal Government and in cooperation with State and local government agencies and authorities, the private sector, and other entities."

USA has National Infrastructure Protection Plan (NIPP) in place under Department of Homeland Security (DHS,2008) with following goal:

"Build a safer, more secure, and more resilient America by enhancing protection of the Nation's Critical Infrastructure and Key Resources (CI/KR) to prevent, deter, neutralize, or mitigate the effects of deliberate efforts by terrorists to destroy, incapacitate, or exploit them; and to strengthen national preparedness, timely response, and rapid recovery in the event of an attack, natural disaster, or other emergency."

The NIPP provides the unifying structure for the integration of existing and future CI/KR protection efforts into a single national program to achieve this goal. The NIPP framework will enable the prioritization of protection initiatives and investments across sectors to ensure that government and private sector resources are applied where they offer the most benefit for mitigating risk by lessening vulnerabilities, deterring threats, and minimizing the consequences of terrorist attacks and other manmade and natural disasters. The NIPP risk management framework recognizes and builds on existing protective programs and initiatives.

Protection includes actions to mitigate the overall risk to CI/KR assets, systems, networks, functions, or their interconnecting links resulting from exposure, injury, destruction, incapacitation, or exploitation. In the context of the NIPP, this includes actions to deter the threat, mitigate vulnerabilities, or minimize consequences associated with a terrorist attack or other incident. Protection can include a wide range of activities, such as hardening facilities, building resiliency and redundancy, incorporating hazard resistance into initial facility design, initiating active or passive countermeasures, installing security systems, promoting workforce surety programs, and implementing cyber security measures, among various others.

The White House issued 'The National Strategy to Secure Cyberspace' in February 2003. The Department of Homeland Security (DHS) established the National Cyber Security Division (NCSD) in June 2003 to serve as a national focal point for addressing cyber security issues and to coordinate implementation of the cyber security strategy in the United States. NCSD's mission is to work collaboratively with public, private, and international entities to secure cyberspace and cyber assets, and to implement the actions and recommendations of 'The National Strategy to Secure Cyberspace'.

According to audit report submitted by Office of Inspector General (OIG) U.S. Department of Homeland Security in June 2007, there are still challenges in securing the cyber space in USA (OIG, 2007). While the National Cyber Security Division has made progress in meeting its mission, according to OIG report it can improve its efforts to secure the nation's cyber infrastructure in following areas:

- Establish priorities to ensure that its mission-critical tasks supporting its programs are completed timely.
- Develop enhanced performance measures that can be used to evaluate the effectiveness in meeting its mission.
- Fully develop its information sharing and communications programs with the private sector.
- Develop and implement enhanced procedures to ensure that all known cyber incidents from across the federal government are being reported.
- Ensure that its support systems comply with all 'Federal Information Security Management Act' requirements, including testing of contingency plans.

In Indian context creation of National Disaster Management Authority (NDMA) under an act of parliament was motivated by similar concerns for mitigating and managing national disasters from natural and manmade causes.

"To build a safer and disaster resilient India by developing a holistic, pro-active, multi-disaster and technology-driven strategy for disaster management through collective efforts of all Government Agencies and Non-Governmental Organizations"

In order to translate this Vision into policy and plans, the NDMA which appears to be nearest to USA's Department of Homeland Security, has adopted a mission-mode approach involving a number of initiatives with the help of various institutions operating at national, state and local levels. The central ministries, states and other stakeholders have been involved in the participatory and consultative process of evolving policies and guidelines.

This Policy framework is also in conformity with the International Strategy for Disaster Reduction, the Rio Declaration, the Millennium Development Goals and the Hyogo Framework 2005-2015. The themes underpinning this policy are:

- Community-based disaster management, including last mile integration of the policy, plans and execution.

- Capacity development in all related areas.
- Consolidation of past initiatives and best practices.
- Cooperation with agencies at national, regional and international levels.
- Compliance and coordination to generate a multi-sectoral synergy.
- From the national vision and aforementioned theme, the objectives guiding the policy formulation have evolved to include:
- Promoting a culture of prevention and preparedness – by centre-staging DM as an overriding priority at all levels and at all times.
- Encouraging mitigation measures based on state-of-the-art technology and environmental sustainability.
- Mainstreaming DM concerns into the development planning process.
- Putting in place a streamlined institutional techno-legal framework in order to create and preserve the integrity of an enabling regulatory environment and a compliance regime.
- Developing contemporary forecasting and early warning systems backed by responsive and fail- safe communications and Information Technology (IT) support.
- Promoting a productive partnership with the Media, NGOs and the Corporate Sector in the areas of awareness generation and capacity development.
- Ensuring efficient response and relief with a caring humane approach towards the vulnerable sections of the society.
- Making reconstruction an opportunity to build back better and construct disaster-resilient structures and habitats.

A quick tour of the NDMA's portal gives a feeling that unless NDMA is unwilling to share its plans with public, a lot needs to be done to achieve same coherence as being practiced by most of the developed world with USA being just an illustrative case. There seems to be no division equivalent to the National Cyber Security Division (NCSD) under DHS in USA. NCSD like organization would formalize our steps towards holistic cyber security.

THE NATURE AND LEVELS OF INTELLIGENCE ANALYSIS

Intelligence analysis requires many of the same analytical methods and techniques, irrespective of domain. From this perspective, intelligence analysis for Internet security is no different from the intelligence task in any other area of national and international security.

The commonality is the concern with those who want to inflict harm and the vulnerabilities they can exploit to do this. Threats can come from many sources: the military activities of hostile nations; inimical economic strategies pursued by adversarial or even allied states; the activities of terrorist groups intent on inflicting harm on society in order to achieve political objectives; transnational criminal organizations pursuing the acquisition of large profits through illegal activities, violence, and corruption; and groups (including any of those just mentioned) and individuals with the ability and desire to distort, disrupt, degrade or destroy information and communications systems.

Whatever their source, threats are inextricably linked to vulnerabilities. Indeed, absolute security could only be achieved if there were no vulnerabilities to be exploited. It is crucial, therefore, not only to identify vulnerabilities but also to understand how hostile groups or individuals might exploit them. Strictly speaking, real security threats only come from those with a combination of hostile intent (*i.e.* a desire to do us harm) and the capacity to inflict harm (*i.e.* exploit vulnerabilities in ways that transform intent into reality).

In the realm of cyber-space, vulnerabilities are inescapable. There are many reasons for this, ranging from the inherent weaknesses in complex systems to specific problems in the creation of software code.

Even if protective security measures were an integral part of information systems rather than being subsequently grafted onto them, problems would remain. Some vulnerabilities stem from the underlying protocols used to communicate on the Internet, which were formulated when the Internet was a relatively small community of trusted systems, with connectivity determined by government contract.

Other vulnerabilities stem from development practices, which may ignore validation of input (or even length checking) and avoid controlling the environment in which programmes execute. Finally, vulnerabilities stem from the rapidly evolving use of software, in which programmes meant for a limited purpose are applied in ways not anticipated by their developers. The intruder community is constantly seeking to find interesting (and, from their point of view, profitable) ways to discover and exploit vulnerabilities.

This behaviour tends to be quite trend-driven. A newly discovered interesting vulnerability exploit in an application will spawn both intensive interest in other vulnerabilities in that application and an intensive search for similar vulnerabilities in other applications.

This results in waves of discovered vulnerabilities that impact both specific vendors and the community in general.

At the same time, the recognition that there are measurable trends in vulnerability exploitation are at least a temporary advantage to intelligence analysis efforts. From a tactical perspective, the recognition of a trend in intrusion tools and their applications may well allow for at least short-term predictive analysis and the potential for limited warning.

One of the greatest challenges to system owners and administrator is determining how much security is enough. Managing risks inherent in information systems is problem that changes as fast as new technologies are brought online. Intelligence analysis of the threats to information systems should, by definition, be a major component of the risk management process. Without application, intelligence analysis efforts are merely an intellectual exercise and have no value. It is only when the results of that analysis, the assessments derived from the analytic process, are provided to operators that they begin to have value.

Obtaining prior knowledge of both threats and vulnerabilities–as well as sensitivity to possible opportunities to exploit the vulnerabilities-is essential. Intelligence analysis, of course, operates at different levels, ranging from the specific to the general, and from short-term incidents and operations to long term patterns and challenges. Each form or level of analysis is crucial, and complements and supplements the others. Nevertheless, it is important to distinguish them from one another and to be clear at which level the activities are taking place.

It is also important to recognize that the most critical insights will be obtained from fusion efforts that combine these different levels. The several complementary levels of intelligence analysis are strategic analysis, tactical analysis and operational analysis. In practice, these categories shade into each other and are not always sharply differentiated, and differing definitions for these terms exist in the intelligence community. Nevertheless, they offer a useful framework within which intelligence tasks and requirements can initially be delineated.

THE CYBER INTELLIGENCE COMMUNITY

This unique, currently ad hoc, community is made up of government, telecommunication and internet providers, CERTs, and other formal information security entities, specialty companies, and vendors. The members of this community engage in a myriad of activities that could be the potential victim of a cyber threat. This "Cyber Intelligence Community" is currently an informal coalition of the willing that collects and analyses unclassified and classified cyber intelligence data and trends. There is no formal mechanism across industry and government cyber intelligence entities that successfully collects, processes, and analyses all identifiable key cyber threat behaviour and reports it at an unclassified or reasonable classification level to all appropriate customers. An effective connection between intelligence provider and the customer means that the customer has understood and internalized the intelligence resulting in action to work the intelligence and mitigate the threat. Good intelligence professionals relentlessly pursue interactions with customers to ensure that: the data is collected, analysed, and conveyed; the intelligence serves customers' purposes; and some action is being taken (or deliberately not taken). This cycle can be referred to as a constant process of story-finding, storytelling, story-updating, storylistening, and story-heeding. A concept to institutionalize this ad hoc community is currently missing.

Investing in Cyber Intelligence Tradecraft

A substantial and continuing investment in cyber intelligence should be a strategic imperative in the information age. It is also imperative to use that intelligence to safe guard our ability to maintain security. We must ensure that stable domestic and international economies are not jeopardized by possible conflict with rival powers, rogue states, failing or failed states, modern terrorists and thieves, and WMD proliferators.

All formal and informal intelligence disciplines contribute to these imperatives, including Signals Intelligence (SIGINT), Human Intelligence (HUMINT), open Source Intelligence (OSINT), geospatial and Measurement Intelligence (GEOINT), and the volumes of unclassified network data and behaviour being watched by global CERTs.

Continuous liaison among all related parties is critical so that sharing is seamless. This ensures an evolving, improved level of insight and reporting to an increasingly secure and highly performing cyber environment for all.

This evolving cyber intelligence tradecraft requires deep and powerful technical and analytic expertise at all levels. Such technical talent and related capabilities remain ill-defined and in short supply across government and industry.

An institution that has made some headway in this regard is the Information Assurance Directorate (IAD) at the national Security Agency.

IAD is the front line of the defensive cyber mission. It commands substantial resources, high performing talent, strong processes, and informed outreach.

It also works hand in hand with military, public, and private partners to ensure that our cyber capabilities and intellectual property are defended and that our defence is informing offence and vice versa. IAD is a good start, but we must emulate their good practices and innovativeness in defining professional attributes, associated education, and training goals for the unique career fields associated with the cyber realm.

TYPES OF CYBER SECURITY THREATS

Nation-sponsored hacking specifically-targeted cyber attacks will incorporate concepts and techniques from the commercial hacker industry. These campaigns will contain a different malware payload than the traditional attacks conducted for monetary gain. However, these attacks will use similar techniques.

These Advanced Persistent Threat (APT) attacks will borrow techniques, such as automation and viral distribution, making them all the more powerful and potentially more successful. An example of such an attack is Stuxnet, which was not searching for data to monetize, rather it was focused on gaining control of crucial infrastructure.

Both classes of attack (hacker industry and APT) are going to use some of the same techniques so some security controls are applicable to both. On the positive side, given you're covered against the cyber mafia you should have some of the controls to be protected from certain APT attacks. As APT is persistent, if a certain attack does not succeed, another one will come into play. The traditional security controls do not deter these relentless, state-sponsored hacker organizations. For the enterprise as well as government, this means increasing monitoring of traffic and setting security controls across all organization layers.

The insider Threat

In this upcoming year, we expect to see a growing awareness to security incidents of an "insider job" nature. Attention will grow as a consequence of an increased flow of incident reports where data theft and security breaches are tied to employees and other insiders. The cause of this trend will be the emphasis put on new regulations covering the act of notification and disclosure (rather on the actual protection of data).

To deter insider threats, organizations should therefore:

- Enforce access controls such that access is based only a business need-to-know level. This includes eliminating excessive privileges.
- Provide the proper access auditing tools to data centres. These auditing tools should monitor who accesses what data.

Man in the Browser Attacks will man Up

Man in the Browser (MitB) attack sophistication is going to increase, as well as moving forward to more types of online applications. As a consequence, more online service providers are going to include this in their list of priorities for 2011, shifting the responsibility for mitigating the risk from the consumers to the service providers.

While avoiding infection by proxy Trojans is presumably the responsibility of consumers, MitB attacks are quickly becoming a concern of online service providers. The actual rate of infection and the proliferation of the many types of MitB malware suggest that providers must be able to serve (and protect) customers who might be infected with one type of malware or another. Just as the evolution of vehicle safety drove manufacturers to include device such as ABS, Air Bags and ESP, rather than rely on us to drive carefully, so will online service providers need to invest in mechanisms that allow them to conduct business with allegedly infected consumers. Among the technologies that we foresee as helpful are strong device identification, client profiling, fast security code evolution, session flow tracking and site-to-client authentication.

Misanthropes and Anti-socials: Privacy vs. Security in Social Networks

In 2011, we will see prominent social networks, and tools, placing more efforts into security over privacy. This is not the result of resolved privacy issues, but rather an understanding of the real threats to the existence and proliferation of social networks. There are two key factors at stake: security and trust. While privacy concerns the ability to keep personal information hidden from other application users, security controls the way in which people use the information of others. Trust impacts our ability to make decisions based on the information we receive through social networks.

In today's social networking platform, both security and trust are in danger. Cross-site scripting (XSS) and cross-site request forgery (CSRF) vulnerabilities are quickly translating into massive worm out brakes.

Next year, we expect social platforms to invest more resources in improving the security posture of the platform. These measures will provide improved protection against application layer attacks, stronger authentication and account control features, as well as better malware detection systems.

SECURITY CHALLENGING

Efforts to identify intruders are critical both to the assessment of the challenge and the nature of the response. Potential intruders run the gamut from young hobbyists engaged in the equivalent of joy riding to terrorist organizations and nations that are intent on maximizing damage to the target. The problem of identification is particularly difficult in a domain where maintaining anonymity is easy and there are sometimes time lapses between the intruder action, the intrusion itself, and the actual disruptive effects. Moreover, the consequences are not always commensurate with the objectives, in some cases falling short of what the intruders hoped to achieve, and in others going well beyond what they had envisaged.

There is a broad spectrum of potential intruders on the Internet and an almost equal number of motives for intrusions against organizations. Not surprisingly, this includes perpetrators conducting operations against other perpetrators. As enticing as this prospect is, it does not mitigate the effects of such internecine rivalry. New and more sophisticated tools are often the result of such interplay. This sort of jousting can also provide valuable insights to analysts once it is recognized, but does not simplify the analytic task and puts an incredible strain on limited analytic/warning resources. With the continuing proliferation of sophisticated computer technologies into the mainstream population, attribution for an intrusion becomes more difficult by the day.

The dynamism of the intruder population is itself a problem. On the one hand, success breeds imitation and the sophistication of readily available tools means that even those with limited skills can become intruders.

On the one hand, there is a certain degree of attrition in the intruder community. Indeed, there are many reasons why intruders might cease their activity, including increased maturity, a need to find gainful employment, and a perception of the rewards of working to increase network security rather than attack it. The implication, of course, is that the mix of agents threatening network security is changing as the nature of the Internet changes.

The vast majority of the intrusions are probably being conducted by nuisance hackers or "ankle-biters" who have limited objectives and are usually satisfied with the actual penetration of the system or conduct relatively harmless cyber-vandalism such as the defacement or alteration of web-sites. While aggravating to the target, no significant or lasting damage occurs. The more serious problem occurs when an intrusion is carried out by a more sophisticated intruder (either an individual or a group) whose objective is better defined and involves malicious intent. Motives for these sorts of intrusions are also as varied as the persons carrying them out. They range from greed to defined military strategy and doctrine, and all that falls in between.

Four of the more dangerous, and less well defined categories of intruder are governments conducting operations against other sovereign states, the organized terrorist group, insurgency or revolutionary groups, and organized crime. All these entities are beginning to appreciate the potential power, anonymity, and effectiveness of the Internet. There are myriad examples of governments instituting programmes for Computer Network Warfare. In the case of Russia, policy-makers consider the security of their information infrastructure so critical that–rhetorically at least-they equate an attack against it with a strategic nuclear strike (and have promised an appropriate response).

As a result of the realization of the criticality of information infrastructures, computer warfare is now a part of the formal Russian Military Strategy and Doctrine. The same is true of organized terrorist groups. In fact, "most of the 30 top terrorist organizations identified by the U.S. government have web pages and use e-mail, and are ``fairly well developed'' at using the Internet."[Casciano] In many cases, dependence on technology is viewed as an Achilles Heel to be exploited by terrorist organizations.

Within the U.S., many of the more militant indigenous groups have discovered the power of the Internet and have well designed and effective Web sites. Indeed, militia and supremacist groups have had significant increases in membership since developing their Web pages. It is a natural progression from using the Internet for propaganda and recruiting to exploiting its potential as a weapon. There is also growing evidence that some of the active insurgency groups around the world are discovering the potential of the computer. It is just a matter of time until they discover the effect of a computer-generated attack against the infrastructure of the government they are fighting. Once that realization is made, cyber-attacks will likely become a weapon of choice for organizations intent on overthrowing an existing government. Disturbingly, Aum Shinrikyo, the group responsible for the Sarin gas attack on the Japanese subway, has increasingly been involved in the Japanese software industry!

Organized crime probably was the first of the sophisticated intruder threats to realize the power and value of the computer. In 1995, it was discovered that the Cali cartel had sophisticated state-of-the-art equipment for electronic eavesdropping, while smaller drug trafficking organizations in Colombia are using the Internet to pressure the Colombian government to change the policy of extraditing traffickers to the United States. Furthermore, the use of computers by organized crime organizations to garner illicit profits is well documented. However, some criminal efforts have gone beyond simple siphoning of funds and money laundering. Extortion of money from financial institutions by threatening to destroy or modify their computer databases is also evident. It is probable that at least some of these extortion operations are conducted by transnational criminal groups. Some of the extortion efforts go wrong–as did the effort to extort Bloomberg. In other cases, however, large payoffs are almost certainly made to the extortionist. It seems likely, therefore, that larger and potentially more dangerous operations should be anticipated.

The obvious challenge is to develop a capacity to identify and track the activities of these potential intruders with the goal of being able to provide predictive analysis and warning of intrusions. Some of the traditional intelligence techniques should apply to these threats, but new methodologies and the ability to contemplate new and complex concepts have to be developed concurrently. This will become even more important (and difficult) as perpetrators of increasing sophistication operate on the Internet. As motivations vary, so will the efforts of the individuals behind malicious operations to either conceal or reveal their responsibility. All of this complicates efforts to track responsible parties determine attribution. Nations and transnational criminal organizations, by their nature, will be diligent in their efforts to maintain anonymity. In some of these cases, identifying the intended victim may give valuable insight into tracking the intruder. Sometimes the target of an intrusion allows the analyst to rule out certain possible perpetrators. A multi-million dollar extortion plot against a major financial institution is probably not the work of a 13-year-old hacker working out of his bedroom. At the same time, however, many victims, especially within government or sensitive industries such as banking or insurance, often complicate the effort to track intruders because of their reluctance to report the incident. In other cases, such as politically motivated attacks, the perpetrators may want their identity known, but not their location. As such operations become more sophisticated, tracking the attack back to its point of origin will be a major challenge to the intelligence analysts involved. What is clear from all of this is that tracking intruders and gaining attribution is much more than just a technical challenge.

One difficulty, of course, is that there are legal constraints on intelligence collection, especially by the military and the national security establishment. Traditionally the focus of intelligence has been on foreign threats, and there are restrictions on intelligence activities directed against individuals or groups that are domestic in nature. Insofar as these groups are the focus of government attention, it is from the law enforcement community. This points to yet another problem: that of coordination and information sharing between the traditional national security agencies and the law enforcement community. Generally law enforcement focuses on individual cases and wants evidence that stands up in court; intelligence agencies in contrast are concerned with protecting the sources of their information so that they can continue to use them. The problem with cyber-threats is that they fall in the gray area where crime and national security merge into one another.

Forms of Intrusion are Occurring

It is tempting to see intrusions in terms of a pyramid that goes from transient vulnerability probing and defacing web-sites at the base to large scale efforts to undermine the critical missions of an organization or the critical functions of a nation at the top-and to suggest that there is an inverse relationship between frequency and significance, with many trivial incidents and comparatively few of the more serious incidents. There are several difficulties with this however. The first is that probes that appear relatively insignificant could be a harbinger of more serious intrusions. The second is that there is sometimes a gap between intent and consequences–the effects and impact of an incident can either fall far short of what was intended, or far exceed what the perpetrator initially envisaged. This lack of congruence between limited intent and far-reaching consequences stems from the capacity of worms and viruses for infinite replication and multiplication combined with the seamless inter-connectivity of systems. Incidents such as the Love Bug cross the public-private divide and have an indiscriminate impact on corporations, governments, and private individuals irrespective of the initial target. In cases such as this, the consequences have less to do with targeting than with the ubiquity of a particular programme such as Microsoft Outlook that is used as the vector of transmission. In effect, the incident takes on its own momentum.

When the consequences are widespread, of course, the incident becomes very public and is the subject of much media and official commentary. In many other cases, however, there is far greater reticence about the scale, type and targets of attack. The analytic effort must successfully build a trust relationship for the collection of data across a broad variety of organizations. This trust relationship allows for observation of incidents from early probing and experimentation through widespread deployment of automated forms of intrusion. For example, in recent months (June and July 2000) CERTÒ/CC has received reports of intrusions involving a wide variety of automated tools, ranging from simple viruses and system corruption toolkits through complex viruses designed to attack relatively hardened sites with low probability of detection and distributed tools designed to crash network infrastructure. Roughly 10%-25% of the CERT/CC reports involve viruses. Roughly 20%-40% are intrusions where the victim site cannot discern the type of the intrusion from available data. The remaining intrusions are a large number of other forms of intrusion, including compromise of system administration accounts, web defacements, reconnaissance attempts and misuse of computing resources.

Being intruded Upon

Determining who are the victims of intrusions is, in some respects, an enormously significant part of the intelligence process. It is important-at least in those cases where attacks are not indiscriminate-to differentiate between public and private targets, to distinguish infrastructure targets from individual targets, to distinguish between intrusions that focus on targets of convenience and those that are much more precise and calculated. For example, existing analysis has shown a link between port scanning and certain types of later intrusions, but this needs to be more fully explored to provide for effective warnings. Profiling victims can sometimes play a critical role in determining the nature of the intrusion and the nature of the intruders. For this to be done, understanding is needed of the level of "background noise", probes and intrusion attempts occurring across the Internet. Once understood, it may be possible to isolate this activity from the more significant activity directed at a particular victim.

Victim profiles will be just as important, in terms of strategic intelligence analysis of the Internet, as profiling potential intruders. The more serious the intrusion, the more critical this sort of profiling will be. One of the potential hurdles to this effort, however, will be the natural tendency of the victim, whether private or public, to withhold sensitive or proprietary information. A few examples of this kind of reticence would be financial institutions withholding information about loses due to intrusions; companies failing to divulge the nature of an intrusion due to proprietary corporate data; or a government agency protecting information that is sensitive or even classified. Beyond simply protecting proprietary or sensitive data, there are also serious legal questions that have not yet been resolved in the courts or in the legislature. These include constitutional guarantees of privacy; contradictory national laws (or lack of laws) as perpetrators use the global network; laws limiting various governmental agency's efforts to track down the source of an intrusion, and the need to determine what is domestic and what is foreign.

If these barriers can be overcome, critical information will become available. Details of the victim's infrastructure, the nature of the intrusion, identity clues left by the intruder, network traffic flow as observed by the victim site, and intrusion tools left as artifacts on the victim hosts can all provide indispensable clues. Without such information, motivation becomes more difficult to define and profiling efforts will be seriously flawed. Some work has already been accomplished in this area by organizations involved in incident monitoring, including the members of the Forum of Incident Response and Security Teams (FIRST) community. Much more remains to be accomplished, however, as new cooperative agreements are forged and additional analytic efforts and methodologies are developed. Furthermore, while it is true that some of the legal restrictions are avoided by the voluntary nature of the cooperative relationships, they are by no means completely overcome. The keys to success seem to be twofold. First, the analytic organization has to prove itself to be a highly secure confidant, never disclosing victim identities while working to assist victims in recovering from intrusions. Second, it must return information that is of value to the victims, including information that might place the intrusion in a larger context as well as providing assistance in dealing with vendors or other sites. More simply put, the exchange of information must be in both directions. Experience with other organizations has shown that neither trustworthiness nor returned value alone is sufficient, but both appear to be required for effective information gathering with victims.

Beyond their reticence, victim organizations are often unaware of critical parts of their security stance. Available data suggests that victims are often not aware that their networks have been intruded upon. The effectiveness of installed security measures is often overestimated. Levels of trust given to users by computing practices are often unwarranted. All of this hampers both analysis and defence.

One of the reasons that profiling the victims is so critical is that it provides insights in to motivations that can greatly assist analysts in predicting future intrusions under similar circumstances. This insight will need to incorporate identification of circumstances that facilitate or hamper intrusion. For example, K-12 educational institutions might offer a significant opportunity for intruders to stage their attacks, since many such institutions lack knowledgeable system administrators. However, such hosts may be removed from the network during summer break and other times when school is not in session. During the Year 2000 rollover, conditions for system intrusion were relatively poor not only because of the active presence of a large number of system administrators, carefully monitoring their systems, but also the significant number of alternative activities available to potential intruders. These examples serve to identify that there exist time-varying circumstances; further analysis is required to delineate these factors more fully.

4

The Changing Trends of Security in South Asia

Post cold war era has witnessed changing trends in security. The traditional concept of security is now being replaced by non traditional security which stresses upon broader view entailing vast concerns of social, political, economic and environmental issues leading to the comprehensive security which is becoming a more popular version of security. This shift in security paradigm is being felt in South Asia also, which comprises of world's 1.5 population, which remains a deprived and a poor region because of the huge defence spendings. But now there is realization that the region needs to divert its resources from military towards economic and social uplift of the people, thus the stress from high politics to low politics. Both Pakistan and India need to go for more cooperative relations as to bring peace in the region which in turn will bring comprehensive security leading to the betterment of the people of South Asia.

In recent times with fast pace of globalization and complicated issues being faced by states, the understanding of security has become crucial for betterment of humanity. New and complex concerns have replaced traditional issues. The same goes for security which is undergoing changes, new concept of security is becoming more acceptable to that of traditional military security, which only stresses on military and defence aspects. But now states so as to secure security need to pay more attention to the present day problems being faced. These contemporary concerns include terrorism, poverty, population growth, health, environment, cultural, religious and ethnic antagonism. In coming years the above mentioned issues will be posing more problems, thus making states more insecure. If we take the most general meaning of security, it implies being secure from threats. Then how much are the states nowadays secure from the number of threats being faced other than military ones?

The concept of security is ambiguous and elastic in meanings. Generally security is taken as to be free from threats. It is a complicated and a contested concept. It is iridescent and manifold if seen in different perspectives or from different angles. Broadly speaking the concept of security can be divided into two categories: traditional concept of security that emphasizes the importance of state security, and non- traditional or broadened concept of security that seeks social security. Before we go into the graphic detail about what constitutes traditional concept of security and non-traditional concept of security and their implication in the South Asian region, let us briefly look into the theoretical evolution of these two concepts.

The traditional military oriented security was seen in world politics in 1940s till the end of cold war, by the then prevalent Realist scholars, who emphasized on attainment of military power. The Realists were the traditionalists who dominated the international relations in 1940s. They believed in 'power politics' with states as the main actors, giving stress on attainment of more and more military power.

Throughout the cold war the traditional concept of security remained dominant paradigm as both policy makers and experts strongly adhered to the conviction that international relations are essentially conflictual and that war is the only solution, a bitter reality that cannot be overlooked or denied. State security remained primary concern and objective of the followers of traditional concept of security. For them state is the pre-eminent actor in world politics and all other actors such as individuals, international organizations, NGOs etc. are either secondary or unimportant. From the Realist perspective, states face security dilemma and national security is achieved through the military means. The core values of traditional concept of security are national security and state survival; foreign policy of any state is formulated around these two basic priorities or values.

A growing number of contemporary writers have sought for an 'expanded conception' of security, including a wide range of considerations. After the end of cold war, the concept of security became a hot subject of debate, dissection and discourse not only among the scholars but also among the strategists, policy makers and economists. The traditional concept that had emphasized the "centrality of state as pivot of political life" or state-centric security throughout the cold war was questioned and post cold war realities rendered it somewhat implausible and untenable. The fast pace of globalization and immense interaction amongst states demonstrated that security stakes of states are interlinked and interdependent, thus requiring role and contribution of all, leading to collective action for satisfaction of human security. However post cold war era and 9/11 incident brought abut shifts in understanding of security. A number of non orthodox approaches have emerged viewing security differently.

Now the concept of security is not confined only to military threats. Non-military threats have gained much more importance and attention, thus leading to emergence of the concept of 'soft' security rather than the 'hard' security which prevailed during the cold war era. Non-military issues such as economy, trade, environment and terrorism etc. have become part of 'low' politics or 'soft' security which is the current broader view, leaving behind the only military issues captioned as 'high' politics or 'hard' security, coming under the narrow view in security studies. In early 1990's a new approach emerged as the 'Copenhagen School' led by Barry Buzan, which believed in a profound widening of security to non-military issues and also made an attempt to include sub- state groups into security analysis. This school has established itself in a decade.

Further beyond the above mentioned school is the 'deepening' approach led by Pluralists and Social Constructionists; these embrace the idea of human security arguing that object of security should be individual people and not the state or sub state groups. In 1990s United Nations Development Program (UNDP) further developed this concept of human security.

'The concept of security must change from an exclusive stress on national security to much greater stress on people's security, from security through armament to security through human development from territorial to food, employment and environmental security.

'The broad goal of security is to enable people to live without fears for their survival, well-being and freedom. Security thus, is not only the absence of war and conflict, but also the control of infections, diseases, the prevention of poverty, the elimination of illiteracy and the protection of sudden reversals that threaten the quality of their daily lives'. Nowadays governments are giving more stress on issues such as drugs, health and global warming, which fall under the 'comprehensive security'. In the late 1950s Prime Minister of Japan Ohira for the first time used the term comprehensive security. The concept was based on the idea that security was comprehensive in nature and should not be restricted only to military issues. It however did not exclude military capabilities. This approach became quite popular.

Later on in 1990s the concept of cooperative security emerged, it carried a few of elements of all others and included cooperative efforts for achieving security. These efforts would be towards issues of common concern. This has become a attractive security concept as it works around the welfare of all parties going for cooperative measures.

There is growing awareness among the people especially of the developed world that international boundaries are a weak barrier to the problems that afflict the poorest parts of the world. No doubt concept of security is undergoing changes. Military oriented security is being replaced by comprehensive and cooperative security, which gives a broader view of security.

NUCLEAR ARMS RACE

India's defeat in war in 1962 was quickly followed by another uncomfortable military development for India, China's explosion of a nuclear device in 1964. This may have been carried out by Beijing primarily with the US and perhaps the Soviet Union in mind. However, one side effect was that India was now faced not only with a territorial foe, but also a nuclear foe, an uncomfortable power imbalance from India's point of view.

There may have been some limited moves toward reducing Sino-Indian hostilities following Rajiv Gandhi's trip to China in 1988, but relations still remained quite cool in the 1990s. Underlying perceptions of mistrust were very clear on India's side, as well as a sense of having been overtaken in the global pecking order and estimation. China was firmly in Indian sights in the late 1990s, as someone to be strategically matched, something of an ongoing quest. At the time, 1997, Mohan felt that given "the national determination in India to liberate itself from the current second class status in world affairs ... New Delhi will find it impossible to give up its search for global status similar to that of China"; in which "New Delhi is most unlikely give up its determination to acquire a functional nuclear deterrent against Beijing ... India will remain committed to building a small but functional deterrent against China." China's installation of CSS-5s medium range missiles in Tibet, with a range of about 1,333 miles, was highlighted in the Indian media during 1997 as targeting India.

Raja Mohan's 1997 predictions were quickly met, as India moved in 1998 toward transforming its implicit 1974 nuclear capability into an explicit realized capacity. The Prime Minister Atal Bihari Vajpayee was blunt concerning China factors behind the Pokhran-II tests by India:

We have an overt nuclear weapons state [China] on our borders, a state that committed armed aggression against India in 1962. Although our relations with that country have improved in the last decade or so, an atmosphere of distrust persists, mainly due to the unresolved border problem. To add to the distrust, that country has materially helped another neighbour of ours [Pakistan] to become a covert nuclear weapons state.

Vajpayee may not have intended this letter to the US president to be publicized; but the sentiments were clear enough, objectively and subjectively. Indian commentators like General Amarjit Kalkat, who had commanded the Indian peace keeping forces in Sri Lanka in 1987, were also clear at the time where the message of India's nuclear explosions was aimed. It was not a local regional demonstration against Pakistan. Instead, Kalkat argued that:

What strikes me as being particularly significant is their effect on India-China relations. These will be put on an even footing … The tests are really an attempt to correct the current military and technological imbalance vis--vis China, which is already in the threshold of being a world super power … Countries tend to respect equals and nuclear parity does help provide the level playing field needed to build such an equalitarian relationship. China has been a nuclear power for long, but India was not till it showed its capability this week. Similar logic was apparent with India's successful testing of an Agni-II medium range (2,500-3,000 kilometers/1,550-1,860 miles) missile in 1999. Dinkar Shukla at the Government of India's Press Information Bureau asserted that "Pokhran-II and Agni-II are a symbol of a resurgent India," in which "the Pakistani threat is only a marginal factor in New Delhi's security calculus. Agni is at the heart of deterrence in the larger context of the Sino-Indian equation." Such considerations were why Chellaney argued in 2000 that "a major motivation for India's 1998 nuclear tests was the growing military asymmetry with China."

IR theory enters the picture with regard to China's differing responses in 1962 and 1998. Whereas China took military action against India in 1962, it initially responded fairly mildly to India's nuclear explosion in 1998. Lei Guang argues that different perceptions were in play. In 1962, China could feel that its identity was at stake through India refusing to negotiate over what China considered was an unequal treaty imposed on it in earlier times of weakness. Guang argues that "given the centrality of territory to the Chinese national identity, what constituted the border between China and its neighbour was no longer simply a matter of administrative marking." Instead, there was a threefold challenge to China, to its perceived territory, sovereignty and legitimacy. Consequently, this "triple assault on China's fundamental identity as a nation-state contributed to its final decision to resort to violence in 1962." Such consideration are rightly seen by Guang as an example of IR constructivism.

Conversely, China took a more subdued and restrained approach to India's nuclear testing in 1998. Guang explains this difference by arguing that

China's core identity was not particularly threatened by this event; India's nuclear explosion "did not constitute a frontal attack on the PRC's identity in 1998. On the contrary, it testified to China's nuclear power and affirmed its position as a major power in the region." This did not mean that China was not concerned about India's nuclear explosion. What it did mean was that China responded in different ways and at a different pitch than in 1962. As Guang argues, "a main thrust of the Chinese reaction to India's nuclear tests in 1998 was geopolitical in nature. Unlike in 1962, what was at stake for China in 1998 was its national security, not its fundamental identity as a modern nation-state." Its power advantages enabled a cooler calculated restraint in 1998.

Nuclear rivalry continues to affect Sino-Indian relations. A nuclear arms race, and its "nuclear security dilemma" dynamics, adds a competitive spiral element to their relationship. Even as the dust from India's Pokhran-II tests was settling, further deployment of Chinese missiles was causing alarm in India, Chellaney pointing out in 2000 that "India's largest neighbor [China] is conducting the biggest expansion of missile capabilities anywhere in the world. The first of these new missiles, the Dongfeng (DF) 31, last tested in July 1999, can reach every corner of India but little of U.S. territory." Chellaney's own sense of the political context of China's nuclear program was stark, "India's existing modest deterrent capabilities will be gravely undermined as China builds up its nuclear and missile armories. The Sino-Indian asymmetry will increase ... India will have every incentive to acquire similar assets that play a primary role in power-projection strategies." An offensive weapons spiral was in the offing from both sides. Whilst welcoming US attempts to develop a AMD (Anti-Missile Defence) system, Chellaney acknowledged and concluded that "nevertheless, the likely response of those states whose security will be directly affected, particularly China, will significantly affect India's interests. This is what India has to worry about"; even though "in due course, the action-reaction cycle triggered by missile defenses could drive India closer to the United States." Strategic alignment between India and the US is Beijing's nightmare.

In terms of power projection, China's control of Tibet has seen its installation of various medium and intermediate range missile systems. These missile systems are irrelevant to curbing domestic discontent inside Tibet, but do literally and strategically point outside Tibet toward India, its capital Delhi and other major Indian cities. Indian analysts are acutely aware of these implications. For Mahapatra, this military buildup in Tibet is "not only aimed at overwhelming India militarily, but to enable Chinese coercive diplomacy in respect of the border dispute." Asymmetrics is in play. Installation of intermediate and medium range ballistic missiles enables China to immediately and easily threaten India; whereas the main centers of China, Beijing, Shanghai, Guangzhou remained far away from India. Back in 1999, Kanwal was lamenting that "realistic deterrence against China can only be achieved by developing a demonstrated capability to target major Chinese cities such as Beijing and Shanghai with nuclear weapons." However, India's successful testing of the Agni-III intermediate range ballistic missile in 2007 and 2008, with a range of 3,500 kilometers (2,170 miles), for the first time brings many of China's main cities within range of India's nuclear strike capability. The Agni-I short range ballistic missile is clearly oriented towards Pakistan, Agni-III is equally clearly oriented towards China, "China-specific" in Pandit's eyes. India's nuclear mobility is strengthened by the submarine based Sagarika ballistic missile launches carried out in 2008. India is set to test its augmented Agni-III+/IV missile system, with a range of 5,000 kilometers (3,110 miles) in early 2009, enabling India to target all of China for the first time. From China's point of view, this increases its nuclear encirclement, in part from India, in part from India in conjunction with the United States.

Of course, India's and China's modernization and expansion of their nuclear and missile capability is not necessarily just aimed at each other. India has its ongoing concerns with Pakistan, China has its own set of concerns with the United States. Nevertheless, India and China also feed off each other's nuclear programs. The final twist in the nuclear relationship is India's drive to establish an effective anti-ballistic MDS (Missile Defence System), in part through collaboration with the United States, but in part under its own efforts. Following successful interceptor missile tests in 2006 and 2007, India claims to have developed an ABM (Anti-Ballistic Missile) capacity, with operational deployment scheduled by 2011. Classic security dilemma dynamics operate here. As admitted by Mohanty, "China would watch India's growing missile defence capability very carefully ... there is hardly any doubt that both China and Pakistan would most likely try to strengthen their missile strike capabilities to maintain the strategic deterrence." From India's point of view, China's close nuclear links with Pakistan remains a further exacerbating and exasperating factor in Sino-Indian relations, and is part of their respective encirclement and alignment scenarios to which we now turn.

DIMENSIONS OF SECURITY IN SOUTH ASIA

The geo-strategic position of the region has enhanced its importance to the world. It is neighbouring Afghanistan, Iran and China and it is very near to Gulf states and Central Asia. It is not only of high interest on the agenda of United States but is keenly watched by rest of the world. But the two major states, Pakistan and India have been foes, thus bringing instability to the region. Considering the security of South Asia, it concerns the well being of nearly 1.3 to 1.5 billion people seeking stability and economic development. Security, which should not be taken as protection in military terms also involves the economic well being of the people for lasting peace, stability and cooperation.

Since inception both the largest but antagonist states of South Asia, India and Pakistan have been indulged in hostile relations leading to crisis, and even wars. Pakistan and India joined the nuclear club as *de-facto* nuclear powers when they crossed the nuclear threshold by conducting nuclear tests in May 1998. The importance of security, peace and stability of the region soared to an all-time high and the region became the most dangerous nuclear flash point in the world. The strategic importance of the region after the cold war and the demise of Soviet Union became a frequent and favourite subject of debates. Rapidly growing economy of India and Pakistan providing access to Central Asian states oil and gas resources have further highlighted the importance of South Asian region, but in this region, peace and security is the pre-requisite. The security approach which is dependent on military is inadequate to deal with the nature of threats to the security of South Asia. Therefore it is now imperative to consider the non military threats. The policy makers of both the countries have been paying more attention to enhance the defensive and offensive capabilities against each other, which have undermined the socio-economic development of both countries. Even though the achievements in missiles technology and nuclear capability have enhanced the image of both the countries in the world but both countries have to divert huge proportion of their resources towards these fields. The question arises that how both the antagonist states can improve their social security without neglecting national security. Both countries can keep both national security and social security well balanced by introducing and incorporating liberal ideas to their policies.

The nuclearization of South Asia in 1998 has further complicated security arrangements between the two rival states and has made the region a nuclear flashpoint. The event of 9/11 has further highlighted the status of the region, nowadays South Asia has become a very sensitive region due to terrorism and nuclearization. With world's 1/5th population, the region provides immense opportunities to its large population. The nuclear neighbours share a long border but look upon each other with hatred, suspicion and mistrust. Pakistan is strategically located at the cross roads of three important ancient civilizations. It can act as a bridge between Central Asia and the Middle East and South Asia. This will only be possible when Pakistan is willing to provide transit facilities to its neighbours specially India due to its growing its economy. This could not be materialized due to the ongoing antagonism between Pakistan and India for the last more than 60 years. Both have been involved in an arms race with huge stockpiles of weapons assuring mutual destruction. The security paradigm of the region is dominated by this dangerous strategic competition.

The traditional hostility has led the decision makers of both the states to adhere to the military security thus spending large amounts of their resources towards militarization. Consequently, already underdeveloped region has failed to enhance the economic and social conditions of its people, as a result this region has lagged behind in over all development. To upgrade their offensive and defensive capabilities, managers of both the countries have been laying more emphasis on military strength and for this purpose, huge expenses on defence expenditure on both sides scored high. Not only this, but huge amounts are being spent on maintenance and research towards military. An expensive arms race is being witnessed especially of nuclear weapons that required immense resources. Testing of new and more devastating missiles are a regular feature. This is all being done by spending a large amount of budget on their military capabilities, as a result, both posses a large, modern and sophisticated military.

Now looking at the other side of the picture, due to the massive spending on military, as a consequence the other side gives a bleak picture of the socio economic conditions of its people which were neglected leading to under development in many sectors. The region is poverty ridden leading to grave social and economic problems.

There have been ups and downs in relations of both countries since their creation. From 1965 war to Tashkent Agreement then 1971 war and debacle of East Pakistan and then Simla Agreement, 1998 detonation of nuclear weapons to the public embrace between the two prime ministers at Lahore; both witnessed high tensions at Kargil and then the serenity of Agra in 2001; the confrontation during 2002 and then the handshake at 12th SAARC Summit in Islamabad and recurrent rounds of CBMs. The latest developments manifest that bilateral relations between the belligerent neighbours have been improving, but any results of the composite dialogue process are yet awaited. "Even though progress has been essentially on softer and less contentious issues, the security environment has improved significantly".

"Although Karl Deutch's 'security community' may not be just around the corner in South Asia, the region could be more peaceful, stable and secure if the countries bring about changes in their attitudes. 'South Asian security could be enhanced by way of making the countries of the region more interdependent and less 'clausewitzian', people to people contacts and the

SAARC could still be the best hope for the socio-economic development and eventually for security". Both need to develop a culture of peace and understanding as there is realization in both the countries that their common enemy is poverty. The defence expenditures are growing but have failed to provide absolute security to either side.

The core issue between the two as repeatedly said by President Musharraf, is Kashmir issue. India and Pakistan could institutionalize the dialogue process on Kashmir by constituting a Joint Working Group, which should include representatives from the government and also from the civil society. This will help to sustain the dialogue process. However, there are certain apprehensions also; "it is taken as even if the Kashmir dispute is resolved in favour of Pakistan's wishes, it remains a moot question whether this can bring much sought amity between India and Pakistan, as the pre and post-partition memories have seared the minds of many people in both countries, which becomes a stumbling block to open a new bright chapter in friendly relationship".

The outcome of any clash, whatever the cause is, going to be disastrous, as now that both of them possess nuclear weapons. As to avert a nuclear confrontation in South Asia both need to institutionalize CBMs. Mutually acceptable solutions need to be found through genuine debate and talks.

The relations between India and Pakistan have been based on fear and mistrust, which both sides have been unable to overcome. It is fundamentally important to improve the relations between the two neighbours through people to people contact. This will also assist in building trust and overcoming mutual fear. But due to its unorganized nature the people to people level contacts have not brought about respective results. These people to people level contacts should be institutionalized at all levels, in particular, exchange of parliamentarians, academicians, journalists, artists, writers and students from both sides will play a vital role in improving the relations. "Freedom of movement in terms of greater people to people contact and now trade and commerce opportunities can act as a catalyst for charge both in the Kashmir as well as between India and Pakistan".

Sincere efforts need to be promoted for bilateral and regional economic cooperation. Trade links need to be exploited to realize full potential of trade between India and Pakistan. As to increase trade between the two, efforts should be made to give each other the status of most favourite nation. At the 12th SAARC summit, the Islamabad Declaration concluded deciding that the member states wanted to strengthen this organization and in this context the role of Pakistan and India is significant. As to make SAARC more effective such acts should be avoided when in 2005 India refused to attend the SAARC summit. Strengthening of SAARC will definitely have a constructive impact over the relations between India and Pakistan.

Public debate should be initiated in both the countries to know exactly what they want from each other and what they are ready to give each other. This debate can be held outside and inside the Parliaments. Both need to show spirit of give and take to facilitate vital decisions. A detailed multi-dimensional approach is to be adopted for conflict resolution in which bilateral dialogue is the only rational option and other alternatives are inconceivable. Both states must show honesty and flexibility in resolving the disputes, since there can be no meaningful negotiations from inflexible position. Conscious efforts are needed by both the countries to lessen popular hostility towards each other. Especially mindset of military establishment needs to be changed. New Delhi and Islamabad should avoid controversial statements that have negative implications. Declaratory statements have significant impact in the confidence building process. Media can play a very important role in this regard, so both the states should direct their media to help the government in moulding public opinion and developing a positive mindset.

Both countries must be watchful of the intentions of hardliners on both sides of the divide as hinted by the Pakistani foreign minister when he said that majority of Pakistani and Indian people wanted peace and resolution of the issue through dialogues, but some hard-liners on the both sides were blocking the way of dialogues, as they wanted war. Both governments should involve the conservative forces in the bilateral confidence building measures. These rightist forces can be tackled better by accommodating them in the process and not isolating them. The governments should consciously work towards facilitating travel of such polarized groups to the other side. The hope of peace lies in the unprecedented developments in the Pakistan-India relations since 2003. They have moved towards rapprochement in a coordinated and cautious fashion, over a fragile foundation of their relationship.

Kashmir dispute has remained the real bone of contention between India and Pakistan. They had wars and serious conflicts over Kashmir. They allege each other for cross border terrorism. Consequently, appalling relationship entails arms race. Heavy military spending incapacitates India and Pakistan's abilities to address their socio-economic problems even to a minimal standard. Arms buildup simply cannot be financed without neglecting economic development at home. The economic development's negligence carries its own dynamics. These dynamics pose a negative influence on the internal security of a state. Therefore, it is imperative that both states should resolve their conflicting issues rationally. More precisely, the CBMs, strengthening of SAARC, regional trade and respecting the sovereignty of each other could shun aside the perils of security dilemma and develop amelioration in Indo-Pakistan relationship, and issues like Baghlihar dam should not be allowed to disrupt the peace process.

Both countries need to harness economic and socio cultural co-operation as to enhance popular support for peace efforts. An increase in trade and cultural exchange will result in enhanced communication between the two thus helping in creating an atmosphere without tensions.

Positive aspect of this process is that for the first time Kashmiris are involved in talks and both sides have realized that they must show some flexibility. India has realized that its pace of economic growth and development cannot afford more conflicts, and India wants to get over its regional conflicts. It's now aiming at a global role i.e. acquiring a permanent seat at UN Security Council. Both states have realized now that they need to resolve conflicts because a little miscalculation or misperception on the part of both states may prove fatal.

The conflict between India and Pakistan has undermined the political, social and economic security in the region which needs to be addressed by dialogue. Lasting peace is also a pre-requisite for the development of the people of the region. It is a positive indication that experts from India and Pakistan are talking about conflicts ranging from Kashmir to Siachen, Wuller Barrage, Sir Creek and nuclear confidence, and both are serious in preventing in outbreak of war. But along with this, it is a fact that both the neighbours are constantly increasing their defence budgets, regularly testing nuclear missiles, developing and procuring new and sophisticated weapons. As to create a more positive security environment in the region there is a need for a working relationship between Pakistan and India. On contentious issues both will have to show compromises. Mutual trust and good will have to be created. Rigidity in their behaviour is to be removed as to lessen, mistrust. Along with official diplomatic relations both need to channelize track II and track III diplomacy. South Asia gives a picture where there is poverty and under development and also is facing intra- state and inter state conflict.

It is therefore vulnerable both from traditional and current definition of security. Thus making the task of the statesmen of both sides is even more difficult. In bringing about lasting and cherished goal of peace and prosperity in South Asia both the states have to develop habit of resolving of conflicts. "Income, education, and health levels are lower in South Asia than in most regions, south Asia includes about 23% of the worlds population but as much as 39% of the worlds poor, where the poor are defined as those whose local purchasing power is equivalent to less then US $1 a day".

Huge resources are required to uplift the condition of people of the region with developing economies, the only way is to ease the tension in the region is to encourage cooperative security thus eventually leading to diversion of resources spent on military towards other sectors as to benefit the people. For a stable and peaceful South Asia, both Pakistan and India need to carry on the peace process by which they can lessen tensions and also may even resolve some of the contesting issues.

SECURITY PLURALISM AND PRINCIPLES

If land forces are to be successfully employed on coalition operations, a high degree of cohesion has to be present from the beginning of their mission. This requirement implies that multinational forces will have established a pre-existing level of understanding and functional interoperability before they arrive in-theatre. Looking for ways of improving the conduct of coalition operations, General RisCassi focused on the factors of doctrine and leadership. He argued that doctrine and leadership are the keys to achieving order in the chaos of battle and that this truism rings doubly true for multinational operations. Nonetheless, he noted that, despite long experience of coalition membership, the United States (and by extension all other states) remained remarkably ill-prepared for combined action. Although his comments focused on warfighting, they apply to any coalition force facing armed opposition. The fog and friction of operations, he wrote, were best overcome by:

> accentuating the commonalities that exist: first, between our national interests; second, between how we intend to deal with threats to mutual interests; and then in how we actually apply our combined forces in battle. Where commonalities are required but lacking, we move quickly to create them... The key to achieving this unity is by promulgating a doctrine for warfighting that is commonly understood and applied. Planning systems must be collective and participatory, yet responsive and unerringly timely.

General RisCassi concluded that the friction inherent in coalition operations was best overcome by rapidly analysing and testing combined tactical integration; command-and-control systems; training; and logistic arrangements. Provision could then be made to 'sew' these coalition systems even tighter. The task of developing coalition doctrinal principles that are both capable of being applied by the states of the Asia-Pacific and politically acceptable to them is a daunting one. However, that task is perhaps not as difficult as we might think. Attitudes to multinational operations are often shaped by experiences of UN-run missions. The past record of such operations does not provide an ideal starting point for a consideration of the most efficient way to deploy coalitions—a fact that the UN is honestly, if belatedly, accepting. The

Report of the Panel on United Nations Peace Operations, which was released in August 2000, frankly exposed the problems that many coalitions faced. Such problems included the overly bureaucratic distribution of responsibility in coalitions; shortfalls in officers qualified to serve in command and staff positions on coalition headquarters; the lack of training and equipment; and the inability of many states to honour the commitments that they had made to the UN.

These findings emphasised the gross disparities that generally exist between forces hurriedly cobbled together for multinational operations. Despite these criticisms of the manner in which the international community currently mounts multinational operations, there is another dimension to the military profession. Whatever their cultural origins, almost every military force recognises a list of principles that guide its actions. Most of these principles are derived from a common body of professional literature and enable officers, despite their own unique backgrounds and disparate force capabilities, to communicate complex concepts to each other. Working from a foundation of commonly accepted principles, professionally trained officers can establish understandings that will form the basis of a coalition and enable command relationships to be formed. Although we often concentrate on the 'bad news' about multinational forces, we should be surprised that they ever work at all. How many other professionals, sent far from home at short notice, could achieve anything in a polyglot team drawn from twenty or more countries?

With coalition operations becoming more common, soldiers can now expect to serve on a number of such missions during their career. The requirement to sustain operations in East Timor has resulted in the rotation of most active-service Australian Army units through that theatre. In addition, many Australian officers have gained valuable operational experience in multinational headquarters or as liaison officers with other forces. Officers from other armies participating in the operation often have even more experience of multinational operations than their Australian counterparts.

From a regional perspective, a middle-level officer in the New Zealand Army is likely to have served on three or four overseas peace operations, and a Fijian soldier may well spend half of his career overseas on operations. If the operational tempo currently maintained by the Australian Army persists, frequent overseas service may well become the norm, not the exception, in a soldier's career.

In these circumstances it makes little sense to reinvent the wheel for each operation. Longstanding, well-trained alliances such as NATO forces, or for that matter the forces of the Warsaw Pact, have demonstrated the value of possessing formed doctrine. The existence of such doctrine does not presuppose a commitment to particular operations, but does demonstrate a capacity to collaborate effectively if required. Different levels of cooperation are achieved within every interstate relationship: military, political and economic connections operate in different dimensions and at distinct levels. For example, the formal treaty-based special relationship with the United States is supported and supplemented by the specific operational synergies with other armies that the Australian Army gains through its participation in the American–British–Canadian–Australian Armies Program. In fact a comparative reading of Australian, US and British doctrinal publications will demonstrate extraordinary conceptual similarities—similarities that often extend to the order of the words themselves. (In the academic world we might call it plagiarism. In the drafting of military doctrine it is considered a full, frank and open exchange of ideas.) The high level of intellectual understanding that English-speaking and other NATO forces can establish only emphasises the problems faced by ad-hoc coalitions, which are often required to coordinate military operations in a matter of days.

Due to their complexity, land forces are particularly reliant on doctrine. Historically, the development of doctrine has reflected the particular national and cultural characteristics of individual forces. Their cultural similarity explains the ease with which English-speaking armies can share operational philosophies. In the Asia-Pacific, where even the simplest level of understanding between disparate forces is difficult to achieve, it is not possible to share common doctrine. In the absence of linguistic and cultural ties, it becomes even more important to seek alternative means of building common understanding. A recent joint US–UK–German–French working group on improving cooperability on coalition operations found that: Coalition partners working with very different doctrines will obviously have problems harmonizing their efforts. Indeed, regardless of the degree of technical interoperability they might achieve, genuine cooperability will be all but impossible to achieve. In simplest terms, forces that operate on different fundamental principles become vulnerable to misunderstandings, poorly coordinated actions, and even working at crosspurposes. Doctrine can, if harmonized, be the glue of coalition operations. Finding ways to harmonize doctrine is, therefore, a priority effort to ensure improved coalition operations.

It is a mistake to believe that the task of improving the level at which land forces can cooperate is fettered to the state of relationships between states in the Asia-Pacific. Nor is it in the long-term interest of regional states that the level of security dialogue should be pinned to formal diplomatic instruments. As Lord Palmerston famously commented: 'There are no permanent friends, only permanent interests.' It is in the interests of states that they be prepared to cooperate at short notice, even if it is impossible to foresee the circumstances that might give rise to joint action.

In a proposal with particular relevance for the Asia-Pacific, Colonel Michael Smith, Director of the Joint Doctrine Directorate in the US Army's Training and Doctrine Command, suggested that: To overcome the problems associated with the lack of common doctrine, regional organizations should develop regional doctrinal publications which identify doctrinal 'considerations' for commanders and planners. The term 'considerations' is used because it is unlikely that anything more detailed or prescriptive would be adopted and endorsed by all potential coalition members from a region.

Unfortunately, the nature of the strategic environment in the Asia- Pacific militates against the creation of a 'strong' security community. The region is simply not ready for developed multilateral cooperation in the way that Europe is. Not only does the region not share a monolithic security architecture, but historically it has not shared many of the presumptions on which international law and the notion of collective security are based. The security implications of the heterogeneous nature of the region are particularly clear in the case of the member states of the Association of South-East Asian Nations (ASEAN). In a paper published in 1996, Nicola Baker and Leonard Sebastian highlighted the extreme reluctance of ASEAN states to commit themselves to formal alliances:

Formal multilateral security agreements and structures were not considered feasible or desirable by the founding member states of ASEAN for three... reasons: they lacked the defence capacity for any form of collective security, their relations were complicated by unresolved territorial disputes, and they had quite different threat perceptions. Regional defence capabilities have since improved significantly but few have reached the point where adequate forces could be committed to, and sustained in, any form of collective action beyond the occasional military exercise.

To a certain extent, operations in East Timor have disproved this last assertion. Regional forces have established a precedent for cooperation on active service. Importantly, both INTERFET and its successor, the peacekeeping force element of UNTAET, have enjoyed regional leadership— in turn generals drawn one each from Australia and the Philippines, and two from Thailand.

Despite initial worldwide and regional support for the US-led 'coalition' against terrorism, we are unlikely to see overtly formal cooperative security structures established in the region in the near future. At the intergovernmental level, such an initiative—particularly if it originated in a Western state—is likely to be unwelcome. Although initially most East Asian governments pledged support for the planned US retaliation against the al'Qa'ida organisation, these governments have often had to face hostile domestic constituencies. The promises made to the United States have placed many regional countries in a difficult position—particularly those countries where the United States does not enjoy domestic popularity. As Bruce Gilley of the *Far Eastern Economic Review* wrote: Domestic pressures in every country will force most governments to keep their cooperation with the U.S. low profile. Anti-American sentiment, and more commonly a lack of support for a U.S. response, runs deep within the region. Some countries—particularly Singapore and Malaysia—are wary of making themselves targets of terrorists. Yet a failure to support U.S. efforts would put a country in danger of being labelled an undependable ally, or a rogue regime. So far, that is providing a formidable incentive to stand up and be counted.

While current circumstances provide indications that regional resistance to security cooperation may not be permanent, we must not be naive about the political constraints on the task of creating the preconditions for military coalitions. Over and above questions of language, culture and technical interoperability, many regional military forces play political and economic roles in their own countries. In some instances they have been implicated in human-rights abuses. The usual Western response to this concern was summarised by the Canadian scholar Brian Job, who made the quite valid point that: expansion of the extent and scope of military to military activities is viewed positively by Asia-Pacific security analysts who see substantial longer term benefits from opening dialogues among national militaries, as preliminary steps toward creating understanding, advancing transparency, and promoting important functional [links].

Nonetheless, liberal democracies cannot afford to be seen to be providing implicit support to the armed forces that might not fully represent the legitimately expressed aspirations of the populations that they are meant to protect. It would be naive to believe that we would never act in concert with such forces; instead, we can expect to belong to coalitions with a diverse composition when our national interests are involved and the particular operation or cause is demonstrably legitimate. Issue-based coalitions— rather than formal, standing defence relationships—will continue to be the norm so long as regional military forces remain active participants in their countries' political and economic affairs. The question that confronts us in the immature strategic environment that is the Asia-Pacific is how to create cooperative synergies with essentially dissimilar militaries.

Although multilateral diplomatic engagement has its place, post-Cold War regional diplomatic initiatives have singly failed to improve conditions of security. As Frederick the Great is credited with saying, 'diplomacy without arms is like an orchestra without instruments'. Security needs to be backed up by potent military force, and in the information age the talisman of military power needs to be transnational. At the level of military-to-military cooperation, US strategic engagement in the Asia-Pacific provides a model that regional forces need to embrace wholeheartedly. The challenge to US Pacific Command and its regional partners that Admiral Blair enunciated requires an information-age response that can only be achieved when armed forces have developed a high level of familiarity with each other. In the Asia-Pacific the US policy has been to support the growing pattern of security pluralism in the region. Admiral Blair has been particularly active in promoting the notion of 'security communities' that will enable specific-issue cooperation between military forces, even if more comprehensive political links do not exist between countries.

The notion of security communities—which was the brainchild of Karl Deutsch, the noted Harvard-based political scientist—is used to describe a group of nations that share dependable expectations of peaceful progress. Recognising that many regions were not yet ready for amalgamated security arrangements, much less shared political and economic systems, Deutsch identified three factors that could substantially enhance the prospects of a pluralistic security community. The first of these was the widespread unattractiveness of war as a means of resolving conflict among the potential members of the community. The second factor was the spread of intellectual movements favouring security interdependence. Thirdly, Deutsch promoted: the development and practice of skills of mutual attention, communication, and responsiveness, so as to make possible the preservation of the autonomy and substantial sovereignty of the participating units, and the preservation of stable expectations of peace and peaceful change among them.

The first factor is almost a foregone conclusion in a region that seeks stability for economic growth and where most countries would regard war as a calamity. The second process is certainly in train, through measures such as the second-track diplomacy of the ARF and the Council for Security Cooperation in the Asia-Pacific (CSCAP). The third process is one that could be substantially enhanced by the practical security collaboration that will arise from preparation for coalition efforts.

The concept of the security community is particularly useful for those states that are likely to come together to form coalitions and that need to prepare their forces to do so. As already demonstrated, land forces require the most preparation for multinational operations, and they have the most to benefit from the sort of cooperation envisaged by regional security cooperation.

Admiral Blair has pointed out that: An attractive feature of security communities for Asian states is the absence of any requirement for security institutions or regimes specified by treaty. Communities may be based on a non-military organization such as the ASEAN Regional Forum; or their membership may be based upon geography or common concerns rather than any multilateral security forum. The key is that the members are committed to policy coordination, including combined military cooperation on a particular regional security issue, or a series of related security issues, to advance peaceful development of their region over time without major conflict.

As far as land forces in the Asia-Pacific are concerned, cooperation can be engendered by practical measures to prepare regional land forces for the most common operations that they will have to carry out. In the current strategic environment, this requirement entails preparing for peace operations and countering transnational threats such as terrorism, smuggling, piracy and other crimes that threaten regional order. In the absence of more formal cooperative instruments, a useful expedient would be the formation of a multilateral army-to-army program, modelled on the highly successful ABCA system and building on the excellent relationships formed in recent regional peace operations.

The ABCA program provides the region with a useful model for inter-army cooperation since it is not an alliance, nor has an ABCA force ever been employed under the program. The program began after World War II to take advantage of the unprecedented levels of standardisation achieved by the American, British and Canadian armies. Australia joined the program in 1963 and New Zealand joined as an associate member two years later. The member armies conduct formation-level exercises on a biennial basis in order to identify technical interoperability issues and to test the abilities of the armies to operate in coalitions should the need arise. These exercises do not, however, imply a commitment to alliance operations; rather, they are a recognition of the common interests of the member states and signify an awareness of the fact that the member armies are likely to continue to serve together in the pursuit of common objectives. The program produces standardisation agreements, advisory handbooks and planning guides that help the armies to operate together when they are called on to do so. Although achieving total technical and doctrinal interoperability between armies from such varied operational environments is not likely, or even desirable, the experience of the synergies that they have been able to achieve demonstrates the value of this arrangement. The adoption of an ABCA-style model in the Asia- Pacific would not commit regional land forces to common doctrine, but it would enable them to harmonise their operational styles. Nascent infrastructure for army-to-army cooperation already exists. The Pacific Armies Management Seminar (PAMS), which is annually cohosted by the US Army and the army of one other Pacific Rim country, has been in existence since 1978. Representatives from 33 countries attended the seminar in 2001. Similarly the biennial Pacific Armies Chiefs Conference (PACC) involved fifteen army chiefs at its second meeting in Kuala Lumpur in September 2001. Although significant adjustments to the circumstances of the Asia-Pacific would be necessary, the adoption of a standardisation program would build on the goodwill and shared experience established by the Australian Army's participation in recent operations in Cambodia and East Timor.

RAW: INDIAN INTELLIGENCE AGENCY, A TERRORIST ORGANISATION

The role of an intelligence agency should be different from that of a terrorist organization. The CIA, the Mussad, the ISI and the Raw must not be mixed up with LTTE, the Black Water Force and particularly the detracted groups of Taliban & Al-Qaida which are defaming not only Islam but also the Muslims all over the world. If an intelligence agency is trying to forget its prescribed aims and objects by surpassing its limits, it should not be ranked as an intelligence agency but a terrorist organization.

A few days back the Federation of American Scientists FAS issued a report which confirmed that the Research and Analysis Wing RAW, was directly involved in the secession of East Pakistan into Bangladesh, and is currently engaged in similar activities in Balochistan. The FAS is a group which is engaged in analysis and advocacy on science, technology and public policy concerning global security, especially about the countries having nuclear capability. It is a privately funded non-profit policy organization whose Board of Sponsors includes 55 American Nobel laureates. The report says '"The assistance provided to RAW by the Russian KGB enabled RAW to arrange terrorist attacks in Pakistani cities throughout the Afghan War.

The defeat of the Soviet Union in Afghanistan did not end the role of RAW in Pakistan, as it established training camps in East Punjab, Indian Held Kashmir, Uttar Pradesh and Rajasthan where agents are trained for terrorist activities." Pointing towards the role of Raw in the formerly East Pakistan the report says, 'The involvement of Raw in East Pakistan started in 1960s when it began with promoting dissatisfaction against Pakistan. Later on Raw funded at a large scale Mujeebur Rehman's general election of 1970. This organization not only funded Mukti Bahini but also trained and armed the workers of Mukti Bahini.' There is another shocking revelation in the report that Raw staged the drama of hijacking a plane of Indian Airlines proceeding to Lahore in 1971. The hidden aim behind this hijacking was to put all blame on the

Kashmiri Freedom Fighters and to introduce them throughout the world as terrorists. In the light of the above disclosure it won't be wise to rank Raw as an intelligence agency. Hijacking of airplanes, massacre of innocent citizens and patronizing training camps of terrorist are certainly never the job of an intelligence agency. These are the actions of a terrorist organization. It is not only Pakistan which has been suffering from the childish misdeeds of Raw since long; the list of the afflicting countries is endless.

A few months back, in one of its editorials the leading newspaper of Sri Lanka, Daily Mirror criticized RAW by saying that this agency is playing a heinous role in the regional countries to destabilize them.. Commenting on the RAW's role in Sri Lanka, the editorial said: "The RAW in Sri Lanka has a pretty colorful record. Having raised, nursed and fortified the Liberation Tigers of Tamil Eelam, it later went through phases where it adopted 'rock the baby, pinch the baby' approach towards the LTTE." The paper is of the opinion that Raw never works on serious grounds because this organization is nothing more than a vase weeded with bitter thorny and discolored wild flowers. Its workers and employers are morally bankrupt and spiritually barren. The newspaper wrote: "In 2007, ripples were created in the spy agency when one of its Colombo-based officers, Ravi Nair of 1975 batch, was found allegedly carrying on an affair with a woman working for another country's spy agency. The 'crime' was considered only second to what was committed by the RAW Joint Secretary, Rabinder Singh, in 2004 when he escaped with copies of several highly-confidential documents and is believed to have passed them on to the CIA. This was after Singh's superiors confronted him with evidence that he had spent time with a Delhi-based female US embassy officer at a resort down the New Delhi-Jaipur highway."

According to the sources RAW and the Indian Ministry of External Affairs are provided Rs. 250 million annually as "discretionary grants" for foreign influence operations. These funds are meant for supporting the organizations fighting Sikh and Kashmiri separatists in the UK, Canada and the US. An Extensive network of Indian operatives of Raw is controlled by the Indian Embassy in Washington DC whose covert activities include the infiltration of US long distance telephone carriers by Indian operatives, with access to all kinds of information, to blackmail relatives of US residents living in India. In 1996, an Indian diplomat was implicated in a scandal over illegal funding of political candidates in the US. Under US law foreign nationals are prohibited from contributing to federal elections. The US District Court in Baltimore sentenced Lalit H. Gadhia, a naturalized US citizen of Indian origin, to three months imprisonment. Gadhia had confessed that he worked as a conduit between the Indian Embassy and various Indian-American organizations for funneling campaign contributions to influence US lawmakers. Over US $46,000 from the Indian Embassy were distributed among 20 Congressional candidates. The source of the cash used by Gadhia was Devendra Singh, a RAW official assigned to the Indian Embassy in Washington. Now Raw is adopting the same philosophy and mode of action in Balochistan by patronizing the so called 'separatist elements' which originally do not belong to the 'soil'.

Talking to the media men, Balochistan Chief Minister Jam Mohammad Yusuf said that involvement of external elements; including the Indian intelligence agency Research and Analysis Wing in the current acts of terrorism in Balochistan could not be ruled out. As long as Kashmir issue is not settled these elements will continue to create difficulties for Pakistan. Jam Yusuf referred to various training camps in which, according to him, terrorists were being harboured and paid huge sums to create trouble. He said that none of the Baloch 'waderas' had the capacity to finance such an operation. RAW had been running terrorist camps in Iran and Afghanistan since long and now it has set up 30 to 40 such camps in Balochistan, each with training facility for 30 people who are paid Rs10,000 monthly.

If we compare the East Pakistan episode and the present situation of Balochistan with reference to the report issued by the FAS, we can very easily analyze the scenario. Raw is repeating the same story of 'divide and disperse' in Balochistan which was once employed in the formerly East Pakistan. The situation calls for a very serious attitude on the part of Pakistani politicians. They must not waste their time and efforts in digging old graves.International forces are trying their best to divert the attention of the Pakistani politicians to some very trivial and valueless issues so that they may not be able to concentrate upon the worsening situation in Balochistan. Raw is craving for giving birth to another 'East Pakistan' out of its old barren and out worn womb. The Pakistani politicians must keep in mind like sensible fathers that we can no more afford another pregnancy.

INDIAN SPECIAL FORCES-CAPABILITIES AND SHORTCOMINGS

India, like any other country does have its own Special Forces – the Army has Para Commandos, which are elite airborne units and the Ghatak Platoons which are attached to each infantry battalion of the Army, the Navy has the Marine Commandos (MARCOS for short), and the Air Force the Garud. Besides, India has the National Security Guards (NSG), a Special Response Unit which is primarily tasked with counter terrorism activities, the Special Frontier Force whose one squadron is responsible for counter-terrorism duties and the various state police have their own Special Task Force for special operations, like for instance Jammu and Kashmir Police has the Special Operations Group to tackle terrorism. Opinion seems to be divided if we really have the intelligence and military capabilities to emulate the operation carried out by the US Navy SEALs in Abbottabad on May 2, 2011 to neutralize Osam bin Laden. In the backdrop of Osama bin Laden's killing in Abbottabad, India's Air Chief Marshal P.V. Naik and Indian Army chief General V.K. Singh declared their forces have the capability and competence to carry out a commando operation outside the country to target terrorists.

'There is no doubt about it. The army, navy and air force are paid to be ready. None of the services chiefs is going to say he does not have the capability,' says retired Commodore C. Uday Bhaskar, director of naval think-tank National Maritime Foundation, when asked about the services chiefs' comments. Brigadier Gurmeet Kanwal, director of army think-tank Centre for Land Warfare Studies, concurs with Uday Bhaskar. 'We virtually have the same capability (as the US Navy SEALs),' Kanwal told IANS, pointing out that the army itself has over half-a-dozen special forces battalions trained to carry out such attacks on strategic targets. Brigadier Kanwal, however added that India should look at energising its external intelligence agency Research and Analysis Wing (RAW) for getting its wanted, rather than use its armed forces.

'To be very honest, it is not possible to disclose if we have these capabilities or not. But, yes, we have the joint strategic capability for any special task that the government assigns to the armed forces, not necessarily in the neighbourhood, but anywhere around the globe,' Air Marshal P.K. Barbora, former Indian Air Force (IAF) vice chief, told IANS.

'But the decision on such operations is not taken by the uniformed personnel. It is taken by the political leadership after receiving all inputs including the implications and fall-out, and after planning for all exigencies, be it a nuclear conflict,' Barbora said.

The Contrary View

According to Lt. General R. K. Nanavatty, who has been involved in planning aspects of Indian Special Forces and has been studying the subject for years, India does not have the capabilities of executing an operation similar to Operation Neptune's Spear. Nanavatty said "We are not capable for a variety of reasons. Political understanding of special operations is very important then only you can commit money, time and technology for nurturing such a force. "Special Operations today are controlled by men who do not understand them". Lt Gen P C Katoch, a former SF officer and a leading expert on Special Operations, said major operations by Indian troops have at various stages demonstrated what was wrong with them. "There are problems of intelligence, logistics etc. Our SF forces are doing what conventional troops can do and there is an overall lack of political willpower to nurture the capability with long term vision," said Katoch, who led an SF unit in Sri Lanka with the Indian Peace Keeping Force in the 80s and has also been involved in planning of Indian SFs. "Our men are ready, but minus intelligence, support etc," Katoch pointed out.

General Katoch pointed out that many of the mistakes of 1988 when Indian troops carried out an unsuccessful operation to capture the top leadership of the LTTE including its supremo Prabhakaran from Jaffna University were there to be seen in November 2008 in Mumbai when NSG commandos were deployed to take on the Pakistani terrorists. A decade back in 1999, a team of NSG commandos tailed hijacked IC814 aircraft to the Gulf region but returned. They couldn't also think of carrying out a surgical operation in Kandahar for a host of reasons including lack of airlift and political will.

According to Colonel Anil Athale, the Indian State does not have the will to carry out such operations and hence has not created the wherewithal to carry out strikes like Operation Neptune's Spear.

The Essentials

The two essential pre-requisites for conducting a successful special operation are availability of hard intelligence and sophisticated technical support. To elaborate, the planners and executors of this type of operation must be fed with concrete real time intelligence about the mission or objective to be accomplished. For instance, when the Israelis executed the raid at Entebbe in 1976, the commandos and the senior military commanders sitting in Tel Aviv were fully aware of the location of the hostages, the number of terrorists, the layout of the terminal building, etc. The commandos knew where their targets were, where precisely the Ugandan troops were stationed and how reinforcements, if any, were to be neutralized. There were no loose ends. In the absence of human intelligence (HUMINT), it may be impossible to carry out a successful operation. America's Central Intelligence Agency maintained a safe house near Abbottabad town for a small team of spies who conducted extensive surveillance on slain Al Qaeda chief Osama bin Laden's compound for months before President Barack Obama signed an order to kill the most wanted terrorist on April 29. It is estimated that the US has had about 3000 operatives active in Pakistan at the time of the Abbottabad raid.

The second essential is the availability of technological support such as satellite imagery of the target area, stealth technology for the purpose of infiltrating and exfiltrating of the operatives undetected and secure communications. India's Imagery Intelligence (IMINT) capabilities are quite limited. India, in April 2009 launched its first dedicated radar reconnaissance satellite Radar Imaging Satellite 2 (or RISAT-2). The radar has an Israeli-built primary sensor which allows RISAT-2 to return images at any time of day, and in any weather conditions. India also has Cartosat-2 launched in 2007, which according to some experts may be used for military purpose. India needs to augment its space-based intelligence gathering capabilities.

Another important essential for carrying out special operations is political will. India lacks the political will to carry out any type of surgical strikes against non-state as well as state actors, notwithstanding the fact India has repeatedly been subject to terror strikes sponsored by Pakistan. In 1999, when IC 814 was hijacked and flown to Kandahar, Indian commandos merely tailed the hijacked aircraft but did not attempt a hostage rescue mission. Again in 2001, in the aftermath of the attack on Indian Parliament, the political masters could not muster the political will to carry out surgical operations against Pak-based terror outfits. It was the same story in 2008. Israel on the other hand, has displayed considerable amount of political will in striking back at its adversaries and has the unique distinction of having struck against non-state actors far from its borders.

India's past experience of special operations (involving its Special Forces) have been limited in its scope. Barring Operation Cactus (1988) in Maldives, the failed mission to nab the leadership of the Tamil Tigers in Jaffna in 1988 and Operation Khukri (June 2000) in Sierra Leone all Special Forces' operations have been carried out within the country, mostly in Jammu and Kashmir and in the North-East. In Operation Cactus a battalion of the Parachute Regiment was air-dropped to rescue and assist the government of Abdul Gayoom against the mercenaries belonging to the People's Liberation Organisation of Tamil Eelam (PLOTE) and Operation Khukri was a daring rescue mission conducted by the Para Commandos in Sierra Leone resulting in the rescue of 21 hostages. In Operation Blue Star (June 1984), commandos of the 1st Battalion of the Parachute Regiment were unsuccessful in reaching the edge of the sacred pool to the Akal Takht. The National Security Guards (NSG) was established pursuant to an Act of Parliament called the National Security Guard Act, 1986. It was set up in the aftermath of the infamous Operation Blue Star wherein apart from the high casualties suffered, the shrine itself suffered severe damage. The operation necessitated the need for setting up a highly specialised and efficient force for counter-terrorist operations. Thus, NSG was deployed initially to combat the militancy in Punjab. In Black Thunder I (April 1986) about 300 National Security Guards commandos stormed the Golden Temple along with 700 Border Security Force troops and captured about 300 separatists. Two years later, in May 1988, the Golden Temple was again besieged and the security forces conducted Operation Black Thunder II and were successful in eliminating about 40 militants and forced the surrender of 200 militants.

Operation Ashwamedh was an operation conducted in April 1993 when NSG commandos stormed a hijacked an Indian Airlines aircraft with 141 passengers on board at Amritsar airport. The lone hijacker, Mohammed Yousuf Shah, was killed in the operation. In September 2002, again the NSG carried out Operation Vajrashakti to flush out two heavily armed LeT terrorists who had caused carnage in the Akshardham Temple, Gandhinagar. In this operation, while the terrorists were killed, nearly 29 devotees and two commandos and one state police officer were also killed. About 79 devotees were also injured in the terrorist attack.

It is important to remember that all operations carried out by Special Forces have not been successful. The US which is lauded today for its operation against the terror master-mind Osama bin Laden had to face embarrassment and political backlash in April 1980 when the then US President Carter authorized an operation to rescue fifty-three American citizens held hostage in Iran ended in disaster. Operation Eagle Claw, as the ill-fated rescue mission was called resulted in the death of eight US servicemen. The fireball in the Iranian desert took the Carter presidency with it.

Concluding Observations

In conclusion, it must be said that though India has Special Forces, they have been largely used as a kind of super-infantry-employing them on missions which the regular army would baulk at. India does not lack brave men and officers, but what it does not currently possess is the right blend of political will, politico-military-intelligence integration and specialized technology that make these operations possible. As former Intelligence Bureau chief Ajit Doval says "What we need is to have a national political will accepting active national self defence as a doctrine to neutralise the enemies of India". "The nature, instrumentalities and deniability quotient of covert actions should be determined by our mission objective, intelligence capabilities and requirements of consequence management," he added.

By their very nature, all Special Forces operations are fraught with not just physical danger, but grave political consequences may ensue from failure. A goof-up in Abbottabad would have led not only to the possible capture and death of the US Navy Seals, but a possible sinking of Barack Obama's presidency as in the case of Operation Eagle Claw.

INDIA, INTELLIGENCE AND SECURITY

Espionage and intelligence appears in the recorded history of the Indus Valley as early as the fifth century. The modern nation of India gained its independence from Britain in 1947. The withdrawal of the British colonial government left India with little governmental infrastructure, and the nation embarked on an ambitious plan to create a new national government. Indian independence, however, also sparked resistance from ethnic groups on the Indian Subcontinent, such as the large Muslim community. As a result of the developing conflict, India quickly established military and intelligence forces.

India's intelligence community is divided into a traditional structure that separates military and civilian, and foreign and domestic intelligence. Though each agency is charged with its own mission, the government has provided a means to facilitate the sharing of information between members of the intelligence community. The Joint Intelligence Committee (JIC) processes and analyzes data gathered by both civilian and military intelligence agencies and coordinates joint operations. The National Security Council acts as liaison between the government's executive branch and the intelligence services, advising leadership on intelligence and security issues.

The main civilian intelligence agency in India is the Intelligence Bureau (IB). The IB focuses on domestic intelligence, but the exact structure and operations of the agency are largely unknown. Political espionage is illegal in India, and police gathered wiretapping information is inadmissible as evidence in court proceedings. However, the IB conducts regular electronic monitoring of telephone communications, and mail surveillance, despite occasional admonitions from Parliament. The Central Bureau of Investigations handles most criminal investigations, often acting on initial information provided by one of the IB's many departments. Increasing political tensions with neighboring Pakistan altered the focus of IB operations in recent years, with increasing attention paid to the protection and surveillance of national borders.

The Research and Analysis Wing (RAW) is India's primary agency responsible for foreign intelligence. RAW operations are largely focused on espionage against Pakistan. With the addition of both India and Pakistan to the growing cadre of the world's nuclear powers, India's RAW conducts counter-intelligence operations, as well as technological and remote espionage, against Pakistani defense and military interests. The RAW is not subject to Parliamentary review, and its actions are highly secret. The Indian government also used RAW resources to aid predominantly-Hindu Bangladesh's 1971 quest for independence from Muslim Pakistan. Most recently, the RAW aided international antiterrorism efforts by providing the United States and British governments information on the al-Qaeda terrorist network and its strongholds in Pakistan and Afghanistan.

Military intelligence is conducted by the Army Directorate of Military Intelligence. The agency is the weakest of India's intelligence community, but often aids civilian intelligence operations. The Army also maintains the Joint Cipher Bureau, the main code breaking department of Indian intelligence. To the northwest, the independent Muslim nation of Pakistan claims the Kashmir region of India. The two nations have never resolved the border dispute, and tensions recently reached a climax when both nations declared themselves nuclear powers and began testing weapons of mass destruction. The nuclear programs of India and Pakistan raise interesting questions about the efficacy of current non-proliferation measures and the increasing global prevalence of industrial and scientific espionage. The increasing instability of the region has aroused the concern of the international community and the United Nations Security Council.

THREATS AND VULNERABILITIES OF THE NATIONAL SECURITY

The illegal presence of foreign military troops on the territory of the country and the phenomenon of political separatism that generated the Transnistrian conflict and loss of control over the Eastern regions are a continuous threat to independence, sovereignty, territorial integrity and national security of the Republic of Moldova. The fundamental rights and freedoms of the population from the left Nistru bank are systematically violated by the separatist regime's structures. Lack of control on behalf of constitutional Moldovan authorities over the Transnistrian segment of the Moldovan-Ukrainian border favors smuggling of goods, which seriously harm the economic security of the country and fuel cross-border organized crime, illegal traffic of ammunition, drugs and human beings.

Military threats are linked to the illegal presence in the Eastern regions of the Republic of Moldova of foreign military forces, ammunition and armaments, as well as to the activity of the factories in the Transnistrian region, that produce armament without any monitoring or tracking, which must be conducted by the competent Moldovan authorities. The presence of the Russian troops and armament on the territory of the Republic of Moldova contravenes the Constitution of the Republic of Moldova, international commitments and the will of Moldovan citizens, thus becoming a political pressure tool and major threat to the national security of the country. The foreign military presence on the territory of Moldova favors the consolidation of the separatist regime.

Threat of Foreign Coercion

The threat of foreign coercion, political or other, to influence the foreign and domestic policy of the Republic of Moldova is real. Such pressure may be exerted by means of economic or other constraints against the Republic of Moldova or through the special services of other states. The EU integration process that facilitates the political, economic and social transformations in the country, cumulated with the civil society consolidation based on democratic values, rule of law and legality shall foster the capacity of the Republic of Moldova to cope with coercions and, whenever needed, to efficiently respond to such types of threats.

External Negative Developments and International Crises

Problems which the Republic of Moldova is confronted with may not be addressed in isolation from the developments in certain areas of Europe, the latter being subject of broader international concerns. The current threats to the national security of the Republic of Moldova may become more imminent if combined with other new threats, including negative external developments and unsolved international crises. Contradictory developments in the pos-Soviet area might conduct to the generation of new threats to the security of the Republic of Moldova. Given the indivisibility of the European security, the Republic of Moldova's national security is influenced by the security issues on the continent and vice versa. Crisis situations and their consequences threaten the security on the continent. Prolonged instability on the sub-regional level negatively impacts the process of promoting lasting development strategies, discourages foreign investments, closes markets for Moldovan products, favors illegal migration and trafficking in ammunition and narcotics.

The Threat of Organized Crime

Organized crime, including the cross-border organized crime, follows the tendency to intermingle with the activity of terrorist organizations and with the proliferation of arms of mass destruction. The persistence of criminal factors creates premises for terrorist activities and proliferation of arms. Without control over the Eastern regions and the Transnistrian segment of the Moldovan-Ukrainian border, the phenomenon of organized crime represents an ascending threat to the national security of the Republic of Moldova. This risk factor may also generate negative effects at the sub-regional and regional levels.

The danger of increasing influence of the cross-border organized crime over the Moldovan society, combined with corruption and eventual penetration of the political, economic and social spheres by the organized crime may undermine the supremacy of law and, implicitly, the national security of the Republic of Moldova.

The Treat of International Terrorism

On the background of diminishing military threats to the national security, non-conventional threats, in particular the globalization of international terrorism and proliferation of chemical, biological, radioactive and nuclear arms, including their acquisition by non-state entities, are growing.

Reduction of the international terrorism threat and prevention of proliferation of arms of mass destruction are possible only by concerted and rapid actions on international level that requires Moldova's participation based on its international commitments.

Additionally to the actions undertaken in the context of international cooperation, the Republic of Moldova is implementing domestic anti-terrorism measures.

Threats that Derive from Human Activity and Natural Disasters

The threats that derive from human activity and that may impact the national security of the Republic of Moldova are: explosions and conflagrations; accidents at power stations, at plants that use radioactive and chemical agents, at transportation enterprises, as well as cross-border effects of such accidents. In the South-eastern European region, where the Republic of Moldova is situated, the potential danger may be caused by the obsolete equipment of several nuclear power stations and large enterprises that use dangerous chemicals in their industrial process. Natural disasters that may determine force major in the Republic of Moldova are earthquakes, floods, landslides and other of a natural origin.

Economic Threats

Because of its small size and increasing economic interdependency between the Republic of Moldova and the global economic system, a global or regional economic crisis or instability on the traditional or priority foreign markets may considerably impact the country's economy. The major risk factors of economic origin that could pose threat to the national security of the Republic of Moldova are generated by the excessive and unilateral dependency of local electric and energy systems as well as of gas distribution networks on foreign monopolies in the filed. This dependency, at the same time, constitutes the internal vulnerability of the state.

Social Threats

Drug addiction, alcoholism, HIV/AIDS spread, and other contagious highly dangerous diseases for the society represent a threat to the welfare, social and political stability of the country.

IT Threat

Instable and dysfunctional information systems may pose threat to the national security. Progressive expansion of electronic information systems in the Republic of Moldova and the high degree of interconnection with the international information systems facilitate the criminogenic factor in the field of IT and increase the vulnerability of such systems, including in the spheres of primordial importance for the national security.

Internal Vulnerabilities

The above-mentioned threats interconnect with the domestic vulnerabilities. The effects of these vulnerabilities may determine accentuation and manifestation of existing threats as well as generate new ones to the national security. Overlapping and combination of such effects may negatively impact the national security. Neglect, cease of monitoring and loss of control over the vulnerabilities may transform them into threats to national security and may trigger domestic instability. The negative effects on the national security caused by domestic vulnerabilities may be multiple, interdependent, dynamic and many-sided.

The main domestic vulnerabilities of the Republic of Moldova are:

- Existence of a range of factors that intercalate and favor the persistence of the aggressive separatism in the context of yet unsolved Transnistrian conflict. These vulnerability constitutes the impossibility to administrate the Eastern territory of the country, lack of control over the Transnistrian segment of the Moldovan-Ukrainian state border, continued illegal and uncontrolled production of military equipment and armament, inability to control and manage the entire air space of the country.
- The excessive and unilateral dependency of the Republic of Moldova on foreign monopolistic energy systems represents a major internal vulnerability. This vulnerability may easily grow into a threat to the national security. Such also include the broad possibilities of accumulation of the foreign capital coming from economic systems where market economy rules are not secured or underdeveloped in the national economic sectors of major importance.
- Continuing problems within the energy system of the country that may cause disruptions in this system. Insufficient protection of energy sector objects.
- Lasting character of the transition period that continues to cause negative economic, financial, social effects and delays in structural reforms.
- Economic migration, unemployment, population aging and low

birthrate phenomena. Lasting and complex character of the reduction of poverty process, existing tendencies of social polarization, as well as upholding of gray economy that may generate tensions and general discontent among people.

- The existing discrepancy between the actual needs and efforts spent by the law enforcement and special agencies to combat criminality, particularly, cross-border criminality.
- Corruption and management deficits within the state administration.
- Slow development of the informational infrastructure and low competitiveness in the IT sector, low quality of information processing and unsatisfactory use of information of national interest, lack of quick react capabilities on information that is bias and distorts the realities of the Republic of Moldova. Internal vulnerabilities also include maintaining the connectivity between national and former Soviet Union informational systems, and perpetuation of inconstancies in protecting classified information.
- Continued use of obsolete technologies that may be hazardous for people and lead to ecological disasters.
- Reduced capacity of preventing ecological disasters and natural calamities (land slides, floods, earthquakes, etc.), as well as addressing the consequences thereof.
- Emigration of highly qualified specialists and wakening of the country's development potential.

Transnistrian Conflict and Foreign Military Forces Withdrawal

As it was mentioned in the present Concept, the Transnistrian conflict, the lack of an efficient control on the Transnistrian section on the Moldovan - Ukrainian border, the presence of Russian troops and armament on the territory of the Republic of Moldova constitutes a major obstacle in the state and society's development and generates multiple interconnected threats of conventional and non-conventional nature to the national, regional and international security. Therefore, the Transnistrian conflict settlement and reintegration of the country is no longer an internal problem of the Republic of Moldova, instead it evolved into a regional security problem and its settlement requires full involvement of external influential factors such as the EU and the USA.

The Republic of Moldova spends efforts to achieve a peaceful settlement of the conflict, secured Moldovan - Ukrainian border and unconditional implementing by the Russian Federation of its commitments made at the OSCE summit in Istanbul in 1999. These are the priority objectives of the foreign and security policy of the country.

Fomented separatism and increased instability are generated by the illegal presence on the country's territory of the foreign military forces and armaments. The Republic of Moldova will use all legal methods to reach the unconditional and complete withdrawal of the Russian military forces, according to the Istanbul (1999) OSCE Summit's decisions.

The full implementation of the Istanbul's decisions will set the conditions for the Republic of Moldova to ratify the Adapted CFE Treaty.

On July 22, 2005 the Parliament of the Republic of Moldova adopted the Law on basic provisions of the special legal status of Transnistria, (nr. 173-XVI) which determines the future autonomy framework of the region within the structure of the reintegrated state.

The Republic of Moldova's authority's vision regarding the ways for Transnistrian conflict settlement actively supported by the Moldovan civil society includes, in particular, the goal of democratization and demilitarization of the Transnistrian region as well as implementing a confidence building measures.

The democratization process requires the establishment of an international mechanism for political reforms that would allow for free and fair elections leading to the legitimate local authorities.

The future autonomy status of the region with the reunified country will be negotiated only with such legitimate authorities and in accordance with the principles stipulated in the above-mentioned law of 22 July 2005. In order not to allow for external pressure on the voters, Moldovan authorities believe that the electoral process must be preceded by withdrawal of foreign troupes from the territory of the country.

The demilitarization means the withdrawal of the Russian troops from the territory of the country, dismantlement of the paramilitary forces and the security structures of the unconstitutional regime, the replacement of the current peacekeeping operation with an international mission of civilian and military observers established in line with the UN/OSCE standards.

An international inspection should take place at the armaments stockpiles of the Russian Federation and an OSCE-led monitoring mission should be organized at the military industrial complex in the Transnistrian region.

The objectives on securing the state border include: drafting and implementing the National Strategy on integrated stet border management in order to adapt the existing border management to the EU standards; further cooperation with Ukraine and the EU border assistance mission (EUBAM); consolidating the cooperation between the national institutions with related competences at the border and international cooperation on combating terrorism, proliferation of mass destruction arms and illegal migration as well as in combating all types of border crimes.

Supremacy of Law and Democratic Institutions

From the perspective of the national security of the Republic of Moldova, guaranteeing the good functioning of the democratic institutions and the rule of law, as well as protecting human rights and fundamental liberties of the people are primary objectives.

The administrative, public order protection and judicial systems are consolidated and developed to ensure the governance functionality based on rule of law. The continuing development of the civil society is essential for the functioning of the democratic institutions and the rule of law.

The preconditions for the development of the civil society are ensured by the constitutional democratic and stable framework, level of openness of the society, promoting civil initiatives and accessibility to the high quality education.

Prevention and Combating Corruption and Organized Crime

The policy on prevention and combating corruption and its successful implementation requires the compliance of the public authorities' activities with the democratic and rule of law standards. The Republic of Moldova worked out a long-term state policy on combating economic crimes and corruption.

These areas are developed through balanced cooperation between the public sector, private sector and the society ensuring, at the same time, the implementation of the international commitments made by the Republic of Moldova in the respective filed. The main tasks of the strategy on combating corruption are improving the legislation and consolidating the institutional system as well as increasing and supporting public information on legal issues. The main state institutions assigned to fight economic crimes and corruptions are:

- *The Centre for Combating Economic Crimes and Corruption* the main body tasked with preventing and combating corruption, with main functions including: a) preventing, identifying, investigating and curbing economic-financial and fiscal infringements and crimes; b) fighting corruption and protectionism; c) combating legalization of goods acquired illegally and money-laundering; d) anti-corruption expertise for the draft bills and the Executive's regulations with the aim at bringing them in line with the state policy on preventing and combating corruption.

- *Anti-corruption and criminal investigation Prosecutor Office* a specialized subdivision within the PGO of the Republic of Moldova. The Prosecutor Office leads and conducts criminal investigations, represents the prosecution in courts, as well as checks the legality of the procedural-criminal activities carried out by the criminal investigation body.
- *Other public authorities, as envisaged by legislation.*

The amendments operated within the national legislation regarding the legalization of the capital and fiscal amnesty are directed to improve the situation in the fields of registration of the private property and taxation and to facilitate the prevention of a legalization of an illegally gained property as well as the gathering of a necessary proofs for the identification of the penal cases.

5

Pakistan's National Security

Armed Forces Overview: The military is formally called the Pakistan Armed Forces, and as of 2004 consisted of approximately 619,000 active personnel in the army (550,000), air force (45,000), and navy (24,000), as well as 513,000 reserves. Under the 1973 constitution, the federal government controls the armed forces, and the president is the commander in chief. The Ministry of Defence has a permanent staff of civil servants headed by the defense secretary general, and the minister of defense is a civilian member of the prime minister's cabinet. The Joint Chiefs of Staff Committee deals with problems concerning military aspects of state security and is charged with integrating and coordinating the army, navy, and air force.

The committee's secretariat acts as the principal link between the service headquarters and the Ministry of Defence. The Directorate for Inter-Services Intelligence (ISI) is of particular importance at the joint services level because it manages covert operations outside of Pakistan (and in internationally disputed areas) and because it has been involved in domestic politics, usually to keep track of the incumbent regime's opponents. The chief of the army staff (COAS) is the key power holder in the armed forces and is also one of the triumvirate that runs the country, along with the prime minister and president. The COAS usually operates from army headquarters in Rawalpindi. General Pervez Musharraf acts as both president and COAS. Musharraf also heads a National Security Council composed of politicians and senior military officers.

Under the constitution, the military is responsible for defending the nation against external aggression and threats of war and is to aid civil authorities only when called to do so. The military is forbidden constitutionally from acting independently of the elected political leadership in domestic matters. However, from 1947 to 2004 military generals have acted as head of state for nearly 30 years, and in times of civilian government the armed forces have routinely intervened on domestic and foreign policy issues. The military justifies its consistent involvement in politics as protection from malign foreign interests and corrupt and incompetent politicians. Although public opinion surveys are rare, it appears that the public dislikes military rule, yet consistently has a more favorable view of the military than of elected officials.

Because the military conducts its affairs with carefully defended secrecy, the degree to which army officers and personnel are religiously motivated is debated. However, Western analysts tend to conclude that whereas the military increasingly sees itself as serving Islam, the institution's decision making is still largely secular.

Military intervention in politics is designed to limit civilian involvement in sensitive matters, such as Kashmir, nuclear disarmament, internal military personnel decisions, and defense spending. The military also is extensively involved in the economy, and military enterprises produce approximately 3 percent of the gross national product. Military enterprises include the Army Welfare Trust (AWT), whose assets include the Askari Bank, one of the country's largest financial institutions, and the Fauji Foundation, which is the country's biggest conglomerate. These and other military financial institutions often are exempt from taxes and regulations covering the manufacturing sector and asset disclosure.

With regard to military strategy, the military's budget and personnel have reduced strategy to largely defensive objectives, such as limited offensive tactics in bordering areas (particularly Kashmir), use of irregular forces, and deterring and countering possible attacks from foreign powers (particularly India). The military's history of far lower military expenditures and capabilities than India has prompted the military to attempt to impose high costs on India to force its withdrawal from Kashmir. Furthermore, the military hopes that its nuclear capabilities can reduce the disadvantages of its conventional forces. However, the theoretical deterrence between nuclear powers has not limited military engagement between India and Pakistan—as exemplified by the 1999 Kargil War—and analysts believe that Pakistan's military strategy historically has suffered from overly optimistic assessments of potential success and underestimations of diplomatic and military losses, as well as a lack of contingency planning.

Foreign Military Relations: Pakistan has sought to become an important actor in international politics, but its foreign military alliances often are intended to address matters with bordering countries. Other countries have established alliances with Pakistan to address their own strategic interests in South and Central Asia, and these alliances have tended to be ephemeral. Pakistan's military relationship with China started in the 1970s as a way of countering India, but China has softened its relations since India's military strength has increased. Still, Pakistan and China maintain a military relationship, including periodic joint military exercises. United States aid in the 1980s was significantly reduced after the Soviet Union pulled out of Afghanistan in 1989 but resumed after the September 11, 2001, terrorist attacks. Moreover, in March 2004 the United States granted Pakistan status as a major non-North Atlantic Treaty Organization ally, which provides access to U.S. military equipment and cooperation. In fact, the United States is one of the largest suppliers of military equipment to Pakistan along with China and Russia. Pakistan's military relations with India have been contentious, and the two countries fought a limited conflict in Kashmir in 1999. However, under the 1999 Lahore Agreement the two countries provide each other with advance notification of missile tests, and in 2003 and 2004 they engaged in several high-level discussions that have eased tensions.

External Threat: The military and public generally view India as the nation's primary security threat, and opposition to India is often a greater source of social cohesion than either Islam or Urdu. India's far greater military capabilities have been a source of both fear and frustration, and many suspect that this imbalance has prompted Pakistan to engage Indian forces indirectly through supporting insurgents morally, financially, or otherwise. Whether Pakistan has done so is debated, but it seems clear that the country's newly demonstrated nuclear capabilities have helped level military differences with its rival neighbor. Yet India is not the country's only security concern, as Pakhtun and Balochi irredentist movements in Pakistan's western provinces have contributed to sometimes-tense relations with neighbouring Afghanistan.

Defense Budget: According to World Bank figures for 1988 to 2003, Pakistan's military expenditures represented 25–29 percent of central government expenditures and 6–7 percent of gross national income. In fiscal year (FY) 2004, military expenditures constituted 18 percent of government expenditures. Historically, Pakistan's governments have used defense spending to stimulate economic growth.

Major Military Units: The army, with 550,000 active personnel and 500,000 reserves, is organized into nine corps located at Bahawalpur, Gujranwala, Karachi, Lahore, Mangla, Multan, Peshawar, Quetta, and Rawalpindi. The Northern Area Command is headquartered at Gilgit and is directly responsible to army general headquarters. The army has 2 armoured divisions, 19 infantry divisions including 1 area command, 9 corps artillery brigades, 26 independent brigades (7 armoured, 1 mechanized, 6 infantry, 5 artillery, and 7 engineer), 3 armoured reconnaissance regiments, 1 special forces group, and 1 air defense command. The navy has 24,000 active personnel—including 1,400 marines and 2,000 in the Maritime Security Agency—and 5,000 reserves. The navy has four commands: fleet, logistics, naval installations in the north of Pakistan, and fleet headquarters at Karachi, the nation's only major naval base. Two bases are under construction at Gwadar and Ormara. The air force has 45,000 active personnel and 8,000 reserves. Air force headquarters in Rawalpindi has directorates for operations, electronics, administration, and maintenance. The air force has three regional air commands: Northern (in Peshawar), Central (Sargodha), and Southern (Faisal).

Major Military Equipment: In 2004 the army had an estimated 2,461 tanks, 1,146 armoured personnel carriers, 1,829 tube-launched optically-tracked wire-guided "TOW" missiles, 260 self-propelled artillery, 52 multiple rocket launchers, 2,350 mortars, 165 surface-to-surface missiles, 10,500 antitank guided weapons, and 1,900 air defense guns. The army also had 80 observation aircraft, 45 liaison aircraft, 2 survey aircraft, 22 attack helicopters, and 131 transport helicopters. The navy had 8 anti-surface warfare submarines, 3 inshore submarines, 7 frigates, 6 missile craft, 3 coastal patrol craft, 6 combat aircraft, and 9 armed helicopters. The air force had 415 combat aircraft and no armed helicopters. Pakistan became a nuclear state in 1998 and periodically tests nuclear-capable short- and medium-range missiles.

Military Service: Military service is voluntary, and active-service personnel are liable for duty eight years after active service ends. Officers are obligated to serve until 50 years of age, other ranks until 45 years of age. Women serve in the military but are a numerical minority.

Paramilitary Forces: The central government (specifically the Ministry of Interior) controls the coast guard, paramilitary forces, and numerous specialized police agencies, such as the Federal Investigative Agency and railroad and airport police forces. However, provincial governments organize paramilitary forces, which often act as an extension of the army to assist provincial police in internal security matters.

In addition, senior government officials often have strong control over security forces and have at times established personal security forces. The largest paramilitary organization is the 185,000-member National Guard, which comprises the National Cadet Corps, the Women Guards, and the Janbaz Force. The Frontier Corps reportedly has 65,000 members and is responsible for Balochistan and the North-West Frontier Province. The Pakistan Rangers has 35,000 to 40,000 members and deals with unrest in Punjab. The Northern Light Infantry has an estimated 12,000 members, and the Maritime Security Agency, which is under the navy's direction, has an estimated 2,000 personnel.

Foreign Military Forces: Pakistan hosts 45 military observers from nine countries stationed in Jammu and Kashmir under the United Nations Military Observer Group in India and Pakistan (UNMOGIP). U.S. military forces occasionally work with Pakistan's military against insurgents supporting the Taliban and al Qaeda in areas of Pakistan bordering Afghanistan.

Military Forces Abroad: In 2004 Pakistan's military participated in United Nations peacekeeping missions in Burundi, Côte d'Ivoire (9 personnel including 3 observers), the Democratic Republic of the Congo (1,092 personnel including 26 observers), East Timor (78 personnel including 5 observers), Georgia (8 observers), Liberia (2,762 personnel including 16 observers), Sierra Leone (3,865 personnel including 15 observers), Serbia and Montenegro (1 observer), and Western Sahara (7 observers).

Police: Provincial governments are charged with police administration in their respective jurisdictions, and provincial police forces operate independently. The federal government is largely uninvolved in provincial police administration but controls police in federally administered and tribal areas. The federal minister of interior supervises police nationwide, and the Police Service of Pakistan (PSP) selects, trains, and assigns senior officers to provincial or central government agencies. Although service in the PSP is competitive and well paid, lower-ranking police personnel often have far lower education, skills, and motivation. Police often are accused of routine extortion, violating civil liberties, and acting to preserve the tenure of government officials rather than the rule of law. The quantity of overall crime and various types of crime (such as murder and banditry) increased steadily from 1992 to 2003, and the extensive availability and use of automatic weapons in Pakistani society is often referred to as the "Kalashnikov Culture." Furthermore, the population generally does not perceive the police to be effective against crime or publicly accountable.

Internal Security and Terrorism: Pakistan has numerous categories of terrorism and internal threats, with most insurgent groups identifying themselves as religious or ethnic separatists. Some political parties represent distinct religious and ethnic communities, and rivalries among these parties have been violent. Violence between religiously identified groups is rarely based solely on differing religious doctrines but rather the different social, political, and economic statuses that correlate with religion. Some Islamic militias have connections to the Taliban and al Qaeda, which was linked to two assassination attempts on President Musharraf in December 2003. Militant organizations have some influence on Pakistan's foreign policy, and militants in Pakistan (such as Harkat-ul-Ansar) have assisted militant organizations in countries whose governments are perceived as oppressing Muslims. There are also concerns that Pakistan's nuclear arsenal could be seized by insurgents in an event such as a coup or assassination of the nation's president. However, the government claims that it has enacted security measures to prevent such a threat and that the numerical and political superiority of religious moderates over religious extremists is a substantial obstacle to the latter's access to Pakistan's nuclear weapons.

The most significant violence between religious groups is between Islamic militias, the Shia militia Sipah-e-Mohammed Pakistan (SMP, "Army of Mohammed") and the Sunni militias Sipah-e-Sahaba Pakistan (SSP, "Army of the Friends of the Prophet") and Lashkar-e-Jhangvi (LeJ, "Army of Jhangvi"). The violence has, at times, disrupted both civil order and the economies in areas of Sindh and Punjab provinces. The violence has resulted in large part from the influx of weapons and returning mujahideen from Afghanistan, as well as financial support from large landowners, drug lords, and some political parties. Tensions between ethnic groups often stem from perceptions that other ethnic groups dominate politics and economics to the detriment of minority ethnicities.

The Muhajir Quami Movement (MQM) was involved in substantial conflict in the 1980s and early 1990s but has since been far more quiescent as a result of internal factionalism and an apparent lack of motivating doctrine. The only other significant ethnic violence involves secessionists in Balochistan, who contend that the government is appropriating the province's mineral wealth while providing little economic benefit in return. There are also long-suspected connections of foreign-sponsored subversion, such as Indian support of Sindhi dissidents and Iranian ties to Shia and Balochi militants.

Human Rights: The government's human rights record is generally regarded as poor by domestic and international observers, although there have been some improvements since 2000. Security forces use excessive and sometimes lethal force and are complicit in extrajudicial killings of civilians and suspected militants. The police and military have been accused of engaging in physical abuse, rape, and arbitrary arrest and detention, particularly in areas of acute conflict. Although the government has enacted measures to counter these problems, abuses continue. Furthermore, courts suffer from lack of funds, outside intervention, and deep case backlogs that lead to long trial delays and lengthy pretrial detentions. Many observers inside and outside Pakistan contend that Pakistan's legal code is largely concerned with crime, national security, and domestic tranquility and less with the protection of individual rights. Provincial and local governments have arrested journalists and closed newspapers that report on matters perceived as socially offensive or critical of the government. Journalists also have been victims of violence and intimidation by various groups and individuals. In spite of these difficulties, the press publishes freely, although journalists often exercise self-restraint in their writing. In 2002 citizens participated in elections for the National Assembly, but those elections were criticized as deeply flawed by domestic and international observers.

Societal actors also are responsible for human rights abuses. Violence by drug lords and sectarian militias claims numerous innocent lives, discrimination and violence against women are widespread, human trafficking is problematic, and debt slavery and bonded labor persist. The government often ignores abuses against children and religious minorities, and government institutions and some Muslim groups have persecuted non-Muslims and used some laws as the legal basis for doing so. The Blasphemy Law, for example, allows life imprisonment or the death penalty for contravening Islamic principles, but legislation was passed in October 2004 to eliminate misuse of the law. Furthermore, the social acceptance of many these problems hinders their eradication. One prominent example is honor killings ("karo kari"), which are believed to have accounted for more than 4,000 deaths from 1998 to 2003. Many view this practice as indicative of a feudal mentality and as an anathema to Islam, but others defend the practice as a means of punishing violators of cultural norms and view attempts to stop it to as an assault on cultural heritage.

PAKISTAN'S INTERNAL SECURITY

Turning to Pakistan's internal situation, workshop participants from Pakistan acknowledged, and shared, the concerns expressed by the other participants. However, it was noted that Pakistan's Army remains essentially loyal and the Government is now facing the insurgencies underway across the country with renewed determination. In response to particular concerns over the fighting underway at the time of the workshop itself, a discussant noted that the Swat valley is "a long way" from Islamabad, in practical and political terms, if not geographically.

Other participants were not so sanguine and expressed considerable fear over the future of Pakistan as a stable state. These fears are accentuated by Pakistan's nuclear status. One Indian participant noted the fear of a "nuclear Somalia" on India's doorstep. Others expressed concern that the growing power of the insurgents was such that, even if they did not take over the Pakistani state, they would make of Pakistan a quasi-failed state which would simply bleed out over time. The concern was also expressed that the strengthening of Pakistani extremists could exert a negative influence on India's own "communal fault-lines" and bolster those Indian groups inclined to the same path, thereby encouraging greater practical cooperation between extremist elements in the two countries. Turning specifically to the issue of how Pakistan would fight the insurgency, several workshop participants noted repeatedly that "90 percent" of Pakistan's Army is "facing the wrong way" – that is, it is deployed and prepared for a conventional war with India and not taking any part in the real threat facing Pakistan: the insurgency. Pakistani participants noted a reluctance on the part of the Army to fight against fellow Muslims and tribesmen. This was not accepted by most workshops participants, who noted that the Pakistani police were also Muslims and seemed to be willing to fight the insurgents. In response, the Pakistani participants also noted that, even though India claims that China is supposedly India's main enemy, some 70 percent of India's Army is facing Pakistan.

Apart from the debate over the intentions of India's military strategy, one Indian participant highlighted the need for India to think seriously about how to create incentive structures, engage moderates, and eliminate jihadis in Pakistan. Several Indian participants noted that while the above-listed initiatives are necessary, it is unclear to Indian officials who should be engaged in Pakistan, both because the official power structure is unfamiliar (given the role of the military) and because there is little sense of who are, in fact, the "moderates". A further challenge lies in determining what kind of Pakistan is envisioned by interested parties. In sum, this discussion revealed considerable disquiet. While some felt that the situation is characterised in an overly dramatic fashion, most were not of this view. But few could think of ways that outsiders could dramatically assist Pakistan – this is a fight that Islamabad will have to wage itself. The Pakistani participants acknowledged this, but argued that pressures on Pakistan to take steps that will serve outside agendas (especially in Afghanistan) are not helpful.

Nuclear and Strategic Matters

Participants discussed at length the nuclear programs and doctrines of India and Pakistan and the implications of these doctrines on broader strategic relations. In response to questions as to why Pakistan pursues such a vigorous nuclear weapons programme, participants outlined key elements of Pakistan's strategic rationale. Pakistan's nuclear development was explained as being primarily driven by nuclear development in India. The term "receptive proliferator" was used to describe the logic behind the country's capability development. Participants also outlined the role of conventional force in driving Pakistan's nuclear agenda. When Pakistan was subject to heavy US sanctions, it sought to develop its conventional military capability through weapons acquired from China; however, China's conventional capability at the time was generations behind the weapons that the US and other Western

European sources were supplying to India. In this regard, nuclear strength in Pakistan constitutes a means of countering India's assured conventional superiority. While Pakistan has not formally released a nuclear doctrine, participants addressed perhaps the most salient feature of Pakistan's unstated doctrine: the absence of a "no first use" (NFU) principle. Instead, Pakistan retains a degree of ambiguity on the matter in order to protect its vital national interests and avoid the vulnerability to which the country would be subject in the event of a drawn out conventional war with India. It was noted earlier that Pakistan's nuclear program is driven, in large part, by the need to counter India's conventional superiority.

This observation drove a discussion regarding the conditions under which Pakistan would consider the nuclear option. No concrete answer was given; nevertheless, participants did indicate that under extreme conditions in a conventional conflict it would be conceivable that Pakistan would deploy nuclear weapons. It was also stated by one Pakistani participant, however, that while such a capability must be asserted by Pakistan, other rational avenues would be pursued to their full extent.

An Indian participant described the degree to which India's political landscape has historically held a distaste for nuclear weapons—a trend which continues in the present-day. To illustrate this, the participant pointed to the lag after China's test explosion before India launched its own "peaceful" test and the subsequent lag following its first test before the country went overtly nuclear. As a "reluctant" nuclear power, India has adopted an accompanying nuclear doctrine which features its NFU principle. This doctrine also characterises India's nuclear posture as being one of "minimum deterrent," but it was noted by several that India has never fully explained what this means in practice, despite some pressure from the US and others to do so. Indian participants admitted that this ambiguity is deliberate and intended to provide India with a degree of flexibility.

Some of the Indian participants noted that the renewed international movement towards nuclear disarmament would have an influence in South Asia. Even if this ultimate goal would not be achieved for decades, South Asia could not stand outside the international trend, particularly if specific agreements, such as the Comprehensive Test Ban Treaty (CTBT) and the Fissile Material Cut-off Treaty (FMCT), were being agreed upon and ratified. Participants on both sides discussed the compatibility of the renewed disarmament agenda proposed by President Obama with their country's existing positions.

One Indian participant noted that the agenda proposed closely resembles the agenda endorsed by India since its 1988 action plan and updated/expanded agenda for disarmament. It was also pointed out that India is a cosponsor of the FMCT and that if the Conference on Disarmament were to generate an agenda including the negotiation of an FMCT, India would negotiate in good faith. For its part, the Pakistani side spoke to the country's *de facto* adherence to the CTBT through a self-imposed moratorium on testing. Pakistan has also expressed support for the initiation of FMCT negotiations provided that the resulting treaty sets out a strong verification regime and addresses the matter of fissile material inventories in a balanced manner.

According to Indian participants, in the context of renewed interest in global disarmament, it is incumbent upon India and Pakistan to consider ways that they could be seen to be contributing to nuclear stability and even, ultimately, arms reductions. While agreeing with the sentiment, several Pakistani participants noted two issues.

First, the asymmetric nature of the nuclear relationship makes formal arms control difficult – India maintains a deterrent for both China and Pakistan, while Pakistan is only interested in deterring India. This means that any future arms control limitations may be perceived to have asymmetric implications for regional balances of power, and therefore may be seen differently by New Delhi and Islamabad. Participants noted that such measures will be a difficult sell in Pakistan under present bilateral realities.

Second, India's overwhelming conventional superiority means that nuclear weapons have different roles in the two countries – they are weapons of last resort deterrence in India (which can therefore afford to espouse a "no first use" policy), while they may have to be used first by Pakistan if there is a conflict and its conventional forces cannot hold.

In this context, some of the Pakistani participants noted that such Indian doctrines as "Cold Start" (a doctrine whereby some Indian formations deployed close to the boarder are kept in a state of readiness such that they can attack quickly and without an observable period of "warmup") are deeply disturbing to Pakistan. In particular, the decision of the Indian Government to test "Cold Start" at a time when Pakistan was in a state of tumult was a source of special concern as the doctrine is seen as Pakistan-centric. The Indian participants noted that "Cold Start" was a response to large incursions across the border which need to be opposed quickly and by force, and do not allow for lengthy logistical warm-up periods for major units. One Pakistani participant proposed that confidence building measures should be introduced with regard to "Cold Start". An Indian participant noted that this would defeat the purpose of "Cold Start".

The day's seminar covered a range of critical issues facing not just India and Pakistan, but the region in general. Participants were reminded, at the close of the day that the backdrop of these issues is constantly changing. Observers described a deteriorating situation in Pakistan as previously stable regions of the country face increasing security challenges. With an upcoming election in India that will bring an opportunity for a revised foreign policy toward South Asia, and an American strategy for the region in transition, the challenge will be to seize opportunities to make positive changes. Most notably, there seemed to be a sense among participants of the need to see India re-engage in the region as a member. On the one hand, it was argued that India has had the tendency to distance itself from the region's problems. On the other hand, there was an awareness that the country's bid as a global power also entails responsibilities with regard to its neighbourhood from which India cannot divorce itself. One participant suggested that the way in which (and the degree to which) India engages in the region will be largely affected by the approach taken by outside actors. Arguably, the same holds true for the international community in seeking to develop policies for the region that take into account India's role and the approaches likely to be assumed by New Delhi. The opportunities for dialogue offered by this seminar was seen as valuable for discussing not only India-Pakistan and South Asia issues, but also the significance of these issues to international actors with an interest in fostering regional stability.

All of the regional participants noted, either in the concluding session or privately to the moderator that the day had gone "better" than they had expected. Given the difficult political situation, especially post-Mumbai, there had been concerns that the day might degenerate into acrimony and squabbling. While some of the exchanges were "testy," the general tone was productive and respectful. Indeed, on a personal level, several of the participants who had not previously met found that they got on well. This was particularly so at the coffee breaks and dinners. Several participants expressed the hope that Canada would take the lead to organise similar discussions in the future.

PURSUING NUCLEAR SECURITY

In an address at the United Nations last September, Pakistani Foreign Minister Hina Rabbani Khar said that her country takes nuclear security "very seriously." Islamabad's efforts in the 15 years since its 1998 nuclear tests give some support to that claim. In February 2000, Pakistan announced the establishment of a National Command Authority (NCA), with the Strategic Plans Division (SPD) as its permanent secretariat. The responsibilities of the NCA include deploying and employing the nuclear force, coordinating Pakistan's strategic organizations, dealing with arms control and disarmament issues, and overseeing implementation of export controls and the safety and security of nuclear installations and materials. The NCA has a three-tiered structure with two committees. The Employment Control Committee and the Developmental Control Committee constitute the first tier, the SPD the second tier, and the three services' strategic force commands the third tier. The SPD is responsible for the daily management of Pakistan's strategic assets, coordinating with all strategic organizations and overseeing the budgetary and administrative aspects of these organizations. The primary responsibility of the services' strategic force commands is to exercise technical, training, and administrative control over the strategic delivery systems. Operational control, however, rests with the NCA.

Islamabad also established the autonomous Pakistan Nuclear Regulatory Authority (PNRA) in January 2001. In 2004, comprehensive export control legislation was promulgated, with control lists meeting the guidelines of the Nuclear Suppliers Group, Missile Technology Control Regime, and Australia Group, which covers exports that are potentially relevant to biological or chemical weapons. Since then, rules and regulations and administrative structures have been developed for the effective implementation of the export control law. In late 2007, an NCA ordinance was issued to regulate the functioning of strategic organizations such as the Pakistan Atomic Energy Commission (PAEC) and the Khan Research Laboratories, which have played a central role in Pakistan's nuclear weapons program. The ordinance also specified criminal activities and the legal powers and procedures to deal with any infringements of the law. The ordinance was passed as an act of parliament in 2010.

From the perspective of nuclear security, however, the most significant organization is the security division of the NCA. The organization has grown exponentially over the years from a very modest beginning and is headed by a two-star general, who currently has 20,000 personnel under his command. This strength is projected to reach a total of 28,000 men in the next few years. The division is responsible for the physical security of all sensitive nuclear sites through a layered system of defence with inner and outer perimeters augmented by electronic sensors and counterintelligence teams. It screens all personnel inducted into any component of the strategic program in concert with other intelligence agencies in the country. It also administers an improved and rigorous Personnel Reliability Programme.

It is useful to recount some of the most significant developments of the NCA Security Division. Initially, the division's security force comprised mostly retired military personnel. More recently, however, it set up a state-of-the-art training academy in Kalar Kahar, comparable to the U.S. Department of Energy's National Nuclear Security Administration's academy in Albuquerque,

New Mexico. The new Pakistani academy provides specially selected Pakistani recruits with training similar to that given to the special forces. These recruits have become the backbone of the nuclear security force and gradually will replace most of the retired military personnel. Through field exercises and war games, Pakistan regularly tests the capabilities of the upgraded security force.

The SPD training academy also is going to house a mock nuclear facility that is being designed and built in collaboration with the PNRA. This will become a "centre of excellence" for security forces training and, under the auspices of the International Atomic Energy Agency (IAEA), will offer training facilities to other countries.

The security division also has constituted an elite response force and an emergency response centre at its headquarters in Rawalpindi to deal with an emergency at any nuclear facility. It has installed radiation detection monitors at various entry and exit points. These portal monitors are in addition to the ones installed by the PNRA.

Pakistan also has taken steps to improve nuclear safety. In his address to the annual IAEA General Conference in Vienna last September, PAEC Chairman Ansar Parvez said Pakistan had been "actively engaged in absorbing lessons" from the March 2011 accident at the Fukushima nuclear reactor complex in Japan. The PAEC has "identified a comprehensive set of safety retrofits" that are "in various stages of implementation," he said.

The PNRA has set up the School for Radiation and Nuclear Safety, where it holds regular courses, workshops, and tabletop exercises to train first responders in handling a radiation emergency. It includes the customs service and other border control agencies. The PNRA also has established a National Radiation Emergency Coordination Centre at its headquarters in Islamabad and has put in place the national Nuclear Safety Action Plan to guide the organizations acting as first responders to a nuclear or radiological emergency.

The Pakistan Institute of Engineering and Applied Sciences has introduced master's degree-level courses with a specialization in nuclear safety, mainly, to train new PNRA personnel. Pakistan also has benefited from cooperation and exchanges of information on best practices with friendly countries, including the United States, and has maintained a vibrant, cooperative relationship with the IAEA.

CHALLENGES FOR PAKISTAN'S NUCLEAR SECURITY

The attack last August against the Kamra military air base in Pakistan reignited concerns about the threat that terrorists could pose to the security of the Pakistani nuclear arsenal. There is no doubt that recent attacks on military targets in Pakistan have increased in number and boldness.

So far, however, the targets of the attacks have not been military installations that contain nuclear weapons or components. Yet, the confluence of increased terrorist activity in Pakistan, the country's ongoing political instability, and the growing size of the Pakistani nuclear arsenal is increasing the challenge to Pakistan's nuclear security. The number of facilities and people that produce and use sensitive nuclear materials and technologies in Pakistan is increasing, raising the bar for personnel screening and infrastructure protection. Last summer, there was a reported threat by the Taliban to attack the nuclear complex at Dera Ghazi Khan, a remote town in southern Punjab, but the attack failed to materialize.

Since 2001, Pakistan, cognizant of the terrorist danger, has taken a number of steps to improve the command and control system for its nuclear assets and the screening and training of employees in its nuclear enterprise. As with all security systems, constant vigilance and a culture of continuous improvement are important to deter and, if necessary, respond to threats. The U.S. government has put forth a message of reassurance regarding Pakistan's nuclear security. President Barack Obama and top administration officials have consistently said since 2009 that they have confidence that Pakistan takes its security mission seriously and that its physical protection and training are adequate and improving. This is in part a result of collaboration between the Pakistani and U.S. governments on best practices for the security of Pakistan's nuclear infrastructure. These interactions have led to better training and equipment. Despite these assurances, a number of specialists around the world remain skeptical of the security steps that Pakistan has taken. There are several explanations for this perspective. One is that foreign experts and journalists have highlighted the danger when reporting on Pakistan's nuclear program. Also, within the country, the media, politicians, and anti-nuclear activists raised a number of questions about the ability of the Pakistani nuclear security establishment to protect and defend its nuclear assets against an intruding force in the wake of the Osama bin Laden raid at Abbottabad by U.S. special forces in May 2011.

In an article written after a 2009 visit to Pakistan, former U.S. Department of Defence official Lawrence J. Korb recounted various doomsday scenarios for Pakistan and argued that "given the strategic location of Pakistan and the fact that it has nuclear weapons, it's easy to see why some might embrace a worst-case scenario. But based on my visit, I don't buy it at this time." Although made four years ago, his point is still valid; the situation on ground is not as bad as it may appear to distant observers.

Yet, there is much that the U.S. and other governments do not know about the Pakistani nuclear arsenal, despite closer cooperation, especially between the United States and Pakistan, over the past decade. The overarching reason for the recurring concerns is the prevailing internal security situation in Pakistan. The nightmare scenario is that, in the event of a political collapse in Pakistan, things could spiral out of control and even the best training and equipment could not be relied on to keep terrorists away from Pakistan's weapons. Understandably, distant observers will find it difficult to accept the notion that the nuclear installations in Pakistan are islands of stability and security in the midst of a generally chaotic security and political environment, especially when so little information on Pakistan's nuclear security regime is available. This is a major reason why the recent attacks on military bases have raised alarm about the security of Pakistan's nuclear infrastructure.

HUMAN SECURITY VERSUS SECURING ENERGY RESOURCES

Since much of Pakistan's minerals are in the sparsely populated province of Baluchistan or in the highly heterogeneous province of Sindh, there are also serious concerns about asymmetric development and benefit trajectories for the country. While it may be considered environmentally fortuitous that the mineral reserves of the country are in a region of lower population density to mitigate aggregate risk, the negative differential distribution of benefits to Baluchis from the minerals has led to serious grievances. Instead of making the minerals appear as a distributive conflict, the government should use the revenues being generated as a means of addressing the economic dispariaties that exist in the province.

Such disparities cannot be alleviated simply by large infrastructure but rather through educational capacity-building for the Baluch to ensure employment security in the long-term. Otherwise, there is a danger of capital flight and a continuation of asymmetric development. Contrary to common perception, mining companies are often willing to operate in politically insecure locations so long as the government is supportive of their economic interests. Unlike other industrial sectors the location of a mine is determined by geology far more than by individual choice. Resource companies are more afraid of nationalization and uncompetitive government behaviour than they are of ethnic tensions. When queried at a recent shareholder meeting about the $100 million investment that Barrick Gold has made in the Reko Diq copper-gold mine in Baluchistan in spite of ethnic tensions, the CEO Peter Munk responded: "If I had my choice between dealing with (Venezuelan President Hugo) Chavez, or (Bolivian president Evo) Morales, or Aziz (the Pakistani prime minister), I know where I would put my money."

However, it is important that the government not misuse this complacence to ethnic strife on the part of mineral investors, since at the end of the day they will still have to spend enormous amounts of money for security which could be avoided by constructive engagement with the community. Furthermore, the demands of the indigenous Baluchis must not be conflated with the insurrection of tribal elite such as Nawab Bugti's family.

The energy factor should also be used as a means of fostering cooperation not only between provinces but also regionally between South and Central Asia. The proposal for various gas pipelines have the potential to not only provide relatively clean and environmentally manageable energy to the region, but also to foster cooperation.

Interdependence is an attractive incentive for cooperation. Nevertheless, in this case, political stability is far more consequential for success than with individual mines. The potential for sabotage along pipelines can paralyze projects and constructive engagement with all players is essential to the success of these projects.

There are lessons which Pakistan can learn from recent projects such as the Baku-Tblisi-Ceyhan pipeline from Azerbaijan to Turkey via Georgia about how to manage such matters. In that case there were environmental challenges that led to conflicts while the political negotiations brought the countries closer.

A willingness to engage with communities and stakeholders, even if this may delay the project, as well as political compromise between countries must occur simultaneously for such projects to succeed. However, if appropriately managed they can indeed lead to greater cooperation and stability. Pakistan's development predicament is emblematic of many countries that are undergoing rapid growth in energy demand from demographic pressures as well as more intense industrialization. While such growth can certainly be a sign of progress and potentially a means of poverty alleviation, it can also lead to errant euphoria and rash decision-making by policy-makers. At such times of ambition and anxiety, environmental concerns are regrettably relegated to "low politics," and dismissed with pleasantries as short-term gains are calculated on the basis of prestige projects such as large dams and sky-scrapers.

Bursts of infrastructure development require enormous amounts of energy and without careful planning such efforts can leave countries resource-depleted without much economic gain. The fate of capitals such as Abidjan or Buenos Aires that might boast superb buildings and roads but distressed economies must be considered by the infrastructure enthusiasts. Similarly enormous energy capacity projects such as the Caborra Bassa dam in Mozambique reflect how infrastructure without proper environmental planning and a resolution of indigenous conflicts can decay and deteriorate and become more of a liability than an asset.

Even in China, which is often considered the hallmark of rapid industrial development in Asia, the connection between environmental harm and long-term economic decline is now being considered by the government. On April 16, 2006, President Hu Jintao made an alarming admission that China is perhaps growing too fast at the expense of its environment. The statement was made during a meeting with former Taiwanese opposition leader Lien Chan, as they discussed prospects for peace in the region. While many Pakistani policy-makers often talk about emulating mainland China's development path, perhaps there are many lessons that they might instead learn from Taiwan in terms of a relatively green growth. A composite environmental performance index developed by Yale University's Centre for Environmental Law and Policy ranked Taiwan two scores ahead of the United States in its environmental performance. China scored 70 ranks below Taiwan. Pakistan, India and Bangladesh were all in the lowest quartile, largely due to poor air quality indicators that are linked to their energy policies. Sri Lanka and Nepal faired slightly better on account of better environmental health indicators but still far below environmentally progressive countries such as Malaysia and Costa Rica, which were in the top quartile.

Taiwan has managed to accomplish growth despite a very large defence budget — the usual excuse for slow development by countries like Pakistan. While the country's economic and environmental performance might have been even better without its massive arms purchases, at least the island state has managed to follow a positive development trajectory. Studies by the Chinese government have shown that asymmetry of development and environmental decline are causing economic losses. One such study cited by the New China News Agency says the country's Western provinces will suffer an annual loss of 15 billion euros, or 13 percent of the region's GDP, because of environmental damages. President Hu Jintao's statement reflects a realization of these economic consequences.

Keeping in views such global comparative perspectives, it is pivotally important that Pakistan's energy policy develop its resources with utmost care for ecological indicators.

THE IMPACT OF POST-9/11 ON SECURITY PERCEPTIONS

After the terrorist attacks on the US on September 11, 2001, the West has expressed serious apprehensions concerning the terrorist groups acquiring weapons of mass destruction and the nuclear-related materials, from the

Indian and Pakistani nuclear facilities. But, the fact remains that the prospects of these non-state actors acquiring WMD materials from the Indian and Pakistani facilities is "extremely low since both countries keep their nuclear arsenals in an unassembled form, and because their components are stored separately."

Therefore, the chances of terrorist groups acquiring nuclear-related materials from within India and Pakistan for terrorism are remote. However, according to Rizvi and Basrur, fears regarding four types of nuclear terrorism cannot be ruled out. These include the sabotage of nuclear facilities, use of a "dirty bomb" to disperse radiation, terrorist takeover of nuclear installations and a threat to blow them up, as well as clandestine transfer of nuclear material for use/assemblage somewhere else.

Rizvi and Basrur have suggested eight measures, which in their viewpoint could substantially enhance the safety and security of nuclear facilities in India and Pakistan:

1. Track-down the groups and the individuals engaged in violent activities and terrorism.
2. Extensive surveillance of the borders and coastlines to contain the movement of goods and people.
3. More use of modern technology to enhance the physical protection of nuclear weapons, material and installations.
4. Thorough scrutiny of the personnel handling the nuclear programmes of the two countries.
5. Acquisition of latest technologies for the transportation of fissile and radioactive materials.
6. Highly trained manpower may be employed for the protection of nuclear facilities.
7. Extensive coordination network amongst all the set-ups dealing with the nuclear infrastructure and, in addition, there should be an independent body to ensure an oversight and accountability.
8. Finally, a disaster management body may be established to handle a security alarm systems, and the actual nuclear-terrorist incidents and emergencies.

Obviously, the US and the Western countries have a strong interest in preventing a nuclear war between India and Pakistan. The military standoff of 2001-2002 between the two countries had visibly brought the two countries much closer to a war, which then prompted the US and the European Union countries to assist them in defusing the tension. Therefore, logically, in future, US and the EU countries should be keen to strengthen the safety and security mechanisms of India and Pakistan's nuclear weapons programmes, because the threat of nuclear-terrorism is global in range and its effects cannot be contained to a single geographical region alone.

On September 17, 2002, the Bush Administration announced *National Security Strategy of the United States of America,* which laid-down a comprehensive policy to combat the WMD, and to defeat global terrorism. This significant document envisaged a proactive counter-proliferation policy to deter, and to defend against the perceived threat of terrorism before it is let loose. Secondly, to strengthen the non-proliferation regimes with a view to interdict the 'rogue states' and terrorist organisations from gaining the technologies, materials, and expertise to assemble the WMD. Thirdly, to effectively contain the effects of the WMD use, whether by the rogue states or by the terrorist networks. The main thrust of this new policy is on pre-emptive actions even in an anticipatory self-defence against such states and the terrorist groups. More significantly, this doctrine considers the Cold War era's deterrence principles (as a weapon of last resort and defence) as ineffective against the present-day deterrence postures, which is primarily premised on threat of retaliation that is not expected to work against the rogue states, and the terrorist organisations, which would tend to risk the lives of their nations. Interestingly, this strategy has an inherent flaw because it would tend to lead to more reliance on pre-emption that would "turn force from an instrument of last resort into one of first resort," comment Ivo H. Daalder, James M. Lindsay, and James B. Steinberg. Moreover, it will accord an opportunity to other states to formulate principles and strategies in accordance with their narrow national interests to have "an unfettered right of pre-emption against its own definition of threats to its security" to act unilaterally. This doctrine instead of rooting out the scourge of terrorism is likely to widen the gulf of alienation between the friends and allies and, at the same time fails to address the question of threat to security.

It would be appropriate to make a distinction between the state and the non-state actors' acquisition and potential to use the nuclear weapons. Since the break-up of the former Soviet Union, the West became apprehensive regarding the proliferation of nuclear materials, equipment, technology, and personnel to the 'rogue states' and terrorist outfits. In 1992, US and Russia, to ensure that nuclear weapons and materials do not fall in the hands of the undesirable elements, established the Nunn-Lugar Cooperative Threat Reduction (CTR) programme. Additionally, in 1999, the Clinton Administration announced a policy to expand the work of CTR by the Expanded Threat Reduction Initiative (ETRI) plan to ensure that WMD-related technologies did not reach the wrong hands, including to the states sponsoring terrorism. But, since the tragic terrorist incidents of September 11, 2001, the US perspective concerning the possibility of nuclear terrorism has undergone marked transformation. Robert Kagan, a leading scholar of US foreign policy, writes,

Europe is turning away from power, to put it a little differently, it is moving beyond power into a self-contained world of laws and rules and transnational negotiation and cooperation. It is entering a post-historical paradise of peace and relative prosperity, the realization of Immanuel Kant's "perpetual peace." Meanwhile, the United States remains mired in history, exercising power in an anarchic Hobbesian world where international laws and rules are unreliable, and where true security and the defence and promotion of a liberal order still depend on the possession and use of military might.... Americans generally see the world divided between good and evil, between friends and enemies, while Europeans see a more complex picture. When confronting real or potential adversaries, Americans generally favour policies of coercion rather than persuasion, emphasizing punitive sanctions over inducements to better behaviour, the stick over the carrot. Americans tend to seek finality in international affairs: they want problems solved, threats eliminated. And, of course, Americans increasingly tend toward unilateralism in international affairs.

Kagan's perspective is widely shared in the United States, including by the Bush Administration, that Washington should pursue a more proactive, rather unilaterally coercive diplomacy, to finally eliminate the scourge of terrorism and to solve the other problems of the world. But, the fact remains that US nuclear non-proliferation policy, and international non-proliferation regimes, still form an integral part of Washington's security architecture to deal with the potential threats of WMD-related terrorism. Therefore, in the foreseeable future, US would be less inclined on the international institutions like the United Nations in order to achieve its national objectives. In this context, the US National Security Strategy and the National Strategy to Combat Weapons of Mass Destruction (NSCWMD) would continue to guide a new strategy for the US Homeland Security, and a fundamental diversion from the traditional concept of deterrence with a view to combat the WMD threats. Because, Bush Administration perceives that its enemies were seeking the WMD, and that the NSCWMD would proactively bolster, interdiction-oriented approach to mitigate the WMD threats. Prima facie, the document is intended to target the 'rogue states,' but it also does not rule out action against the other states as well who sponsor or harbour terrorism.

The NSCWMD also envisages bolstering of US conventional, nuclear, intelligence/surveillance, interdiction, and domestic law enforcement capabilities to improve its overall deterrent posture vis-à-vis the WMD threats. This includes capabilities to detect and destroy adversary's WMD arsenals before their use. Therefore, US would consistently endeavour to formalise new agreements, which could cater for its non-proliferation objectives. In addition, strengthen the existing non-proliferation regimes to promote its security interests. Moreover, in parallel conceive a comprehensive sanctions policy as a tool of diplomacy to support its overall strategy of NSCWMD. But rightly in the view of some experts, the question of nuclear terrorism by states is fundamentally different from the issue of the "acquisitions and use of such weapons by non-state actors." Thomas Badey writes,

It is highly unlikely that countries with a desire to acquire nuclear weapons, such as Iran, Iraq, Libya, Sudan and North Korea, would spend millions of dollars and years of research to acquire nuclear weapons, only to sell or hand them over to non-state actors, knowing that they might be held accountable for the actions of potential clients.... It is much more likely that states, particularly those targeted by export controls and economic sanctions, may use non-state actors to acquire nuclear materials for them rather than the other way around.

The use of nuclear weapons by the 'rogue states' with an inadequate backing and accompanying capabilities would be counter-productive rather than proving of any strategic gain. Because, in the case of use of nuclear weapons by the 'rogue states' and their sponsored non-state actors, it would certainly eclipse the potential benefits and, the consequences would be more horrendous to contemplate. Besides, it is highly improbable that any single individual could equip a group to have an access to fissionable material or even to crude a form of nuclear device without the assistance of a reliable delivery system, which is otherwise only feasible with the collaboration of a major industrial enterprise. In the views of the former head of nuclear weapons development programme at the Los Alamos, J. Carson Mark, it requires a team of a mechanical engineer, nuclear physicist, a chemist, and explosive expert, a mathematician, and along with other auxiliary staff, and at least a year to develop a nuclear device. Besides, it would be highly unlikely for the non-state actors to hire the services of highly qualified and experienced scientists; the requisite industrial infrastructure; the financial resources; weapons-grade uranium or plutonium; and an access to clandestine transport or to a delivery system, that too, for terrorism, appears to be incredibly implausible. However, the security of nuclear installations, personnel, and the fissionable and radiological materials in possession of the *de jure* and the *de facto* NWS, should be made foolproof. Secondly, the existing non-proliferation regimes can be made vibrant to ensure that nuclear technology and material does not pilfer into the possession of non-state actors and the 'rogue states,' which could jeopardise the stability of international peace and security. Though, the non-state actors can easily assemble the chemical and biological elements for terrorist attacks, therefore, rationally the emphasis should be to check the proliferation of chemical, radiological and biological agents, which the terrorist organisations may acquire from the international black-market, and then convert the same into a 'dirty bomb'. In this connection, US President Bush in a statement on May 31, 2003, during his visit to Poland, referred to the Proliferation Security Initiative (PSI) of the US in collaboration with ten other countries, including its allies, to employ all the legal, diplomatic, economic, military channels, including searching planes and cargo ships, to interdict illegal weapons, nuclear, missiles, and radiological materials. Such measures would go long way in deterring the terrorist organisations from implementing their nefarious designs, provided PSI is reconciled within the parameters of the international law. In addition, the nuclear-related CSBMs between the *de jure* and the *de facto* NWS, and other developed countries, could also collectively evolve a strategy to seize the transfer of sensitive technologies to 'rogue states' in order to minimise, if not exclude completely, the possibility of such technologies, nuclear and radiological materials falling in the wrong hands.

Unfortunately, in the South Asian context, since the Lahore Declaration of February 1999, both India and Pakistan have not been able to start talks on nuclear-related CSBMs. In August 2003, Pakistan had offered India the resumption of a dialogue on nuclear-related CSBMs that were agreed in principle in the Memorandum of Understanding (MoU) signed by them at the time of Lahore Declaration, in order to establish the strategic restraint regime. India instead of responding positively to the Pakistani proposal accused it of foot-dragging on resumption of a dialogue and other diplomatic and peace initiatives between the two countries. In this connection, again on December 18, 2003, President Pervez Musharraf, repeated the offer to India for improving bilateral relations by resolving the Kashmir dispute:

We are for United Nations Security Council Resolutions…now we have left that aside. If we want to resolve this issue, both sides need to talk to each other with flexibility, coming beyond stated positions, meeting halfway somewhere…. We are prepared to rise to the occasion; India has to be flexible also…. We have come to a stage where there is a thaw in relations, where there is expectation on both sides in the people…. If the leadership doesn't rise to the occasion, it is a pity and I think we'll disappoint our public again…. Unfortunately, magnanimity has to come from the bigger and the stronger.

President Musharraf's realpolitik and rational diplomatic proposal placed the ball squarely in India's court. It was up to India to capitalise on Pakistan's constructive initiative to resolve the neuralgic dispute over Kashmir, and to set in motion the process of improvement of bilateral relations. During the three-day 12th South Asian Association for Regional Cooperation (SAARC) Summit in Islamabad, the Indian Prime Minister, A. B. Vajpayee, urged the member states for "bold transition" from mistrust to trust, discord to concord, and tension to peace in the region. Moreover, Indian External Affairs Minister, Yashwant Sinha, in a statement also "expressed satisfaction on the progress in bilateral relations and discussed various ways to increase this momentum." While Pakistan's Foreign Minister, Khurshid Mahmud Kasuri, too, reiterated that, "We have developed a good relationship, which is good for the people of both countries. Our relations with India have improved. We will continue to improve our relations." Musharraf and Vajpayee in a bilateral meeting on January 5, further agreed to "maintain the momentum" generated by the confidence-building measures and diplomacy on the sidelines of the SAARC Summit. Therefore, in the second phase, if the proposed CSBMs can take a concrete shape once both countries resume a comprehensive dialogue and initiate further confidence-building measures process with a view to ensuring peace and security of the region, it could help lay the basis to eliminate the probability of terrorists' access to their nuclear, missile, chemical, biological, and radiological materials and facilities. If the momentum resulting out of the thaw in bilateral relations is sustained, it could enable them to find a mutually acceptable solution to all their outstanding disputes, including over Kashmir.

PAKISTAN'S NUCLEAR TRAJECTORY

Pakistan's nuclear program has been at the center of attention for nonproliferation pundits for several decades for a variety of reasons. For them, the acquisition of nuclear technology, even for non-NPT states, both for peaceful and military applications (self-defense), is the divine right of the chosen few who are either unable or unwilling to recognize the legitimate security concerns of states in regions mired in a perpetual cycle of hostility. Faced with the traumatizing separation of its Eastern Wing in 1971, Pakistan resolved never to witness such an event at the hands of India again, and was forced to respond to India's nuclear challenge only three years later in the wake of Pokhran-1. Pakistan had taken the lead in calling for nuclear restraint in South Asia even before India's 1974 test when it first proposed a Nuclear Weapon Free Zone in 1972. This call was repeated twice, once after Pokhran-1 and again in 1978 when Pakistan proposed that both countries simultaneously renounce the acquisition or manufacture of nuclear weapons. The following year, Pakistan again offered India mutual inspection of each other's nuclear facilities and also proposed a simultaneous accession of India and Pakistan to the NPT and full-scope IAEA safeguards. In 1987, it expressed willingness to enter into a bilateral nuclear test-ban treaty with India and proposed a missile free zone in South Asia in 1994. None of these proposals were given any serious consideration. Since 2007, India has consistently rejected six nuclear-related Confidence Building Measures proposed by Pakistan on one pretext or another. Regrettably, India has rejected each one of these proposals in the past four decades even though there have been a few successful CBM's which have stood the test of time such as the agreement of non-attack on each other's nuclear facilities and the agreement of pre-notification of flight tests of ballistic missiles. However, proposals for a strategic restraint regime that would include a commitment not to build missile defences and include prior notification of cruise missiles were not accepted by India.

Therefore, when in the backdrop of a deep history of mistrust Pakistan resorts to indigenous efforts to build its nuclear deterrent, based on its own force goals and resources, it stands accused of following a "mistaken trajectory" and is seen as "punching above its weight." A dispassionate assessment of Pakistan's nuclear trajectory vis-à-vis India and the size of its nuclear fuel cycle in terms of the production capacities of various plants and facilities shows that while it has consistently built up its nuclear capabilities over time, there has been no abrupt or exponential increase in fissile material production comparable to India (for both existing or projected capacities). It is also a fact that Pakistan has reached this stage in its nuclear capability only after four decades of sustained effort and progressive indigenization in its nuclear and missile programs. It has learnt to brace sanctions, find solutions and improvise, and mastered all aspects of the fuel cycle at a fraction of the cost of producing any nuclear plant or facility of the same type or size anywhere else in the world (such as plutonium production facilities). A closer look at Pakistan's nuclear trajectory demonstrates that while India has been producing plutonium from CIRUS since 1963 and from Dhruva-I since 1988 and has a much larger infrastructure outside safeguards to produce more plutonium in addition to its considerable advantages in existing stockpiles of plutonium.

Pakistan is using infrastructure to produce plutonium from 1998 onwards which PAEC was able to build over a period of 25 years (1973 to 1998), save for second, third and fourth 50 MWt production reactors at Khushab (the fourth one nearing completion), all of which were initiated during the fifteen years after the 1998 tests. Thus, Pakistan's pre-1998 plutonium infrastructure comprises a fuel fabrication plant at Kundian (completed 1976-80); the New Labs reprocessing plant at PINSTECH (1973-1981); the 50 MWt Khushab-1 reactor, heavy water and tritium production plants (1985-1997); and the partially completed Chashma reprocessing plant (1978) which has recently been retrofitted and reportedly commissioned. After Khushab-1 was commissioned in 1998, Pakistan was able to add three additional reactors of the same type and size only because it was developing indigenous design and manufacturing facilities in parallel with work at Khushab Nuclear Complex in the 1980s and 1990s.

For comparison's sake, it would be useful to recall that Pakistan has built only two unsafeguarded reprocessing plants since the 1970s; one pilot-scale plant (New Labs) with 20-40 (completed in 1981-82) and the other commercial-scale plant (Chashma) with 40-100 tHM/yr capacity which the French had abandoned in 1978. At the same time, India has built five commercial-scale reprocessing plants (all outside safeguards); one at Trombay (50 tHM/yr) two at Tarapur (100 tHM/yr) and two (100 tHM/yr) at Kalpakkam (the second one nearing completion in 2014).

But Pakistan has no Fast Breeder Reactor and no unsafeguarded heavy water power reactors on its soil. India already has 100 MWt Dhruva-I in operation coupled with 125 MWt Dhruva-II nearing completion along with another 30 MWt reactor being planned. Its 40 MWt CIRUS reactor had already produced 500 kg of weapon-grade plutonium up to 2006 (IPFM 2006) and an additional 45 kg before it was shut down in 2010. Dhruva-I continues to produce 20-25 kg of weapon-grade plutonium every year. India's 8 heavy water power reactors kept outside safeguards under the Indo-US nuclear deal can produce 1250 kg of weapon-grade plutonium each year, even though India claims that the unsafeguarded reactor-grade plutonium produced by them during normal operations would be used as fuel (MOX) for its breeder reactor program (also unsafeguarded). India's 500 MWe EFBR can produce 145 kg of weapon-grade plutonium each year.

Comparisons in highly enriched uranium capabilities and stockpiles show a similar trend. Pakistan has not increased or expanded its uranium enrichment capacity in the past 20 years, where as India is doubling its existing enrichment potential (floor space) at its Rare Materials Plant (Rattehali) in Mysore. In fact, Pakistan's HEU stocks might be less than the known estimates since it is difficult to determine the precise SWU capacity of an enrichment plant and its UF6 feed production. That Pakistan is not engaged in, nor aims at entering into a fissile race with India, is exemplified by the following comparison of unsafeguarded fissile material stockpiles and production capabilities (existing and projected).

Curiously enough, Pakistan's plutonium quest has been at the heart of western non-proliferation efforts since the 1970s when the country was striving to complete the nuclear fuel cycle. It is intriguing that towards the late 1970s when Pakistan was completing research and development work on various plants and facilities for the enriched uranium route (uranium processing, conversion and enrichment) as part of the fuel cycle, and was also quietly building other unsafeguarded facilities for the plutonium route, the United States had used its full diplomatic pressure to secure a major non-proliferation objective in order to force France to cancel the deal for the safeguarded commercial-scale reprocessing plant in August, 1978 (which was never intended for Pakistan's weapons program anyway).

Only a year later, a June 6, 1979, a de-classified US State Department cable stated that Pakistan might be "allowed" to complete its gas-centrifuge program while the United States (in its misplaced opinion) had succeeded in stopping Pakistan's plutonium program in its tracks. This might have been so as the United States was probably not sure that Pakistan could build uranium processing, hexafluoride gas (UF6) production, and gas-centrifuge plants for the enriched uranium route anytime soon, but more significantly because plutonium was and still is the major non-proliferation concern for Pakistan since it provides the capability to develop miniaturized, boosted fission, tactical and thermo-nuclear warheads—the basis of a first-class operational nuclear deterrent.

Thermonuclear weapons is yet another area where Pakistan has shown restraint and has been punching below its weight, even though the capability exists to build these weapons, but perhaps boosted-fission warheads might suffice for existing force goals.

Pakistan's ballistic missile program was largely driven by the effects of the Pressler Amendment. Yet its missile development and testing trajectory does not reflect any arms racing with India in this field with both countries pursuing divergent pathways in the field. For instance, Pakistan's missile development and testing is solely geared towards the consolidation of its existing capabilities designed to achieve greater accuracy, reliability against increasing Indian ballistic and planned cruise missile defences and survivability of its strategic forces. This has been explained in a recent Carnegie study, which states that "*An analysis of aggregated missile test data since 1998 reveals that the armament dynamic is far more complex. The Indian and Pakistani nuclear programs are largely decoupled. The data show little correlation between the adversaries' testing behaviour contrary to what would be expected in a classic arms race. In fact, the types and ranges of missiles under development provide concrete evidence of the divergence in their nuclear objectives and security strategies. Pakistan is building weapons systems to deter India from conventional military operations below the nuclear threshold. India is developing systems primarily to strengthen its strategic deterrent against China....*"

This fact was reiterated when Pakistan did not respond to India's 5000-7000 km-range Agni-V ICBM. in kind, but conducted tests of improved versions of its 1000-1300 km-range Shaheen-1A ballistic missile as a potential substitute to the liquid-fuelled Ghauri. Pakistan also has no ballistic or cruise missile defense programs; no ICBM projects like *Agni*-V which is being armed with MIRVs and no SSBNs like India's *Arihant* armed with the 700 km-range *Sagarika* SLBMs. Pakistan's defense budget has largely remained static at around 2-3% of GDP ($5-7 billion) in the past decade compared to India's which has increased to around $ 40 billion. Similarly, a growing imbalance in conventional forces (which Pakistan can never bridge) is exacerbating with India becoming the world's largest net importer of conventional arms for several years in a row in the past few years.

This then brings forth the logic of Pakistan's recent development of battlefield or tactical nuclear weapons designed to deter limited conventional war below its nuclear threshold. TNWs would be used only as weapon of last resort in case of deterrence failure and collapse of conventional forces or the crossing of its perceived nuclear thresholds, whichever comes first. In case of deterrence failure, there would be no escalation control would become impossible and ineffective resulting in the employment of every means available to Pakistan to defend itself against aggression. Pakistan opted to build TNWs (presumably in limited numbers for deterrence only and not for war fighting) as means to supplement conventional defences.

Nonetheless, when Pakistan tested a 60-km range nuclear capable battlefield missile (Hatf-IX) *Nasr* in 2011, it caused considerable consternation in India and elsewhere. However, when India tested the 50-150 km-range *Prahaar* shortly thereafter,, and dubbed it a "tactical surface to surface missile capable of carrying *different types of warheads*, which operates as battle field support system to the Indian Army" or has recently added another 60-170 km tactical missile *Pragati*, to its missile arsenal, no one raises a finger. That is mainly because India has stopped short of declaring these systems nuclear capable and have declared them to carry conventional warheads only. But if India can develop unconventional warheads for the nuclear capable *Prithvi*-I and II, then it is only a matter of time before nuclear warheads for *Prahaar* and*Pragati* are developed, especially given their deployments against Pakistan and China.

So how many warheads would then suffice for credible minimum deterrence? Pakistan is being placed ahead of India in warhead count by a number of international publications and experts. What is astonishing is the basis of such estimates unless they have had the privilege of having done a warhead count themselves or been able to determine the exact amount of fissile material and the corresponding non-nuclear components developed to produce warheads. Warhead count and the amount of fissile material weaponized would invariable depend on various weapon designs (boosted fission, composite core, two-stage etc.) This in any case would be any nation's most classified information and neither India, nor Pakistan have declared their respective inventories of fissile stocks or warheads.

Since some of India's leading strategic analysts such as K. Subrahmanyam have called for the development of a strategic triad comprising a 400-warheads, Pakistan should settle for at least a triad consisting of a 200-250 warhead force that might include different types warheads required to maintain a credible minimum deterrent, designed to absorb an Indian first strike and respond—a capability needed for any country to maintain strategic stability with a nuclear armed neighbor.

However, any such force goals would depend on the availability of fissile material (especially plutonium and tritium for miniaturized warheads) whose production would be limited by the finite domestic reserves of natural uranium, unlike that of India who is being lavishly furnished by the NSG countries with the means of making the most optimum use of all its natural uranium stocks for weaponization.

When Pakistan attempts to consolidate its strategic forces and ramp up plutonium production—which has enabled it to operationalize its nuclear deterrent—it is accused of punching above its weight. It knows what it is doing within its capabilities and resources. Its force goals have been quantified and its fissile material production will continue till those targets are achieved so as to develop a triad-based assured second strike capability that can withstand massive retaliation and prevent the exploitation of strategic space at the tactical level.

Pakistan is in no way competing with India in pursuing regional and global ambitions through ballistic missile nuclear submarines, ICBMs or space weaponization or retaining huge stocks and production capacity of fissile material outside safeguards—a fact accepted by the NSG countries which accorded India the unique distinction of being the beneficiary of an NPT signatory state without any obligations and allowed it to retain a substantial part of its fuel cycle outside safeguards for producing more fissile material in the future.

Given these realities, if India today were to ask to sign the FMCT and the CTBT, it is most likely that it won't agree to be a part of either of these treaty arrangements and is conveniently taking cover behind Pakistan's stance on the FMCT at the CD. Some Indian scientists doubt whether all the Pokhran-II tests were successful, while many others question Pakistan's claims of having built a miniaturized nuclear warhead for*Nasr* without hot tests. So should both India and Pakistan jointly announce a second round of tests purely for technical reasons in addition to ensuring the reliability and "one-point safety" of their respective warheads and then unilaterally or jointly sign the CTBT, depending on their respective security calculus?

Finally, Pakistan is accused of abetting terrorists and non-state actors when it has been fighting a war on terror on its soil for over a decade and has suffered more than 40000 casualties (including high-ranking civil and military officers) and incurred financial and economic lossesamounting to tens of billions of dollars. Such insinuations are used to justify India's appetite for limited conventional war in the region. So should the recent admission by India's former army chief, that it has been involved in sponsoring and abetting terrorist activities in Baluchistan be used by Pakistan to warrant its own version of Cold Start or proactive operations across the border?

Nonetheless, the silver lining is that a certain degree strategic stability in South Asia might be achieved in the foreseeable future when both India and Pakistan acquire assured second-strike capabilities. In fact, they are steadily moving on the path of technological maturation and once Pakistan is able to deploy a highly survivable triad-based credible minimum deterrent, then it would be irrelevant whether India adds to its capabilities for global reach and power projection beyond South Asia that might one day have the potential to target Europe, North America or Australia.

PARTICIPATION IN GLOBAL EFFORTS

Despite an impressive inventory of actions, Pakistani efforts to provide information about all these developments domestically and internationally have not been adequate. This has contributed to the continued skepticism about Islamabad's ability to protect its nuclear assets.

Yet, one avenue through which Pakistan has been able to play an active role in advocating for and taking action on global nuclear security issues is the nuclear security summit process, in which Pakistan is one of the more than 50 countries that have participated. There have been two nuclear summits, in Washington in 2010 and in Seoul in 2012. A third is planned for The Hague in 2014.

Participants at the summits endorsed a number of important steps, including President Barack Obama's goal of securing all vulnerable nuclear material in four years. The national leaders who attended the summits underscored the importance of maintaining effective security over all nuclear materials on their territory; encouraged the conversion of reactors that use highly enriched uranium (HEU) to low-enriched uranium; and recognized the importance of the International Convention for the Suppression of Acts of

Nuclear Terrorism and the Convention on the Physical Protection of Nuclear Material and its 2005 amendment. (The amendment would extend protection requirements beyond the original agreement, which covers nuclear material while in international transport, by expanding the coverage to apply to nuclear facilities and to materials in peaceful domestic use and storage.) Pakistan has acceded to the convention on physical protection but not to the 2005 amendment or the nuclear terrorism convention.

Summit participants also supported full implementation of UN Security Council Resolution 1540, which requires all countries to enact legislation to prevent the proliferation of nonconventional weapons and their means of delivery, and recognized the continuing importance of the IAEA and its nuclear material security guidelines and activities. The participants also supported the actions of the Global Initiative to Combat Nuclear Terrorism (GICNT). Other ambitious objectives of the summits included the removal and disposal of nuclear materials no longer needed for operational activities and the minimization of the civilian use of HEU. The participants also agreed to consider plans to consolidate nuclear material at fewer national storage sites.

Pakistan has submitted four reports to the UN committee overseeing the implementation of Resolution 1540, thus meeting an international nuclear nonproliferation and security obligation that a number of countries have not met. Islamabad is an active participant in the GICNT, especially on issues related to nuclear forensics and efforts to upgrade the international community's ability to detect nuclear and other radioactive materials in order to prevent nuclear trafficking. At the Washington and Seoul summits, individual countries made commitments to improving domestic regimes for nuclear security. Approximately 80 percent of these national commitments were fulfilled between 2010 and 2012. Pakistan did not make any unilateral commitments at the 2010 summit, but it did at the summit in 2012, when it pledged to open a nuclear security training centre and signed the Joint Statement on Nuclear Security Training and Support Centers. The centre is intended to serve as a regional and international hub for training in nuclear security; in the joint statement, Pakistan joined with 22 other countries in forming what will amount to an international network on that issue.

In Seoul, Pakistan also agreed to continue deploying portal monitors to detect special nuclear material as a means of impeding the illicit trafficking of nuclear and radioactive materials. In addition, it offered to provide nuclear safety and security assistance under IAEA auspices to interested states.

In its progress report at the Seoul summit, Pakistan noted its steps to improve export controls, secure radiological sources, and prevent nuclear smuggling. In these areas, it revised its national export control lists and operates mobile laboratories for technical assistance to law enforcement and first responders.

Pakistan also reported that, under its renewed Nuclear Security Action Plan, originally established in 2006, it is upgrading the physical security at its 11 nuclear medical centers. Medical facilities utilize high-intensity radioactive sources that can be used in a "dirty bomb."

Pakistan has taken a number of actions related to nuclear security and safety beyond those it pledged at the summits. It has intensified collaboration with the IAEA by joining "collaborating centers," which are designed to standardize technology, disseminate information, and facilitate research and learning on a range of issues related to IAEA activities, including nuclear safety and security.

It also is participating in the development of the IAEA Nuclear Safety Action Plan.

It has incorporated some of the lessons of the Fukushima accident, including holding an international seminar on nuclear safety and security and developing a radiation emergency response mechanism and a Nuclear Security Emergency Coordination Centre. It also is considering a program for upgrading physical protection of civilian nuclear power plants. It is not yet clear how the Pakistani steps on nuclear security and safety should be seen. On one hand, if they represent the limits of Pakistan's movement toward transparency and cooperation, they are disappointing. On the other hand, they represent an evolution from Pakistan's previous opaqueness, and that may lead to further progress.

Conclusion

Pakistan is located in a very dangerous neighborhood; it has a history of political instability; and terrorist activity in and around the country remains significant. Control of the nuclear program resides primarily with military authorities, which are not very transparent about nuclear security and weapons operations. There is only modest civilian oversight.

These distinguishing features make the security of the Pakistani nuclear weapons program and its infrastructure a global concern, which is unlikely to diminish anytime soon. As a result, all acts of terrorism in the country, especially those directed at military targets, are going to raise concerns and invite scrutiny and skepticism of official assurances of control.

Pakistan has taken its responsibility for nuclear security seriously. It has collaborated with the United States on best practices, training, and personnel screening. It is participating in international forums devoted to preventing nuclear terrorism and improving nuclear security. It has made strides domestically to improve the legal and regulatory system for preventing proliferation of sensitive materials and technologies. Not least, the authorities in Pakistan, the first Islamic country to possess a nuclear weapon, recognize that the nuclear weapons program is deeply intertwined with national identity and that security of its nuclear infrastructure is a top priority. Domestically or internationally, it cannot afford a loss of control. Yet, there is more that Pakistan can and should do to provide confidence to the international community that its nuclear program employs the highest level of safety and security.

First, there is the need to accept all international instruments that underpin the current nuclear security regime, including the nuclear terrorism convention and the 2005 amendment to the convention on physical protection. Also, as the Fukushima nuclear accident highlighted, the decision by any country, developed or developing, to remain insular and opaque on matters of nuclear safety and security can be harmful to that country and its neighbours.

Although the sovereign control of nuclear assets remains the dominant model at present, there is an increasing recognition that countries have an international responsibility to prevent the unauthorized release of radiation or the theft of materials from their facilities. Both dangers directly affect other countries. These concepts of sovereignty and international responsibility should not be in competition. Both are important and need to be balanced.

There should be a commitment to the highest levels of nuclear security at home and a willingness to provide nonsensitive information on these actions to the global community. This process could begin with the actions listed above, first as a voluntary activity and then evolving into a codified requirement for all countries over time. These steps offer the best combination of assurances and can improve international confidence in Pakistan's nuclear security.

6

Strategic Intelligence Analysis

Strategic analysis is perhaps the most important form of intelligence. It provides a framework within which other forms of intelligence collection and analysis take place, offers an overall assessment from the top down rather than from the bottom up, and helps to provide a basis for policy formulation, strategic planning, and resource allocation. Its weakness is its focus on macro-level issues rather than the more detailed levels of analysis.

On the Internet, such analysis is even more problematic, due to the rapidly evolving nature of Internet usage. Prior to 1994, for example, Internet commerce was illegal. Today it is a multi-billion dollar economic force. New methods of organizational and economic cooperation are constantly evolving, with greater or less security.

Maintaining continuity on this constantly shifting environment is one of the greatest challenges to conducting effective strategic analysis of cyber-threats. Furthermore, for many consumers, strategic intelligence is irrelevant to day-to-day tasks and needs. At the end of the day, however, the importance of strategic intelligence analysis is undeniable. Such an effort helps to discern and make sense of trends, to identify and extract patterns that would otherwise not be visible, and to provide an overall picture of the evolving threat environment and the level of damage that might be occurred in certain specified contingencies.

Analytical initiatives that would fall under the rubric of strategic intelligence analysis include:

- *Overall threat assessments.* These include in the analysis the vulnerabilities of critical missions (including levels of dependence), the kind of disruption and damage that could be caused to the implementation of these missions, the kinds of weapons/instruments that could be used to cause such disruptions, and the likelihood of such attacks and intrusions taking place

- *Sector threat assessments.* Such analyses focus on vulnerabilities and threats either in particular areas such as national infrastructure, or in particular sectors of the economy such as banking or e-commerce. In effect, a strategic analysis of this kind has to take account of changes in what can be a very dynamic environment.
- *Trend Analysis to highlight changing threats and vulnerabilities.* These might include base-line assessments so as to better recognize departures from the baseline. Alternatively, they might focus on future threats and vulnerabilities in an effort to determine in what ways the problem is evolving–and what can be done to anticipate and contain future challenges. The way in which e-commerce has become a major issue suggests that the pace of change in the cyber-space environment is posing novel challenges that can best be understood through strategic intelligence analysis that is very forward looking. Indeed, trend analysis is likely to be most effective when it is linked with careful attention to drivers, *i.e.* fundamental trends in the political, economic, social and technological sectors that will shape the future threat and vulnerability environment of the future.
- *Potential Damage Assessments.* Because of the macro-level view taken by strategic analysis, it also offers the best approach for assessing potential cascade effects of intrusions. The specific target of a an intrusion might be a regional electric power grid, but the effects of a failure to that system can cascade to include telecommunications, public emergency services, water systems, etc. The potential for such wide-spread effects will be recognized most readily as a result of in-depth strategic analysis–which in turn would offer opportunities to develop both defensive and mitigation strategies. Crisis management, contingency planning, mitigation strategies, and disaster management would all be enhanced by strategic analysis of potential damage assessment. Indeed, the capacity for effective and rapid reconstitution might depend on such analysis.
- *Categorizing and differentiating attacks and attackers.* Intrusions in cyber-space can emanate from individuals, whether insiders or outsiders; from hacker groups intent on displaying their skills and capabilities; activist groups using direct action on the Internet to publicize their political cause; terrorist organizations using intrusions to create massive disruption or other forms of large-scale harm, and seeking to obtain widespread publicity and create a climate of fear; transnational criminal

organizations responding to law enforcement pressure with cyber-retaliation, and states using attacks on, or through, information systems as a form of asymmetric warfare. One of the most important tasks of intelligence analysis for the Internet is to discover ways of differentiating among intrusions from these various sources. This will be especially true as groups or individuals develop intrusion strategies that mimic other forms and thereby lessen their chances of identification or, in the case of nation states, provide plausible deniability of their actions. From the perspective of strategic intelligence analysis, this is critical in efforts to determine appropriate responses that might go beyond simply defensive or mitigation strategies. How specific attacks are categorized, of course, will also be an issue at the tactical and operational level. But the differentiating and categorization methodologies, initially at least, are a matter for strategic analysis.

- *Identification of Anomalies*. Searching for anomalies that provide indicators of emerging threats and problems is an important task of strategic intelligence analysis (albeit one that both feeds into and relies on tactical and operational efforts). Anomalies in this context can be understood as developments or events that do not fit typical or known patterns. The detection of anomalies or novel patterns can be a major element in anticipating new methods of intrusion, new targets, or even new classes of intruders. It is a macro-level task that requires careful and systematic "environmental scanning" as well as the coalescing of tactical and operational intelligence reports that identify and highlight specific aberrations from the norm.
- *Analysis of Future Net Environments*. The greatest constant about the Internet is change. Strategic intelligence analysis must take that into account and attempt to provide assessments of potential future environments on the Net and the potential impact of malicious activity within those environments. Given the dramatic changes in technology within the recent past, and seeing the rapid pace with which innovation continues to grow, it seems a reasonable assumption that the Internet (in one form or another) will become more and more integrated into the fabric of society. As this occurs, intrusions or attacks will have far more wide-ranging consequences. Considerations of social as well as political and economic impacts will have to be factored into intelligence assessments.

It is clear from this discussion that not only does strategic intelligence analysis provide a framework for tactical and operational assessments, but that work done at these levels in turn helps to shape the strategic intelligence focus. As for the strategic assessments themselves they should be useful for consumers, providing forecasting estimates that help to reduce uncertainties in ways that feed into policy processes, providing a basis for more informed decision-making and more effective resource allocation.

As strategic analytic methodologies mature, they will also offer the basis for predictive or anticipatory assessments that can serve to provide warning of potential hostile operations.

In effect, strategic intelligence assessments provide a basis for the development of high-level policy and strategy and for strategic responses to vulnerabilities, whether actual or potential.

Tactical Intelligence Analysis

Tactical analysis is a necessary and important complement to work done at the strategic level. It is the natural linking element between macro-level analysis and the micro-level focus on individual cases. *Among the kinds of studies that come under the level of tactical analysis would be:*

- Cluster and pattern analysis designed to discern temporal patterns, the use of particular intrusion methods, commonalities of targets, and attempts to build profiles of perpetrators, whether hackers or insiders.
- Stimulus-response analysis designed to identify potential actions that could be taken by intruders in response to specific known or predicted events. This analysis could be used both proactively in development of warnings or reactively in lending significance to otherwise-unrecognized activity.
- Network environmental analysis methods will have to be developed. It is probable that in-depth analysis of the Internet will reveal patterns similar to those in the physical world. Net weather is already being discussed, and network terrain is a viable concept. Unlike physical environments, however, the Internet environment will probably be subject to much more rapid shifting. That places this sort of analytic effort squarely in the realm of Tactical Analysis.

In physical space, geography helps to differentiate tactical from strategic, but on the Internet this component is lacking, an absence that makes the distinction between strategic and tactical somewhat more tenuous than in other domains. At the same time, the strategic and tactical levels are mutually reinforcing: although strategic intelligence analysis provides the framework for tactical assessments, these assessments in turn help to feed strategic analysis. With a highly dynamic inter-relationship among the various levels of analysis, each level is strengthened by and strengthens the others.

UNPACKING INDIA'S INTELLIGENCE AGENCIES

India's premier civilian intelligence agencies are the Intelligence Bureau (IB) and the Research and Analysis Wing (R&AW): the former deals with domestic intelligence, the latter with foreign intelligence. In addition, there are the intelligence directorates of the Armed Forces. Upon independence in 1947, the IB was the only real intelligence organization that India possessed. Set up in 1887, this agency had been responsible for political surveillance during the British Raj.

After India achieved independence, it was entrusted with additional responsibility for foreign intelligence. Between 1951 and 1968, the agency struggled to meet a very broad mandate in a deteriorating regional security environment, as India's relations with its neighbours plummeted. China and Pakistan launched unexpectedly audacious attacks in 1962 and 1965 respectively, prompting a realization among the Indian political leadership that a specialized agency was needed for foreign intelligence. Thus, in 1968, the R&AW was created. Both agencies have had impressive successes and some rather nasty intelligence failures. The IB in particular is considered as one of the most professional intelligence agencies anywhere in the world, and has achieved a remarkable measure of success in counterterrorism.

Logically it would. In practice, however, the West wishes to retain a modicum of goodwill from the Pakistani Inter-Services Intelligence (ISI), which alongside the Pakistani army, is the main sponsor of terrorist groups in South Asia. This is to be expected, since the ISI is rationing out counterterrorism cooperation to those states that avoid criticizing Pakistan too harshly for its Janus-faced policy of supporting some terrorists while fighting others. With its large and restive Pakistani-origin population the United Kingdom in particular, is vulnerable to Islamabad's blackmail in maintaining homeland security. British security officials privately admit this. Even so, the West's intelligence partnership with Pakistan is a tactical affair borne not of mutual trust and goodwill, but out of the negative leverage that Islamabad retains through its dalliance with radical Islamist groups.

As such, Indian intelligence agencies share a strategic interest with their Western counterparts in dealing with the threat of Pakistan-sponsored terrorism that transcends the divide-and-conquer games that the ISI tries to play. There is already an informal intelligence-sharing network where security agencies compare notes on the kind of dissimulation efforts that Pakistan engages in. Also, India's intelligence services make reliable long-term partners for the West since they operate under full civilian control and within a democratic framework.

The general consensus in India is that Zawahiri's call is part of an effort by the ISI to regain plausible deniability for its sponsorship of terrorist attacks, which was partially lost after the Mumbai 2008 attack. Knowing that Indian political and public opinion would push for strong retaliation in the event of a future terrorist onslaught from Pakistani territory, the ISI is trying to preemptively deny responsibility by floating the idea that 'non-state actors' are responsible.

It has used the same tactic in the past, when in 2007 it created the so-called 'Indian Mujahideen' group, using a small number of jihadists locally recruited from within India to carry out urban bombings. Even if one assumes, however, that Zawahiri's call for jihad against India was made independently of ISI prompting, the fact remains that the core leadership of Al Qaeda is increasingly dominated by Pakistani nationals. A decade-plus of Western counterterrorist operations has badly weakened the Al Qaeda command structure in Pakistan, making it vulnerable to a creeping takeover by local jihadists. So there is no way that Pakistani involvement in a future terrorist attack on India cannot be traced back to that country's borders. What remains an open question is whether the ISI itself can escape international condemnation, which it is hoping to do.

The Indian security establishment has a well-developed doctrine to combat political subversion, and counterinsurgency and counterterrorism are subsets of a larger effort to preserve the democratic framework of the country. This means that working together with communities that are potentially marginalized or disaffected is essential. India's most powerful defense against terrorism has been the consistent patriotism of its Muslim population, which largely recognizes that the ISI is keen to falsely implicate them in cross-border attacks so as to provoke a larger conflict within the country. During the 2008 Mumbai attack for instance, the farcical manner in which Pakistani terrorists tried to masquerade as locals under the moniker of 'Deccan Mujahideen' showed how amateurish the ISI's false-flag operations can be. Indian Muslims are wary of the larger design behind such antics.

Human intelligence from deep-penetration agents, mostly operated by the IB, has been one of the reasons why foreign jihadist groups like Lashkar-e-Taiba have been unable to make any headway in Kashmir over two decades, despite the terrain favouring guerrilla warfare. Likewise, resistance from mainstream Islamic seminaries in India has been a barrier to Pakistani subversion. A classic example was the May 2008 fatwa against terrorism issued by the Dar-ul Uloom seminary in Deoband, the most prestigious in South Asia. Pakistani Islamists were greatly upset by this development, and also by the manner in which the seminary called upon Indian Muslims to show complete solidarity with their Hindu countrymen after the terrorist attack on Mumbai.

Neither the IB nor the R&AW is a law enforcement agency. They need to cooperate with Indian police forces as a matter of routine. This is helped by the fact that both agencies are dominated by career police officials. In particular, the IB draws its senior cadres exclusively from the Indian Police Service (IPS) which makes for a strong sense of camaraderie. Even so, competition between various state police forces, or within a police force, is an unfortunate reality and this has in the past, led to some counterterrorist operations being bungled by the implementing agency. Generally, the focus is on preventing terrorist attacks in large cities, where the police have extensive local intelligence networks based on human sources. The IB and R&AW possess significant technical interception capabilities which can be used to generate strategic intelligence on Pakistani and other foreign threats. However, while coverage might be higher in some regions rather than others, this has to do with the inevitable need to optimize resource allocation towards the most pressing concerns. The fact that numerous Pakistani spies and terrorists have been arrested in remote rural areas, often close to international borders, demonstrates that coverage can be quite extensive.

That there are competing priorities among different ministries is only to be expected in a country with a unique policy problem: how to ensure equitable and sustained economic growth by integrating with the global economy, while at the same time acquiring the structural integrity that strong Western states have in policing their borders. Indian intelligence agencies have been badly hit by economizing trends in the past, and this has usually resulted in information gaps. Projects to streamline data collation and storage have been stymied by the reluctance of some agencies to share information which their counterparts do not need for operational purposes. While I would agree that bureaucratic rivalries are unhelpful, it is also worth remembering that even supposedly efficient intelligence services such as those in Israel have suffered from turf warfare (known colloquially as 'The War of the Jews'). In Northern Ireland, British intelligence agencies have competed for local sources, going to the extent of undermining national counterterrorist efforts in the pursuit of narrow organizational interests. And prior to 9/11, the US intelligence community was no different – counterterrorism coordination meetings were intended for show rather than substance.

THE DEFENSE INTELLIGENCE AGENCY

The early weeks of this month have seen the formation of India's Defense Intelligence Agency (DIA). Lt. Gen. Kamal Davar was appointed as its first chief. Much of the public debate on this development has swung between extreme viewpoints and focused intensely on the publicly stated fissures in the intelligence system. This chapter will attempt to examine some of the issues confronting this newly formed agency in a more secular light. The 'Intelligence Process' involves seven basic steps: collection, analysis, production (assessment), dissemination, coordination, action, and evaluation. A sufficiently advanced intelligence handling system divides responsibility for these parts to independent groups of people, thereby maximizing oversight and minimizing overlap. In India we are still in the process of building such a system. Collection, analysis, and action are relatively easier steps to carry out. Production, dissemination, coordination and evaluation however are immensely complicated. If one carefully reads writings about intelligence issues in India, the difficulties experienced in these steps become apparent.

The bulk of intelligence work in India is carried out by the Research and Analysis Wing (R&AW) and the Intelligence Bureau (IB). The various services intelligence directorates namely the Directorate of Military Intelligence (DMI), the Directorate of Air Intelligence (DAI), Directorate of Naval Intelligence (DNI) and some other agencies are involved also but their activity is smaller by comparison. The R&AW and IB agencies are composed largely of civilians. Military personnel are often deputed to these agencies, but the letter of the law and concerns of deniability limit the use of serving military officers in some types of activity (especially collection and action). Democratic countries look down upon excessive involvement of military personnel in intelligence activity. The role of serving officers on deputation is therefore limited mostly to helping with 'production'. In cases where greater involvement of Military personnel becomes necessary, they are asked to resign from the forces and re-hired as civilians. As the Defense Intelligence Agency will be comprised largely of serving officers, the 'rules' will limit its role in physical collection of secret intelligence. The DIA may however choose to expand the existing Open Source Intelligence (OSINT) collection capability. Similar 'rules' apply to several 'action' related issues. It appears at first glance that the DIA personnel will be involved only in creating a support structure for various 'actions'.

In India repeated complaints have surfaced from various sources over the quality of intelligence production. As the military is one of the biggest consumers of the intelligence product, its complaints have been the most visible. It is impossible to dismiss all complaints as being parochial. A Defense Intelligence Agency does offer certain advantages in terms of quality of production. These are stated below:

a) The composition of the Indian military reflects the immensely diverse Indian society. Only a member of the military with years of service can truly comprehend the complex social divisions and hierarchy in the armed forces. Consequently this detailed knowledge should in theory enable the member to better mould the intelligence product to suit the needs of others in the military.

b) Understanding military technology requires considerable specialization. Such specialization exists in the military. With the growing use of technology in warfare there is a greater need for specialist participation in higher-level assessment.

c) Post-Chagai there is an emphasis on speed and reliability in all parts of the intelligence chain. At lot of the activity in this area will require the kind of discipline largely available in military service. Though in India, the entire responsibility for this targeting cannot be given to the DIA, its inputs will be critical.

In order to avoid becoming narrow and insular in its approach, it is strongly advisable that the DIA hire civilians to assist with the production process as well. Presently the country has a large surplus of trained professionals, a good number of universities and research centres. With suitable encouragement at least some of these could be induced to help with the task at hand. The author feels its it also a good idea to routinely farm out small production tasks to private think tanks and strategic forecasting companies. Such a measure will do a lot to improve the standard of public debate on security and strategic issues in India. The task of 'dissemination' of intelligence offers many challenges. The DIA should hopefully attempt to address some like:

a) The battlefield awareness of the Indian soldier could do with some improvement. Modern technology has improved the ability to reach the soldiers in the battlefield, but knowing exactly what information to give to them is important. This is in part a production issue as well, however any steps taken to improve the ability of the lowest rungs of the military to comprehend intelligence briefings is most welcome.

b) Dissemination of information in the field has its vulnerabilities; modern technology does not overcome all of them. Here too the exact way in which the information travels from source to destination will need much more thinking. There are SIGSEC and COMSEC capabilities but more agile management is always desirable.

c) The sharing of information once it is collected with other agencies is a contentious issue especially in areas of 'concurrent responsibility'. This was the *Achilles heel* of the old system. Whether modern technology can address some of this only time will tell.

'Coordination' at the DIA (local) level will involve managing the exact division of responsibilities between the various service intelligence directorates. Given the diversity of the theatres of operation, it will be a challenge to integrate the service intelligence directorates while maintaining an emphasis on corroboration. The DIA will also act as the liaison between the MOD sub-units and other intelligence centres. At a higher level, the DIA will have to brief the CDS and, and 'coordinate' its production activity with other agencies under the supervision of the Intelligence Coordination Group. This part may take time to settle down. This brings us to the last and most important step of 'evaluation'. This step deals with ensuring accountability within the intelligence handling system. Without this critical step, the entire process of intelligence can become skewed. Indian intelligence agencies have suffered a fair bit because of a lack of transparency in their evaluation procedures. Most of these are cloaked in the same veil of secrecy that surrounds other operations. The result is that any public motifs about the agency subsequently color perceptions about accountability. There is a great deal to be learnt from the mistakes made by other agencies in the past. Undoubtedly the new system of intelligence management involving the Intelligence Coordination Group etc… will have evaluation methods built into it, but a mechanism for auditing and reviewing performance within the DIA itself is highly advisable.

In conclusion, it is important to bear in mind that none of the problems have evaporated merely with the formation of the DIA and 'old enemies' may reappear even in the new setup. However in the past the formation of such agencies was overshadowed by severe economic crises. The crises skewed the development of these agencies. The DIA has been born at a relatively calmer time. This should have a very positive impact on the DIA. While all the items above seem within reach, it is important to realize that all of them are big challenges. It is also vital to bear in mind that the DIA is not some magic wand capable of conjuring instant geopolitical victory. The DIA will eventually be a sharp tool, most effective in skilled hands. The formation of the DIA is many years overdue and Lt. Gen. Kamal Davar has an enormous task ahead of him, so with that in mind, the author congratulates him and wishes him and the staff of the DIA the very best of luck on their endeavour.

EVOLUTION AS AN INTELLIGENT PROCESS

God reveals himself in the harmony of what exists.

Spinoza

A central tenet of AI is that we, an intelligent species, can create intelligent machines. At present the machines we have created, while having better memories and greater speed, are clearly less capable than we are at most intellectual tasks. The gap is shrinking, however. Machine intelligence is rapidly improving. The same cannot be said for human intelligence. A controversial question surrounding AI is whether the gap can ultimately be eliminated. Can machine intelligence ultimately equal that of human intelligence? Can it surpass human intelligence? A broader statement of the question is, Can an intelligent entity be more intelligent than the intelligence that created it?

One way to gain insight into these questions might be to examine the relationship of human intelligence to the intelligent process that created it-evolution. Evolution created human and many other forms of intelligence and thus may be regarded as an intelligent process itself.

One attribute of intelligence is its ability to create and design. The results of an intelligent design process-to wit, intelligent designs-have the characteristics of being aesthetically pleasing and functionally effective. It is hard to imagine designs that are more aesthetically pleasing or functionally effective than the myriad of life forms that have been produced by the process we call evolution. Indeed, some theories of aesthetics define aesthetic quality or beauty as the degree of success in emulating the natural beauty that evolution has created.

Evolution can be considered the ultimate in intelligence-it has created designs of indescribable beauty, complexity, and elegance. Yet, it is considered to lack consciousness and free will-it is just an "automatic" process. It is what happens to swirling matter given enough time and the right circumstances.

Evolution is often pitted against religious theories of creation. The religious theories do share one thing in common with the theory of evolution-both attribute creation to an ultimate intelligent force. The most basic difference is that in the religious theories this intelligent force *is* conscious and does have free will, although some theologies, such as Buddhism, conceive of God as an ultimate force of creativity and intelligence and not as a personal willful consciousness.

The theory of evolution can be simply expressed as follows. Changes in the genetic code occur through random mutation; beneficial changes are retained, whereas harmful ones are discarded through the "survival of the fittest." In some ways it makes sense that the survival of the fittest would retain good changes and discard bad ones, since we define "good" to mean more survivable.

Yet let us consider the theory from another perspective. The genetic code is similar to an extraordinarily large computer program, about six billion bits to describe a human, in contrast to a few tens of millions of bits in the most complex computer programs. It is indeed a binary code, and we are slowly learning its digital language. The theory says that changes are introduced essentially randomly, and the changes are evaluated for retention by survival of the entire organism and its ability to reproduce. Yet a computer program controls not just the one characteristic that is being changed but literally millions of other characteristics. Survival of the fittest appears to be a rather crude technique capable of concentrating on at most a few fundamental characteristics at a time. While a few characteristics were being optimized, thousands of others could degrade through the increasing entropy of random change. If we attempted to improve our computer programs in this way, they would surely disintegrate.

The method we use to improve the programs we create is not the introduction of random code changes but carefully planned and designed changes and experiments designed to focus in on the changes just introduced. It has been proposed that evolution itself has evolved to where changes are not entirely random but in some way planned, and that changes are "tested" in some way other than overall survival, in which a change just introduced would be competing with thousands or even millions of other factors.

Yet no one can describe a mechanism in which such planning and isolated evaluation could take place in the process of evolution. There appears, therefore, to be a gap in the theory of evolution. Clearly, the fossil and biochemical evidence is overwhelming that species have indeed undergone a slow but dramatic evolution in complexity and sophistication, yet we do not fully understand the mechanism. The proposed mechanism seems unlikely to work; its designs should disintegrate through increasing entropy.

One possible perspective would state that the creator of an intelligence is inherently superior to the intelligence it creates. The first step of this perspective seems to be well supported in that the intelligence of evolution appears vast. Yet is it?

While it is true that evolution has created some extraordinary designs; it is also true that it took an extremely long period of time to do so. Is the length of time required to solve a problem or create a design relevant to an evaluation of the level of an intelligence? Clearly it is. We recognize this by timing our intelligence tests. If someone can solve a problem in a few minutes, we consider that better than solving the same problem in a few hours or a few years. With regard to intelligence as an aid to survival, it is clearly better to solve problems quickly than slowly. In a competitive world we see the benefits of solving problems quickly. Evolution has achieved intelligent work on an extraordinarily high level yet has taken an extraordinarily long period of time to do so.

It is very slow. If we factor its achievements by its ponderous pace, I believe we shall find that its intelligence quotient is only infinitesimally greater than zero. An IQ of only slightly greater than zero is enough for evolution to beat entropy and create extraordinary designs, given enough time, in the same way that an ever so slight asymmetry in the physical laws may have been enough to allow matter to almost completely overtake antimatter. The human race, then, may very well be smarter than its creator, evolution. If we look at the speed of human progress in comparison to that of evolution, a strong case can be made that we are far more intelligent than the ponderously slow process that created us. Consider the sophistication of *our* creations over a period of only a few thousand years. In another few thousand years our machines are likely to be at least comparable to human intelligence or even surpass it in all likelihood, and thus humans will have clearly beaten evolution, achieving in a matter of thousands of years as much or more than evolution achieved in several billion years. From this perspective, human intelligence may be greater than its creator.

NATIONAL MILITARY STRATEGY

Before proceeding there are three terms which should be addressed: strategy, national security strategy, and national military strategy.

Strategy. Strategy is an easy word to use but is difficult to define. Most standard dictionaries are more confusing than enlightening on that particular entry because a strategy refers to a holistic system and process. Our interest in the word strategy will focus on its component parts because of their utility in analyzing the whole. The U.S. Army War College utilizes a simple but powerful formula to express what a strategy is and what its critical component parts consist of: *Strategy = Ends + Ways + Means*. In this equation "ends" are our objectives or goals, "ways" are the courses of action we choose to achieve those goals, and "means" are the resources either at hand or which must be developed to enable the courses of action.

There are three important aspects of this model to keep in mind. The first is that the three components of a strategy—ends, ways and means—are interdependent. All of the components must be appropriate to the whole and in proper balance with the others if the strategy is to be successful. The second point to keep in mind is that when we attempt to study someone else's strategy, such as the PLA's, focusing on only one component of the strategy without an understanding of the other two may lead to incorrect or incomplete conclusions. The third point is the utility of this model as an analytic tool. It is almost universal in its applicability and is not limited to military affairs. One can easily use this equation to craft, describe or analyze political or economic strategies.

Also, in the realm of military planning it is applicable across the three levels of warfare—the strategic, operational and tactical levels.

National Security Strategy. American analysts often use the term "national security strategy" or "security strategy" in the context of a nation's military concerns or military-related issues. This chapter adopts a variant of the much broader definition used by the U.S. Joint Chiefs of Staff. A National Security Strategy (NSS) will refer to the development, application and coordination of all the elements of national power (political/diplomatic, economic, informational, military, sociological/cultural) to achieve a nation's objectives in domestic and international affairs in peace as well as in war. In pursuing the national objectives set forth in a NSS, multiple strategies co-exist: an economic strategy, a political strategy, a diplomatic strategy, a social strategy, and a military strategy, at the very least. There are two points to make about this definition. First, Lykke's equation is still a valid construct. A national security strategy will have to articulate ends (objectives), ways (courses of action), and means (resources). Also, it should be noted that the military element of national power is a subset within the broader national security strategy. This brings us to a description of a national military strategy.

National Military Strategy. A National Military Strategy (NMS) is the military component of a nation's overall National Security Strategy. Its objectives are derived from those within the overarching NSS. It is the role of the national military leadership to ensure that the military element of national power will be available to contribute to the NSS in both peace and war, in the here and now and in the future. The NMS is the vehicle through which the national military leadership articulates, revalidates, and adjusts the ends, ways, and means of the armed forces to comport with changing NSS objectives, a changing security environment, or changes in the availability of national resources to be applied to the armed forces. A national military strategy is usually influenced by civil political and economic decisions. Consequently, national military strategies are dynamic and require constant review, revision and updating. At the national level of military planning—the level at which a NMS is generated—direction, guidance and policies are articulated in broad terms to steer the armed forces in the correct direction. Specific decisions, programs and detailed planning follow in due course.

Once again, the equation is still valid. A NMS must articulate ends, ways and means. In the case of a NMS, the equation is rewritten to reflect the national level of military strategy: *National Military Strategy = National Military Objectives + National Military Strategic Concepts + National Military Resources*. National Military Objectives (NMOs) will be derived from the NSS. The National Military Strategic Concepts (NMSC) will articulate the courses of action that will be undertaken to achieve the ends. The National Military Resources (NMRs) describe the types of capabilities that will be required to be on hand or be developed to enable the NMSCs.

The starting point for crafting a NMS is the articulation of NMOs. From these are developed NMSCs and NMRs. But before articulating NMSCs strategic planners first must use a critical "strategic filter" that identifies the imperatives of conflict and the possible constraints planners may have to consider. At minimum, the strategic filter: (1) considers political decisions handed down to military planners or brokered between military and civilian leaders; (2) assesses the current and projected security environments (conflict with whom? when?); and (3) performs an analysis of the operational environment (what kinds of conflicts?).

The synergistic relationship between the three elements of a NMS is readily apparent. If the resources are not available to enable the NMSCs, then weighty political-military decisions are in order: either adjust the NMOs and NMSCs or commit the resources (usually funding) to develop the NMRs. But such a zero-sum set of decisions is usually unacceptable for political reasons and impractical for reasons of national security. Consequently, at the national level of military planning, the NMS often encompasses multiple substrategies for different time frames. At a minimum, one strategy must be focused on current capabilities and near-term contingencies. Another should consider the requirements of coping with future potential security problems. Crafting military strategies for the here and now while accounting for over-the-horizon problems is a conundrum that is encountered almost exclusively at the national level of military planning and, save success in war, is probably the ultimate test of a nation's generalship.

With the preceding discussion behind us we can now move on to consider the case of China. To do so we will take the iterative and dynamic process that is used to *craft* an NMS, which is a cyclical process, and artificially stretch it out in linear fashion in order to be *descriptive* of its components.

China's National Military Strategy

The national military strategy that will now be discussed finds its roots in the late 1970s and early 1980s, when Deng Xiaoping reassessed the international security environment and made the decision to make economic modernization the central task for the coming decades. Deng's decisions not only sent the Chinese nation down a new and different path, but sent the PLA down a new road as well. It stands to reason that a modernizing, outward-looking China seeking a leading role in the mainstream of the international order would require a new type of defence establishment and a new military strategic direction than that of a previously autarkic China seeking to lead the "Third World." What follows then is a description of what Chinese strategic planners might term the general thrust of the national military strategy "during the new historical period" and into "the cross-century period." It is current to the extent that the latest policy decisions coming out of the 15th Party Congress and 9th National People's Congress are incorporated as adjustments. But we should bear in mind that the general direction of China's NMS has been evolving for more than a decade. Consequently, there is both continuity and change to report.

National Military Objectives

China's national military strategy seeks to achieve three sets of national military objectives: *Protect the Party and Safeguard Stability*, *Defend Sovereignty and Defeat Aggression*, and *Modernize the Military and Build the Nation*.

These three objectives not only define what it is the PLA must achieve as a military force, but highlights the unique role it plays in the political economy of the PRC. Significantly, these three national military objectives are derived from and are mutually supportive of China's three national security objectives. The formulation of these three national military objectives are strictly those of the author's and not authoritative PRC formulations. However, they should be familiar to students of the PLA because China's top military leaders often allude to them or aspects of them in public statements.

For example, in the April 1998 issue of *International Strategic Studies*, Deputy Chief of the General Staff Lieutenant General Xiong Guangkai states that the "basic objectives" of China's armed forces are to "consolidate national defence, resist aggression, defend the nation's sovereignty over its territorial land, sea, airspace as well as its maritime interests, and safeguard national unity and security." In May 1998 Chief of the General Staff Department (GSD) General Fu Quanyou provided this iteration: "the PLA's mission is to strengthen the national defence, fend off aggression, safeguard territorial sovereignty and the rights and interests of territorial waters, and maintain national integrity and safety." As yet another example, in 1996 Defence Minister Chi Haotian offered that the "basic objectives" of China's national defence are to "solidify the defensive capacity, resist foreign invasion, and safeguard the unification and security of the country."

Although the three national military objectives that this chapter posits are seemingly self-explanatory, it is worthwhile to briefly discuss each because through them we achieve a greater appreciation of just what it is the PLA is attempting to achieve, the challenges it faces, and a flavor for the organizational culture of this massive defence establishment.

Protect the Party and Safeguard Stability. The first and foremost mission entrusted to the PLA, and a national military objective, is to be the guardian of the CCP. The past two decades of professionalization and modernization have not altered the fundamental fact that the institutional loyalty of China's armed forces and the personal commitment of it top leaders is to the maintenance of the regime and the primacy of the CCP. The PLA remains the party's army. China's "national command authorities" are the leaders of the Central Military Commission (CMC), which is a party organization under the Central Committee. It is worth remembering that it has only been 71 years since the "Red Army" was founded. The revolutionary heritage of that army and its roots as a communist insurgent force that saved the fledgling CCP from annihilation in the 1920s and 1930s is not too distant a memory for some of the current PLA leaders. Minister of Defence and CMC Vice Chairman General Chi Haotian (66 years old) joined the PLA as a young man in the early 1940s during the "twin struggles" against the Nationalists and the Japanese and he spent a good part of his later career as a senior political commissar. The constant self-propagandizing within the PLA to remind the troops that the party is the focus of their loyalty has not abated as the Chinese armed forces have attempted to become a more proficient military force. Indeed, the first among the "Five General Requirements" issued by Jiang Zemin for all PLA soldiers is to be "politically qualified."

It is often argued that today the party and ideology mean less and less in China. For the general populace and even some civil cadre that may be truer than not. However, the party and ideology still count for quite a lot in the PLA. The "new nationalism" that has been ascribed to the PLA is not necessarily at the expense of the Party and it may just be that in today's China the PLA is the only institution over which the CCP "centre" in Beijing still has near total control from one end of the nation to the other. The constant public affirmations of the PLA's top leaders of the primacy of the Party is no more empty rhetoric than the statements of the top U.S. military leadership affirming the primacy of the Constitution and the principle of civilian control over the military.

In August 1997, PLA Academy of Military Sciences Commandant General Xu Huizi encapsulated many of the above thoughts in an article in *China Military Science.*

> After entering the new historical period, Deng Xiaoping repeatedly stressed that our military situation is that of the party commanding the gun, instead of the gun commanding the party; the military must follow the party's instructions, and must not at any time wave its own flag.... Comrade Jiang Zemin referred to the principle of the party commanding the gun as our military 'soul.'

For these reasons, the PLA must be prepared to defend the CCP with military force against domestic challenges as well as external threats. Over the past few years much of the internal security mission of the PLA has passed to the People's Armed Police (PAP).

However, the PAP is ultimately under the control of the CMC and the "regular" PLA has not been absolved from its requirement to provide for the defence of the party. One of the many reasons the PLA was called upon to converge on Beijing in the Spring of 1989 was because the PAP was incapable of handling a situation that was viewed by the CCP leadership to be burgeoning into a direct threat to the rule of the regime and the CCP. The PLA also pursues the related military objective of safeguarding internal stability. Some domestic challenges and threats may be aimed at the state, not the party per se. Examples would be acts of violence by separatist factions in non-Han China such as in Tibet or Xinjiang. Still other threats to stability with which the PLA must deal are natural disasters and manmade disasters. In these situations the PLA is often called upon to provide disaster relief, internal humanitarian assistance, as well as fight back the forces of nature such as floods or large-scale fires.

At the risk of being guilty of unsubstantiated generalization, I would offer that the top leadership of the PLA remains a very conservative group, which is virulently opposed to any domestic circumstance that could lead to instability (*luan*). The up-and-coming generation of leaders (colonel and above) are probably no less so. The chaos of the Cultural Revolution touched many of this latter generation personally and tragically and they fully understand the cost China paid in terms of development and modernization. And if in their hearts some dismiss as irrelevant Communist ideology, they may still see the CCP as the only political force in China that can successfully keep the nation together and lead it into the future.

Defend Sovereignty and Defeat Aggression. This national military objective brings us to the classical warfighting mission of the Chinese armed forces. Militaries exist to fight and so does the PLA. It is worth pointing out that the PLA considers itself a defensive force. Its leaders often declare that China since 1949 has never fought a war of aggression and has gone to war only when other nations have attacked China first or threatened its territory. Officially, Chinese will argue that their intervention in Korea (1950), the war against India (1962), the Sino-Soviet clashes of the late 1960s, and the incursion against Vietnam (1979) were all conflicts foisted upon China in defence of its sovereignty. Hence, they would couch their warfighting objective in terms of defence against aggression and the preservation of the nation's sovereignty. Moreover, the PLA rejects the notion of fighting as part of a formal alliance, proudly claiming that no Chinese combat troops are stationed on foreign soil, nor does Beijing desire to do so.

However, as mentioned earlier, China's definition of "sovereignty" is much broader than just the sanctity of its borders. The PLA defence of China's sovereignty also includes being capable and prepared to employ force to achieve national unification and assert Beijing's maritime rights. Chi Haotian has commented directly on these points in the past. In a May 1996 interview he was reported to comment that China's national defence policy "is aimed at protecting China's territorial land, waters, and air space as well as China's maritime rights and interests against foreign aggression. It is also aimed at safeguarding China's unity.... In the last decade, Beijing's use of the PLA to assert its claims to resources in the South China Sea has raised a great deal of concern within the region and beyond. As far as China's unification goes, only the issue of Taiwan remains unresolved. Although Beijing claims it prefers to settle this issue in a peaceful manner, China's leaders will not renounce the use of force. This puts a tremendous amount of pressure on the PLA for obvious reasons. As we review China's analysis of its security environment later in this chapter, it will become clear just how much the PLA must accomplish as a professional military force.

Modernize the Military and Build the Nation. The modernization of the military deserves its own place among the PLA's national military objectives. The top civilian and uniformed leadership of the PRC consider China's overall modernization and the modernization of the military (often referred to as "army building") to be mutually dependent and supporting national objectives. "Strengthening national defence and army building," declared Jiang Zemin at the 15th Party Congress, "is the basic guarantee for national security and the modernization drive."

The Chinese believe that without a modernizing and capable military the nation will not be able to enjoy the security from external threats it requires to continue to concentrate on economic reform. Without a capable military China cannot secure the internal stability it requires to modernize in the civil sector. Without a capable and modernizing military China cannot hope to secure any of its national security objectives in the realms of sovereignty or unification.

Finally, without a modern PLA whose capabilities ultimately comport with China's (anticipated) economic, technological, and political strength, the PRC will not be able to take its seat at the table of world leaders in Beijing's much hoped for multipolar international order.

While both civil and military leaders subscribe to these views, the tension in the system revolves around the fact that military modernization is not proceeding at the same pace as economic modernization. Moreover, by long-standing political fiat going back to the beginning of the Dengist period, the decision *not* to invest state treasure in military modernization at the expense of economic reform still stands. Jiang Zemin reaffirmed this tenet at the 9th NPC in March 1998. Speaking to a full session of the PLA's delegation to the NPC, Jiang lectured that:

It is also very important to correctly handle the relationship between economic development and the building of national defence. Building a modernized army and national defence is a guarantee for the country's safety and modernization drive.

This is something the whole party and the whole nation always care very much about. The level of China's productive forces is still not high, and our economy is not that strong. Therefore, we must concentrate our energies on economic development. *Without a highly developed economy, it is also impossible to promote the modernization of national defence and the army. We must always insist on taking economic development as the central task while paying adequate attention to modernizing national defence...*

Outwardly, at least, the top PLA leadership supports this basic line and does not question its validity. A serious challenge to the party leadership on this account should not be anticipated. Yet, as the men who are responsible for modernizing the military in a world (as we will later see) which they view as basically hostile, they do evince concern about how far behind economic development military modernization can lag. For example, General Xu Huizi has cautioned that "we must also understand that national wealth does not equate to military strength; there are many examples both past and present, in China and overseas, where a nation has been wealthy while its military was weak. We must try to keep our military quality development level at a level compatible with national defence security; keeping it at a level appropriate to China's international status as a great nation is a choice on which we must insist." Defence Minister Chi Haotian made a more direct commentary on this point in 1996 in a lengthy article in *Qiushi*. "The building of national defence," stated Chi, "cannot exceed the limitation of tolerance of economic construction, *nor can it be laid aside until the economy has totally prospered.*"

As a result of this contradiction, the leadership of the PLA is going to have to be very focused in how it approaches the modernization of the military. The decisions they make (and are making) in this regard will to a large extent drive some of the major national military strategic concepts in their overall NMS.

The corollary to "modernizing the military" is "building the nation." Not only is the PLA's modernization expected not to be a drain on the state's coffers, but military modernization is also expected to enhance the economic, scientific and technological level of the state. The military, says Chi Haotian, is expected to do so by leading and participating in "key state projects," by bringing science and technology to the rural areas of China, by transferring superior military technologies to the civilian sector, by providing the nation with a pool of PLA veterans who are technically advanced relative to their civilian counterparts (the PLA as a "big school"), and providing infrastructure to the hinterlands.

These, then, are the broad national military objectives the PLA seeks to achieve. To achieve these goals China's military planners need to articulate strategic concepts, or courses of action. Before they can do that, however, they must think through the environment in which they must operate, now and in the future. They must employ a "filter" that highlights both challenges and opportunities.

China's National Security Objectives

China's national security strategy has been apparent and quite public for over two decades and there is no need to detail it here. The political reports from the 13th,14th and 15th Party Congresses, the work reports associated with meetings of the National People's Congress (NPC), and a good number of key decisions and policies emanating from Central Committee plenums and NPC Standing Committee meetings have all become increasingly public over the years. From the time Deng Xiaoping consolidated his power in the late 1970s, observing and analyzing the ends, ways, and means of that strategy has defined the essence of China-watching. The "Four Modernizations," "Reform and Opening Up," "Economic Construction as the Central Task," and other phrases coined by the Chinese to describe *aspects* of their strategy are all quite familiar even to the casual student of Chinese affairs. But because we are slowly working toward developing a national *military* strategy for China, we must posit and articulate Beijing's national security objectives since they will drive the PLA's national military objectives. If one were to distill all of the statements of China's national security objectives, both explicit and implicit, that have been publicly declared or adduced over the last few years they could be distilled to three simple words: *sovereignty, modernity,* and *stability*. These words encompass the totality of everything the Chinese nation is determined to achieve. Moreover, these objectives are not only those of the People's Republic of China (PRC), but capture the essence of the Chinese Revolution.

That revolution has been in motion since the last decades of the Ch'ing (Qing) Dynasty. The Chinese proudly proclaim over five thousand years of continuous civilization, and rightly so. But China is new to the business of developing a nation-state—less than one hundred years, less experience than the United States. The history of the Chinese Revolution has been, and continues to be, the story of the difficult transformation of an ancient traditional civilization into a modern nation-state. Every stage of the revolution has more or less sought the same three objectives: sovereignty, modernity, and stability. From K'ang Yu-wei to Dr. Sun Yat-sen to Republican China under Chiang Kai-Shek, to Deng Xiaoping and now Jiang Zemin— all have attempted to achieve these goals. Where there has been divergence has been in the "ways" to achieve those "ends." The great exception was, of course, Mao. While he embraced sovereignty and modernity as legitimate national security objectives, he rejected stability as a goal in his later years. By substituting "perpetual revolution" for stability and by making "class struggle the key link," Mao set back China's progress immeasurably. Consequently, the history of China under Deng Xiaoping is in great measure the story of Deng's efforts to reverse the damage and find a new path to progress. And there is little doubt that China under Jiang Zemin embraces these three national security objectives as well. Let us explore each a bit further.

Sovereignty. One would think that sovereignty, "freedom from external control" to cite *Webster's*, is so fundamental to nationhood that it need not be articulated as a national security objective. For China, this is not the case. Beijing's right to assert and defend its sovereign prerogatives as a nation-state is an enduring preoccupation that even today's leadership brings with them to office. It is not surprising of his political report to the 15th Party Congress in September 1997 Jiang Zemin made explicit references to the Opium War (1840), the Eight Power Intervention (during the Boxer uprising, 1900), the war against Japan (1937–1945), and China's "Hundred Years of Humiliation." The prominent position of these references is not mere rhetoric. It underscores that sovereignty is one of the enduring national objectives of the PRC under the Chinese Communist Party (CCP) just as it was for Republican China under the Kuomintang (KMT). This is the result of more than a century of foreign military, political, and economic intervention from without, warlordism and regionalism from within, and the difficulties all Chinese regimes since the fall of the Ch'ing have experienced in just defining and securing the geographical scope of the Chinese nation-state. Consequently, as portrayed by Beijing, Hong Kong's retrocession to China in July 1997 was as much an emotional event for the people of China as it was a political event.

In the context of 1998, how Beijing defines sovereignty is now much broader than merely being the master of its own nation. Today, issues related to sovereignty encompass at least six categories of issues. First, of course, is concern over the return of territories Beijing considers part of the PRC, but over which it exercises no jurisdiction—Taiwan and Macao, for example. Second are issues related to border disputes China still has with some of its neighbours and the problems of demarcation and control.

This encompasses a series of bilateral problems. Issue number three concerns areas of China over which Beijing does exert control but whose indigenous non-Han population oppose China's rule, such as in Xinjiang and Tibet. A fourth category is one of multiple competing claims such as in the South China Sea, not just for atolls, reefs and islets but for maritime resources. A fifth issue involves what Beijing views as unwanted and unwarranted foreign concern over, or meddling in, Chinese domestic social and political issues. A sixth category relates to international pressure for China to accede to multilateral instruments and protocols which might constrain Beijing's freedom of action whether or not the instrument in question is or is not problematical.

The constant lectures on China's sovereignty to which foreigners, official and private, friends and adversaries, are subjected are tedious, formulaic and almost archaic. But it would be a mistake to dismiss the seriousness of the message because of the medium.

Modernity. During the last two decades China's quest for modernity has probably been the most studied, analyzed and scrutinized of Beijing's three national security objectives. This is especially the case in economic matters. Modernity, of course, encompasses much more than economics. It includes social change, political reform, cultural adaptations, intellectual change, and technological and scientific innovation, to name just a few of the aspects of the modernization process. The leadership in Beijing understands this and in fact does have separate objectives and strategies for each of these areas. But for the purposes of this short discussion, we must condense this vast subject to its essential elements.

In the final analysis, the objective of modernity as defined by today's PRC leadership means increasing the economic strength of the nation, enhancing the technological and scientific capabilities of the state, and raising the standard of living of the population. China's leaders have come to believe that its sovereignty and its place among the leading nations of the world in the future will be secured by, and a function of, its economic and technological strength. Hence the centrality of this objective and the emphasis it receives in China's national security strategy.

The 15th Party Congress and the 9th National People's Congress were devoted in the main to articulating the latest adjustments to China's modernization strategy. The Party Congress provided broad statements of "ends" and "means." The NPC, in turn, announced specific plans and policies to enable them. It is worthwhile to quote Jiang Zemin at the NPC in his role as State President for he offers an excellent example of a broad statement of a national security objective in general and a specific "end" or objective for the national security objective of modernity.

The goals we have set are as follows: When the People's Republic celebrates its centenary, the modernization program will have been basically accomplished and China will have become a prosperous, strong, democratic and culturally advanced socialist country. At that time, our country will rank among the moderately developed countries of the world, the Chinese people will have achieved common prosperity on the basis of modernization and the great rejuvenation of the Chinese nation will have been realized.

Stability. This last of China's three national security objectives is as sacred as the other two. A large dimension of the history of Chinese civilization through the millennia is the history of periods of peace alternating with periods of unfathomable social chaos and violence. Moreover, during the last two centuries stability has been the exception, not the norm. It has been a period of *nei luan wai huan* [domestic disorder and foreign calamities]. The legacies of the White Lotus, Taipings, Nien, Miao Tungan, I-ho ch'uan, warlords, civil war, Red Guards, right through to Tiananmen in 1989 represent what every Chinese regime has feared the most, including the current inhabitants of *Zhongnanhai.* They do not take internal stability for granted.

Today the greatest challenge for Beijing's leaders is undoubtedly the need to balance their bold plans for modernization with the risk of instability, for it is clear that economic modernization has been accompanied by tremendous social dislocations. Over the past year and a half, one is struck with the frequency of press reports citing labour unrest, worker protests, and acts of civil disobedience. The Chinese leadership is acutely aware of the *maodun* (contradiction) which they have set in motion. Again, we quote Jiang Zemin at the 15th Party Congress:... it is of the utmost importance to correctly handle the relations between reform and development on one hand and stability on the other so as to maintain a stable political and social environment. *Without stability, nothing can be achieved.*

But the objective "stability" does not just refer to maintaining the internal peace. A second aspect of stability means regime maintenance; that is, maintaining undiluted the authority and monopoly on power held by the Chinese Communist Party (CCP). The third aspect of "stability" has an outward dimension. It is the firm belief of the Chinese leadership that only a peaceful and stable international environment will permit China to successfully pursue its national objectives. Or, as Jiang Zemin put it, "We need a long-term international environment of peace for carrying out socialist modernization, especially a favourable peripheral environment." And it is precisely because of Deng Xiaoping's great "strategic decision" shortly after the Third Plenum of the 11th Central Committee in 1978 that the world security situation had relaxed and a world war was a remote possibility that he decided the time was right to launch China on its grand experiment in modernization. It is clear that how Beijing chooses to pursue its objective of sovereignty while seeking to preserve a peaceful international environment will also pose a challenge in the future.

These, then, are the three key national security objectives posited as the driving forces behind China's current national security strategy. By striving to achieve these objectives the PRC hopes not only to enhance the state of its domestic conditions but also to be able to strengthen its desired role as the preeminent nation in Asia and as one of five key actors in the future multipolar world order that Chinese theorists argue will revolve around the PRC, the US, Russia, Japan, and Western Europe. We now turn to the question of how the military element of national power is developed to support these security objectives.

The Strategic Filter

At a minimum, the "strategic filter" for military planners at the national level must address three issues. First, they must account for political decisions that have been handed down to them or that have been brokered with civilian counterparts. These decisions usually encompass fiscal decisions and affect allocation of resources. Political decisions can also dictate or constrain military courses of action. Second, military planners must survey the security environment and assess what threats, current and future, must be addressed. Third, the nature of warfare must be examined to determine what kinds of engagements on the spectrum of military conflicts are most likely to occur. We attempt to use a "strategic filter" to look through Chinese eyes and attempt to see their strategic planning environment as they do. In some cases, we have definitive Chinese statements on these issues. In others, we can only try to transform ourselves into a PLA staff officer (*canmouguan*) sitting in the General Staff Department and speculate in an informed manner.

Political Decisions. Three key political decisions made by the top Chinese leadership affect what strategic military concepts are acceptable or possible for the PLA's national planners. These political decisions are not recent developments but long-standing policies. The first is that China does not participate in formal military alliances. This means the PLA must plan on being a "go-it-alone force" when it does go to war or when the military element of national power is employed. It also means that PLA planners do not have to concern themselves with questions of interoperability with potential allies or even temporary coalition partners. This goes for doctrinal issues as well as hardware and combat systems which, in any case, the Chinese would prefer to produce indigenously. It explains as well the deep reluctance of the PLA to accept invitations from foreign militaries to participate in combined training exercises even when these events are couched in terms of serving as confidence-building measures.

A second political decision in effect is that the PLA will not station combat forces abroad (trans., stationed on foreign soil). The reasons for this are a combination of geopolitical reality (who would invite the PLA to permanently station combat troops on its soil?) and budgetary considerations (it is expensive to station troops abroad). Moreover, since China does not engage in formal military alliances, such an eventuality is difficult to imagine. Of greater significance, this policy also dictates that the defence of China must take place close in, on, or near China's actual land borders or off the Chinese littoral. These decisions make "forward presence" for the Chinese a relative concept. It also dictates that the PLA must maintain a certain scale or size, especially in its ground forces, to compensate for vast borders and the need to fight close to them.

The third political decision with which PLA planners must grapple has already been mentioned—that the funding the PLA requires to operate, train, maintain and especially to modernize the armed forces will be subordinated to other national priorities. We will not enter the great PLA budget debate here. The jury is still out on the real value of investments China makes in national defence, especially given the opaque nature of their system, the multifurcated streams of funding that find their way to the armed forces, the obviously low official figures, and the issues surrounding the "hidden budget" that is the result of PLA domestic and global enterprises. The numerical spread in foreign estimates of the real value of the Chinese defence budget continues to inspire an awe of its own. For 1994, the range of estimates ran from about $10 billion U.S. to $149 billion U.S. For our purposes the trend is what matters. The recent "official" defence budget increase the PLA received during the 9th NPC (12.8 percent, for an official budget of 90.9 billion Yuan) indicates that while defence spending is going up yearly, no fundamental political decision has been made to reverse national priorities and provide the armed forces with a massive infusion of state funds. The PLA leadership undoubtedly does not receive the funding it would like (in this regard they have much in common with their brothers-in-arms across the globe). The question that we still have difficulty answering is: Are they getting what they need to fund their key current programs and underwrite their future requirements?

The PLA Analysis of the Security Environment. The basic and oft-repeated Chinese articulation of the nature of the world security environment is well known. Beijing sees the next two or three decades as a period in which the possibility of world war is negligible. The basic trend is toward "peace and development." China faces no immediate major direct military threats and the world is generally at peace. It is this assessment, originally made by Deng Xiaoping, that has impelled China to concentrate on economic reform as its primary national security objective. China continues to have, and continues to need, a window of relative peace to experiment and move forward in this endeavour. Jiang Zemin revalidated this assessment at the 15th Party Congress:

The international situation at present as a whole continues to move toward relaxation, and peace and development are the main themes of the present era.... For a fairly long period of time to come, it is possible to avert a new world war and secure a favourable, peaceful international environment and maintain good relations with the surrounding countries.

At the same time, Jiang also pointed out that there are serious security problems that require China's attention: However, the Cold War mentality still exists, and hegemonism and power politics continue to be the main source of threat to world peace and stability. Strengthening military alliance between various military blocs is not conducive to safeguarding peace and ensuring security. The unjust and irrational old international economic order is still infringing upon the interests of the developing countries, and the gap in wealth is widening. It is still serious that human rights and other issues are used to interfere in the internal affairs of other countries. Local conflicts due to ethnic, religious and territorial factors crop up from time to time. The world is not yet tranquil.

Jiang's "caveat" is a relatively subdued echo of PLA concerns. For their part, Chinese military strategists seem to view the world as a place basically hostile to Beijing's national interests, especially China's sovereignty. It is a world where dangers to national security lurk everywhere. The strategists view competition between nations for advantage as the norm and as a zero-sum equation (*ni si wo huo*). Change in the global and regional security environment is viewed as constant and usually dangerous. The absence of war does not mean the absence of hostility toward China. And, over the horizon, today's much-needed trade partners can slowly transform into serious economic, political, and military rivals. China's Defence Minister General Chi Haotian is Beijing's top military spokesman on these issues and he continues to be quite straightforward and frank in publicly highlighting the dangers that PLA planners see bubbling beneath the surface of a relatively peaceful world. As recently as March 1998, he underscored that pockets of antipathy toward China continue to require military vigilance:

Hostile international forces have never abandoned their strategic plot to westernize and split China, and the great cause of the motherland's ultimate reunification has yet to be accomplished. Under the long, peaceful environment and the situation centering on economic construction, we must be prepared for danger in times of peace and enhance our awareness of hardship. We must not become intoxicated by songs and dances in celebration of peace.

Fair enough. It is the job of defence ministers around the world to remind the troops that preparedness is why they are paid. What is interesting is that in this particular talk to PLA delegates at the 9th NPC Chi couches the need for preparedness not just as a matter of general professional responsibility but as a result of clearly identified security challenges.

In April 1996, General Chi spoke of the competitive nature of world relations when he wrote that "Major countries successively take contending for economic and technological superiority and enhancing comprehensive national strength as their development strategies and try by every possible means to gain the strategic initiative in the 21st century." These types of official statements set the analytic tone for PLA strategic planners. But what are the specific concerns these planners see that might affect the formulation of national military strategic concepts, especially those that must be incorporated into their national military strategy? We will now survey them briefly. What we will find is that if one were a Chinese military planner contemplating the various possible contingencies for which military force might be required now or in the future, there would be very little reason to feel complacent. What does the PLA planner see when he looks around the map? What are the major near-term, mid-term, and long-term concerns and shaping factors?

Geography. Geography continues to be a critical factor for Chinese military planners. China shares land borders with fourteen other nations. All told, the Chinese claim more than 20,000 kilometers of land boundaries and 18,000 kilometers of coastline that must be defended. Moreover, these borders encompass almost every major type of climate and terrain known in the habitable world. Just being able to secure its land borders is an almost staggering proposition for the PLA. It should be pointed out that since 1949 all of China's wars or military campaigns (Korea, India, Indochina-Vietnam, Soviet Union) have been fought either to secure control over disputed portions of those borders (India, Soviet Union) or to preempt a potential threat to those borders (Korea, Indochina-Vietnam). But the new international security environment and proactive diplomacy by Beijing have guaranteed that threats to China's land borders remain minimal. Rapprochement with Russia has alleviated a tremendous pressure on the PLA. Moreover, the dissolution of the USSR broke up what was previously the longest land border in the world. Cautious but steadily improving relations with Hanoi continue to keep the Sino-Vietnamese border pacific. The 1996 five-nation agreement between China, Russia, Kazakhstan, Tajikistan, and Kyrgyzstan is addressing problems in the northwest. If China still has a major potential border security problem it is with North Korea, which we shall come to shortly. But for the most part, China's land borders have never been more secure than they are today.

Defence of the Economic Centre of Gravity and the New Maritime Imperative. The same cannot be said of China's coast. In the last twenty years there have been two significant changes in China's security environment. The first is rapprochement with Russia.

The second, ironically, is the result of two decades of successful Chinese economic modernization. China's economic centre of gravity has shifted from deep in the interior, where strategic industries were sequestered in the 1960s to protect them from a possible Soviet invasion, to its current location on China's eastern coast, where Beijing's new market economy is strongest. This "gold coast," from Dalian in the north to Hainan in the south, defines the current economic *schwerpunkt* of China and its likely future location as well. And, arguably, Beijing's ongoing and future potential success in developing this coastal economy will be a major factor in defining China's importance in the future international order.

This shift has resulted in a profound change in the PLA's security calculus. Previously a large land force was required to protect the Chinese interior and its industries against a protracted land war with invading Soviets. Today, however, this pronounced shift in the economic centre of gravity presents China with a littoral and maritime defence requirement that it probably has not had since the mid Ch'ing Dynasty. For the PLA today (and more than likely tomorrow) *the essence of defending China will be defined by the PLA's ability to defend seaward from the coast in the surface, subsurface and aerospace battle-space dimensions*. This is precisely the type of warfare that the PLA is currently least well postured to conduct. Hence, the emphasis in military modernization over the past few years has been on naval forces, air forces, and missile forces—the three services whose force projection capabilities are required for and best suited to defend the new economic centre of gravity. Because of this shift it could be argued that even if the PLA did not have a Taiwan "problem" to consider, it would still emphasize force projection capabilities with a maritime (and maritime airspace) control and denial focus.

Defence of Maritime Sovereignty. In line with China's new coastal defence requirements, it is clear that the PLA has other maritime issues to contend with. Besides their 18,000 km of coast, the Chinese claim to have "more than 6,000 islands, and three million square km of territorial waters..." to defend.

The PLA must develop the capability to enforce Beijing's claims over disputed areas in the South China Sea and other maritime claims. While the waters have been relatively calm since the "Mischief Reef" incident, China could decide to employ the military element of national power once again if, from its perspective, it feels provoked by the other claimants in the region. Besides the Spratly Islands, China has competing claims with Vietnam over the demarcation of the Gulf of Tonkin and with Japan over the Diaoyu/Senkaku Islands. The issue of the South China Sea also highlights the importance China places on maritime resources (oil, fishing, and minerals) as it proceeds with economic modernization. And it is worth highlighting again that in his articulation of China's national military objectives earlier in this chapter Defence Minister Chi Haotian specifically cites the need of the PLA to safeguard China's "waters and maritime rights and interests." These two requirements—defending China's maritime territorial claims and defending its maritime resources—are specifically included in the articulation of the objectives of the PLA Navy by its commander, Lieutenant General Shi Yunsheng.

Close to Home: The Prospect of Instability. PLA and PAP military planners cannot discount the possibility that their classic internal defence mission will become more important in the next decade. As mentioned earlier, the social dislocations attendant to China's economic modernization are becoming greater and greater. Over the past few years worker protests, sit-ins, and physical attacks on local party officials and headquarters have been reported in the press with increasing frequency. As the social safety net continues to erode, by political mandate or by virtue of poor management, the possibility of increasing social instability cannot be discounted. China already has a "floating population" of some several millions which the state security apparati blame for increasing crime. If Jiang Zemin and Zhu Rongji actually implement the reforms of the state-owned enterprises as they have promised at the 15th Party Congress and 9th NPC, then over the next three years some three to five million additional Chinese could become unemployed and be without any social benefits at all. The "Great Amway Riots" of April 1998, as I like to call them, could be a harbinger of worse situations to come. And should the Asian financial crisis eventually hit China hard, the social chaos could be totally unmanageable.

But beyond the social unrest that could take place, China has other internal problems that must certainly keep PLA planners alert. In Xinjiang, the Uighur separatist movement has not been crushed. It is difficult to determine just how large or minuscule the problem is in fact. Last year several "terrorist" attacks in Beijing and other parts of Han China were reportedly tied to the East Turkistan freedom movement. We do not know if that linkage is true. But for the first time that one can remember (or that has been reported outside of the mainland) China now has a terrorist problem and the Chinese certainly believe the Pan-Turkic problem is potentially serious. This means that the PLA will need to have contingency plans on file if the PAP and other state security forces cannot handle future unrest in Xinjiang Province.

And always there is Tibet. The on-again, off-again unrest in that region is certainly a part of the PLA planning calculus. The issues of Xinjiang and Tibet directly attack Beijing's national security objectives of sovereignty and stability. Consequently, there is no reason to think that Beijing would not employ the PLA in either combat or military operations other than war (MOOTW) in either of these locations if its capabilities were needed to quell serious unrest.

Taiwan. Taiwan represents both a near-term contingency and a long-term readiness problem for PLA planners. Beijing will not renounce the right to use military force against Taiwan. Consequently, the PLA must develop a serious conventional deterrent capability vis-à-vis Taipei. The problem, of course, is that the only credible military deterrent is real conventional capabilities (we assume the political will is there). The next question must be, capability to do what? Whether the March-April 1996 mini-crisis in the Strait was a success or failure for Beijing is still being debated abroad. But one thing is certain; if one were a Chinese military planner, it should be painfully obvious that the PLA needs to develop a more diversified set of conventional military capabilities to employ as flexible deterrent options (FDOs).

Relying heavily on missiles as a FDO runs the risk of being too provocative (witness the U.S. reaction). This is true whether the PLA must act against Taiwan or in defence of its claims in the South China Sea. In the 1996 affair, the PLA quickly escalated from "forward presence" (large military exercises on the coast) to "demonstration of force" (missile launches). It appears that either the PLA did not have many other options in between with which to *slowly* escalate or they totally miscalculated the external response. My own inclination is that it was both.

Russia. Russia should probably be viewed as a long-term potential problem for the PLA. In spite of increasingly friendly relations and their new "cooperative strategic partnership," there is no dearth of mutual distrust between Russia and China, especially in Siberia and the Russian Far East. China is still viewed by the Russians as a threat and these views have their political champions on the far right in Moscow. Beijing's economic strength at a time when Moscow is relatively supine is felt most sharply in Russian Asia, and the Maritime Provinces recoil at what they see as Moscow's kowtowing to Beijing at their expense. For their part, Chinese military planners likely view Russia as a possible "over the horizon" problem. They may worry about the day when the Russians recover their national strength and the imperatives of geography and the legacies of historical animosity act to unleash rivalries anew, not just on their common border but perhaps in Central Asia. These rivalries will probably be driven by competition for natural resources: lumber, oil, minerals, and food from the sea.

Korea. Chinese military planners discount the possibility of an all-out war in Korea á la 1950. Nevertheless, they should be worried about the security problems China could face if the economic and political situation in North Korea deteriorates to the point of a total meltdown. An implosion in the north has the potential to send tens of thousands of North Korean refugees streaming over the border into China's ethnically Korean provinces. This type of chaos on China's border is precisely the type of situation for which the PLA is historically deployed. But in this sort of scenario the PLA would not be fighting a classic war. China's armed forces would be engaged in MOOTW. They would have to secure their borders, deal with thousands of refugees, and possibly keep the Korean People's Army at bay simultaneously. The scenarios are endless. The point is, the PLA must be prepared to intervene unilaterally to secure China's own interests in the event of total chaos on its border with the Democratic People's Republic of Korea (DPRK).

Japan. The Chinese view Japan as the only Asian nation that has the political, economic, technological, and (potential) military strength to challenge Beijing for regional dominance in the next century. Japan is likely viewed by the PLA as the primary mid-term strategic concern. While it may seem irrational from an American perspective, Beijing believes that under the veneer of a generally pacifist Japan lurks an undercurrent of unrepentant Japanese militarism and a strong desire on the part of the Japan Self-Defence Forces to overturn constitutional limits on their roles and missions. Tokyo's reluctance to directly confront its role in World War II and Japanese military participation in United Nations Peace-Keeping Operations (PKOs) in Africa and the Middle East fuel these Chinese suspicions. However, *the* most worrisome development from the perspective of the PLA is the recent promulgation of the revised U.S-Japan Guidelines for Defence Cooperation. This instrument is viewed as a codicil under which the Japanese armed forces, especially the navy, will justify operating even further out from Japan proper while still claiming to be a force purely for the defence of the Japanese home islands. Even more damning, China considers Tokyo the "other black hand" behind Taiwan's drift toward independence. This is because of a variety of reasons that go back to Taiwan's status as an Imperial Colony (1895–1945) and Lee Teng-hui's ties to Japan. These two factors (Chinese suspicions of Japanese military expansion and the Taiwan factor), when combined with maritime territorial disputes, makes for an imposing set of military planning requirements for PLA staff officers.

India. Up until the May 1998 nuclear detonations by India and their accompanying barrage of anti-China rhetoric, relations between Beijing and New Delhi seemed to be on the road to mending. The fact that the nuclear detonations occurred shortly after the visit to India of GSD Chief General Fu Quanyou was a double slap in the face. It is still too early to say what impact these events will have on overall Sino-Indian relations or what impact the Indian detonations will have on China's nuclear policies. These questions notwithstanding, the Indians have handed PLA planners a set of potential problems that encompass both a readiness issue on land in the disputed border areas and possibly a mid- to long-term maritime-aerospace planning problem in the Indian Ocean. At a minimum, India will continue to be viewed as an enduring security concern.

The United States. The United States poses a special conundrum for the PLA. China needs good relations with the U.S. to achieve its overarching national security objective of modernization. But this should not be confused with a shared vision of how the post–Cold War security regime in Asia should unfold. For one thing, the Chinese do not subscribe to the U.S. argument that Washington's bilateral military alliances in the region are necessarily stabilizing. Moreover, from the viewpoint of PLA planners, the forward presence of the American armed forces throughout the Pacific and Asia on land, sea and air cannot be a happy fact of life. The Pacific Ocean is still an American lake and the looming shadow of the U.S. Navy casts a pall over all others. It is in the interests of China and the PLA to see the U.S. military presence in Asia reduced at some point in the future. There is probably little debate in Beijing on this basic point. Where there may be significant debate is on the timing of a U.S. force withdrawal.

Some Chinese security analysts could argue that the American military presence has some utility for China by acting as a guarantor of the regional stability Beijing must have. They might argue that a quick drawdown by the U.S. would result in Tokyo filling the military vacuum quicker than the PLA could be prepared to credibly face down the Japanese. Others might see utility in the continued U.S. military presence in Korea as a check on instability close to home, although that argument will disappear after Korean unification or reconciliation.

Yet, there is a residual distrust and apprehension in some circles in the PLA about the true intentions of the United States in Asia and the role of its armed forces in the Pacific. The United States, through its forward military presence, has the *potential* to act as the great spoiler to two of Beijing's *core* security concerns: Taiwan and Japan. Because the United States underwrites the security of Taiwan, some Chinese security analysts argue that Taipei can continue to be recalcitrant in negotiating cross-Strait political issues and reckless to the point of provocation in its foreign and domestic policies. Moreover, it is the United States, some PLA planners would argue, that is goading the Japanese to rearm and pressuring Tokyo to expand its military role in the region under the false flag of increased host-nation burden sharing. Moreover, the "China Threat" theory that was in vogue in the U.S. a couple of years ago had its

Chinese analogue. Some PLA analysts seriously believe that the U.S. is attempting to contain China militarily using Japan as the "northern anchor" and Australia as the "southern anchor." And Chinese opposition to NATO expansion is borne of a fear that the Partnership for Peace might spread to Central Asia and exponentially enhance U.S. influence on China's western doorstep.

Consequently, PLA views of the U.S. are highly dichotomous. On the benign side, the U.S. is probably viewed by PLA strategists not so much as a *direct* military threat to Beijing, but as a lumbering but lethal giant that can wreak havoc on China's various national security interests because of (as viewed through Chinese lenses) vacillating American domestic political tacts and ignorance of the greater strategic implications of Washington's ever-changing policies. On the more cynical side, the U.S. is seen as capable of undermining core interests concerning Japan and especially Taiwan. More than likely, the PLA must constantly factor the potential reaction of the U.S. into almost every military contingency plan it may have. Assuming there are a variety of PLA contingency plans targeted against Taiwan, the "U.S. factor" is a significant unknown variable for the PLA. Beijing's suspicions about Tokyo's future path and the vagueness of the phrase "areas surrounding Japan" in the U.S.-Japan Guidelines for Defence Cooperation have probably only heightened concern about the U.S. role.

Nuclear Threats. Beijing's decision to develop nuclear weapons decades ago was in part a function of the desired status that capability conferred upon the PRC in the world order. However, Chinese security analysts are also quick to point out that China had no choice but to possess atomic weapons because China had been subjected to "nuclear blackmail" in the past—first by the United States during the Korean War and later on by the Soviets. For the past thirty years, Beijing has adhered to a nuclear strategy of minimum deterrence and has publicly declared a no-first-use policy.

It would appear that China's leadership has been satisfied with this approach. But whether this will remain the case indefinitely may be open to debate, certainly within China. One reason is the recent nuclear detonations by India. Second, over the past few years there has been growing concern among

China's nuclear scientists and Beijing's security policy establishment over the possibility that the U.S. might in fact develop a national ballistic missile defence system and concerns about what China views as U.S. pressure on Russia to amend the Anti-Ballistic Missile Treaty to allow high-capability Theater Ballistic Missile Defence systems.

The prospect of India having offensive nuclear capabilities, and the U.S. possessing highly capable high-altitude ballistic missile defenses cannot be a comforting combination for those charged with responsibility for China's nuclear strategy.

7

Strategies in Defence and Intelligence

Defence Intelligence (DI) is a member of the United Kingdom Intelligence Community, but differs from the agencies (SIS, GCHQ, and the Security Service) in that it is not a stand-alone organisation, but is an integral part of the Ministry of Defence (MOD). The organisation employs a mixture of civilian and military staff and is funded within the Defence budget. Like the rest of the MOD, Defence Intelligence was subject to the 2008 'Streamlining' initiative in which 20–25 percent of Central London staff were cut and it has had to continue to find additional savings since. The organisation was formerly known as the Defence Intelligence Staff or DIS, but changed its name in 2009.

The primary role of Defence Intelligence is that of 'all-source' intelligence analysis. This discipline draws information from a variety of overt and covert sources to provide the intelligence needed to support military operations, contingency planning, and to inform defence policy and procurement decisions.

The maintenance of the ability to give timely strategic warning of politico-military and scientific and technical developments with the potential to affect UK interests is a vital part of the process.

DI's assessments are used outside the MOD to support the work of the Joint Intelligence Committee (JIC) and to assist the work of other Government Departments (OGDs) and International partners (such as NATO and the European Union). It is this 'all-source' function which distinguishes Defence Intelligence from other organisations such as SIS and GCHQ which focus on the collection of 'single-source' Human Intelligence (HUMINT) and Signals Intelligence (SIGINT) respectively. As such Defence Intelligence occupies a unique position within the UK Intelligence Community.

Defence Intelligence also performs an intelligence collection function, primarily through the military capabilities lodged within the Joint Forces Intelligence Group (created in 2012 from what was formerly known as the Intelligence Collection Group or ICG).

History

Defence Intelligence can trace its ancestry back to 1946, when the Joint Intelligence Bureau (JIB) was established under the direction of General Sir Kenneth Strong. The JIB's was structured into a series of divisions: procurement (JIB 1), geographic (JIB 2 and JIB 3), defences, ports and beaches (JIB 4), airfields (JIB 5), key points (JIB 6), oil (JIB 7) and telecommunications (JIB 8).

When the Ministry of Defence was formed in 1964 the three (Naval Intelligence, Military Intelligence and Air Intelligence) were combined to form the Defence Intelligence Staff (DIS).

Although the DIS focussed initially on Cold War issues, more recently its attention has moved to support for overseas operations, weapons of mass destruction and international counter-terrorism activities. It changed its name to Defence Intelligence (DI) in 2009.

DEFENCE INTELLIGENCE ROLES

To support its mission, Defence Intelligence has four essential roles:

Support to operations: DI plays an integral part in the planning process throughout all stages of military operations, by providing intelligence collection and analysis at the tactical, operational and strategic levels. Examples of the support DI has provided to operations are:

- Coalition action in Iraq
- NATO led forces in Afghanistan and Bosnia
- UN humanitarian and peace-support operations in Sierra Leone, Liberia, Cyprus, Eritrea and the Democratic Republic of Congo

DI has deployed intelligence analysts, linguists and reservists overseas, and provide geographic support by supplying both standard and specialised mapping to overseas theatres.

Support to contingency planning for operations: DI provides intelligence data and all source assessments that assist in preparations for future situations with the potential to require the commitment of UK Armed Forces. These products, which cover political and military developments, country and cultural information, critical infrastructure and internal security, all aid contingency planning.

Provision of early warning: A fundamental responsibility of Defence Intelligence is to alert ministers, chiefs of staff, senior officials and defence planners to impending crises around the world. Such warning is vital for short and medium term planning. DI meets this responsibility by focusing on current areas and topics of concern, highlighting the effects of changing circumstances, predicting security and stability trends, and assessing how these trends may develop. The assessments are distributed to decision-makers throughout the MOD, the Armed Forces, other government departments, allies, and UK Embassies and High Commissions.

Provision of longer-term analysis of emerging threats: Defence Intelligence provides longer-term assessments of likely scenarios around the world where UK Armed Forces might need to operate and of the equipment that they might face. It also provides technical support to the development of future military equipment and to the development of countermeasures against potentially hostile systems.

How Defence Intelligence does its work

Direction: The Chief of Defence Intelligence (CDI) receives direction from the Chief of Defence Staff (CDS) and Permanent Under Secretary (PUS) on MOD's Intelligence needs and draws national guidance from the Cabinet Office Joint Intelligence Committee (JIC).

Analysis and production: Intelligence assessments are written to meet the needs of customers and must be timely and relevant. The assessment process involves judging the authenticity and reliability of new information and its relevance to existing intelligence. Assessments focus on probable and possible outcomes, to provide the best available advice for developing a response or resolution. They are continually adjusted in light of new intelligence or events.

MILITARY SCIENCE

The system of knowledge about the preparation for and waging of war by states, coalitions of states, or classes to achieve political purposes. In Soviet military science the nature of possible wars, the laws of wars, and methods of waging war are investigated. Theoretical principles and practical recommendations on questions of building the armed forces and preparing them for war are worked out and the principles of the art of war and the most effective forms and methods for groupings of the armed forces to wage military operations and for thoroughly sup-porting them are defined. Proceeding from political goals, the evaluation of the probable enemy and one's own forces, and the scientific and technical achievements and economic capabilities of the state and its allies, military science, with practical experience, determines ways to improve existing means of armed combat and create new ones. The component parts of current Soviet military science are the theory of the art of war (strategy, operational art, and tactics), in which principles and recommendations on preparation for and waging military operations are worked out; the theory of building the armed forces, in which questions of their organization, technical supplies, recruitment, and mobilization are studied; the theory of military education and training for personnel of the armed forces; the theory of Party political work in the armed forces; the theory of military economics, in which is studied the use of material, technical, and financial means to support the activity of the armed forces; military geography; military history, in which the history of wars and of the art of war are studied; and technical military sciences, in which the types of weaponry, war materiel, and means of material support of the armed forces are developed. Soviet military science serves the interests of the armed defence of the Soviet socialist state. It is based on Marxist-Leninist theory and is supported by the progressive Soviet state and social systems, whose guiding and directing force is the CPSU.

The fundamental difference between bourgeois military science and Soviet military science lies in the reactionary ideological foundation and the class essence of the former. Bourgeois military science serves both the aggressive foreign policy and the reactionary domestic policy of the dominant exploiting classes of the capitalist states; it is at the service of aggressive imperialist policy, which is directed primarily against the socialist countries and the national liberation movement of the peoples of the countries of Asia, Africa, and Latin America.

The modern scientific and technical revolution is causing intensive differentiation and integration of scientific knowl-edge, which leads to the appearance of new branches, directions, and disciplines in most of the sciences. A similar process is also natural for military science. Military science is developed from conclusions drawn from historical experience in the waging of wars, analysis of all types of practical activity by troops during peacetime, prediction of the development of new means of warfare and probable methods and forms of waging war in the future, and thorough study of the probable enemy and of trends in the development of international relations.

Military science took shape and developed over the course of a lengthy historical period. Its elements were conceived far back in ancient times during the period of the slaveholding society in Egypt, Persia, China, Greece, and Rome when military leaders and theoreticians formulated and solved certain questions related to strategy, tactics, military geographical conditions, and the organization and education of troops and when these military leaders and theoreticians analyzed and drew general conclusions from their experience in battles and campaigns. Military science continued to develop during the period of the Middle Ages. As the productive forces of society increased, weapons and war materiel were improved, troop control and the art of war as a whole became more complex, and military historical experience accumulated. All this led finally to the formation of military science as a definite system of knowledge.

Modern military researchers assign the formation of bourgeois military science to the 18th and beginning of the 19th centuries, when on the basis of the developing capitalist method of production there was a speedy development of the political, economic, and natural sciences. At this time military theory was also further developed in various countries. One of the first representatives of foreign bourgeois military science in the 18th century was the English general G. Lloyd. He outlined certain general principles of the theory of war, pointed out the links between war and politics, and emphasized the importance of the moral and political factor. However, he believed that military science was applicable only in preparing the army for war. The course and outcome of the war, in his opinion, depended entirely on the genius of the military leader, since there were no observable operating laws in this field and, consequently, it had no relationship to military science.

Major progress in the development of Russian military science at the beginning of the 18th century is linked with the name of Peter I, the government figure and military leader who carried out military reforms and established a regular army and navy. Peter I was the creator of the new *Military Regulations*, which outlined generalized conclusions drawn from experience in large and small battles and various questions of military administration and troop education. It marked the beginning of an independent Russian national military school. A great contribution to military science was made by major Russian military figures of the second half of the 18th century, including P. A. Rumiantsev, A. V. Suvorov, and F. F. Ushakov. Rumiantsev devoted a great deal of attention to improving the organization of the Russian Army, increasing its mobility, and improving troop combat training. He introduced the principle of decisive battle as the primary way to achieve victory. His work *Order of Service* (1770) was adopted as the manual of the Russian Army, and his *Report to Catherine II on the Organization of the Army* (1777) became the basis for further improvement in the organization of the army. Suvorov had a great influence on the formation of the art of war of the Russian Army and on the improvement of troop education and training. He sharply opposed the cordon strategy and linear tactics that prevailed in the West. In his *Science of Victory* (1795-96), Suvorov worked out a number of important rules on questions of military training, education, and combat operations. Ushakov worked out and applied in practice new forms and methods of combat action at sea, proving the superiority of mobile offensive tactics over the linear tactics prevailing in foreign navies.

The experience of the wars in defence of the Great French Revolution exerted a decisive influence on military theory. V. I. Lenin pointed out: "Just as the French revolutionary people then manifested within the country a maximum of revolutionary energy unprecedented for many centuries, so in the war at the end of the 18th century the people manifested equally gigantic revolutionary creativity, reshaping the entire system of strategy, breaking old laws and customs of war, and creating in place of the old armies a new revolutionary people's army and a new conduct of war". The French military leader Napoleon I made a significant contribution to the theory and practice of the art of war. He gave divisions and corps a more orderly organization and cut back sharply on transports, as a result of which the army acquired greater mobility. Napoleon I established the utter defeat of enemy personnel in one all-out battle as the primary goal of combat action and he strove constantly to destroy the enemy by parts, achieving maximum superiority of forces on the axis of the main effort.

Very significant in the development of Russian military science was the leadership skill of M. I. Kutuzov, who was able to crush Napoleon's army, which was one of the leading armies at the beginning of the 19th century.

Among the military theoreticians of the 18th and beginning of the 19th century in Germany, a prominent place was occupied by H. D. von Biülow, who attempted to write a theoretical summary of everything new that had been created during the age of the Great French Revolution. He considered correctly that military strategy is subordinate to politics and carries out its demands, but he did not understand the class content of politics. He divided military science into strategy and tactics and thus reduced it to nothing but the art of war.

The development of bourgeois military science in the first half of the 19th century is closely linked with the names of A. Jomini (Swiss by origin) and K. von Clausewitz (a German theoretician). They served for a significant length of time in the Russian Army and made full use of its experience in their historical and theoretical works. Jomini felt that the art of war could and should have its own scientific theory, but at the same time he recognized the predominance in the art of war of "eternal principles" inherent in all wars at all times, and thus he deprived the theory he had created of a truly scientific basis. He mistakenly asserted that the impact of politics on strategy is restricted to just the moment of decision-making, whereas during a war strategy supposedly did not depend on politics. Jomini's theoretical principles and ideas, which emphasized the significance of military theory, found followers in various armies of the world. The service of Clausewitz was that he profoundly revealed the link between war and politics and explained many phenomena of war (the nature and essence of war, armed forces, attack, defence, the war plan, and others). He attached great significance to the material, geographical, and moral factors in war, as well as to the role of the military leader. Being a bourgeois military thinker, Clausewitz was not able to reveal the class content of politics; he defined politics as an expression of the interests of the entire society and did not tie it to classes and the class struggle.

The question of the subject and content of military science constantly attracted the attention of Russian military theoreticians. As early as 1819, Major General I. G. Burtsov pointed to the relationships between politics and war in his article entitled "Thoughts on the Theory of Military Knowledge". He felt that military science could not be restricted to the art of war but should include the study of the laws of military affairs in its subject matter. Major General A. I. Astaf ev in his book *On the Current Art of War* (part 1, 1856) also considered that the subject of military science was broader than the art of war. Astaf'ev criticized Lloyd, Btilow, and other foreign military theoreticians for their endeavor to turn the art of war into a code of invariable rules. Prominent Russian theoreticians in the second half of the 19th century who influenced the development of military science were Minister of War D. A. Miliutin, Admiral G. I. Butakov, Generals G. A. Leer and M. I. Dragomirov, and Rear Admiral S. O. Makarov. Under Miliutin's leadership the military reforms of the 1860's and 1870's were carried out to overcome backwardness and conservatism in the army. In his book *First Experiments With Military Statistics* (1847-48), Miliutin was the first in military science to lay out the fundamentals of military statistics (including military geography). In his work *The New Foundations of Steamship Tactics* (1863), Butakov drew generalized conclusions from the experience in combat operations of ships of the steam fleet and suggested rules for changing their formation in the squadron for the waging of naval combat. These.principles were acknowledged in all the navies of the world. Leer recognized the unity of politics and strategy and placed politics in the leading role. In his works *Notes on Strategy* (1867), *The Method of the Military Sciences* (1894), and *Applied Tactics* (1877-80), Leer summarized critically the most common views on solving many questions of strategy and tactics and developed a military theory based on generalizations drawn from military historical experience. Dragomirov gave an extensive explanation of the question of tactics and troop training and education. His *Textbook of Tactics* (1879) served as the basic text at the General Staff Academy for 20 years. Makarov's works had a significant influence on the development of domestic and foreign naval thinking. Makarov's *book Discussions of Questions of Naval Tactics* (1897) was the first major work on the naval tactics of the armored steam fleet. At the turn of the 20th century a definition of military science was given in the Russian encyclopedias *Encyclopedia of Military and Naval Sciences* (vol. 2, 1885) and *Military Encyclopedia* (vol. 6, 1912). The latter establishes that "military science engages in a comprehensive investigation of wars. It studies: (1) phenomena in the life of society and (2) forces, means, and methods for waging battle".

In the second half of the 19th and the beginning of the 20th century with further development in engineering, lines of communication, and signal methods and with the appearance of improved armament for ground forces and the armored, steam-powered navy, there was intensive development of naval art and of the strategy and tactics of ground forces. The increased complexity of troop control required the establishment of general staffs, which began to determine the general direction of development of theoretical military views and of military science as a whole. Assessing the military capacities of their own and of other states, to some degree they influenced the policies of their own states.

Along with the development of bourgeois military science in the second half of the 19th century the foundations of a military science that viewed phenomena from a dialectical materialist point of view began to be laid. Discovery of the materialist understanding of history by Marx and Engels caused a revolutionary change in the social sciences, including military science. For the first time the relationship of methods of waging war, army organization, the armament of the army, and strategy and tactics to the economic structure of society and its political superstructure was scientifically revealed. F. Engels was one of the first Marxist military theoreticians. His works are devoted to the development of the doctrine of war and the army and their origin and class essence and to questions of military science and the history of the art of war. In the manuscript entitled "Possibilities and Preconditions of the War of the Holy Alliance Against France in 1852" he presented theoretical principles on the development of the art of war in different socioeconomic structures, especially during the period of proletarian revolution and classless society. As Marx and Engels showed, the proletarian revolution demands the destruction of the old, bourgeois state apparatus and the establishment of a new one, which means, consequently, the establishment of a new, socialist military organization in the interests of armed defence of the dictatorship of the proletariat. In the articles "Army," "Infantry," and others, which were written for the *New American Encyclopedia,* Engels gave the first materialist explanation of the history of military theory and practice. He showed that the development of the art of war depends on growth in productive forces, the development of social relations, and major revolutionary upheavals in society. In opposition to the theory of the "free role of the military leader," which prevailed at that time, Engels formulated the law that "the entire organization of armies and the methods used by them to wage combat, as well as victories and defeats, are dependent on material, that is, economic, conditions: on human material and on weapons and, consequently, on the quality and quantity of population and on matériel".

World War I (1914-18) had a great influence on the development of bourgeois military science. During this war technical military means of combat continued to develop and new combat arms (aviation, tank, and chemical troops) appeared; rich experience was gained in the fields of the organization of wars, operational art, and tactics. After the victory of the Great October Socialist Revolution the main task of bourgeois military science became the development of methods of waging war that would ensure the rapid defeat of the Soviet state and the revolutionary movements in the capitalist countries.

During the 1920's and 1930's theories of waging war were being created that took into consideration the possibility of equipping armies with qualitatively new, more effective war materiel and replacing the human being with the machine. At that time the bourgeois military theories of the "small army" (J. Fuller and Liddell Hart in Great Britain and H. Seekt in Germany) and of "air war" (G. Douhet in Italy and W. Mitchell in the United States) became widely known. Fuller first presented his views in the book *Tanks in the Great War, 1914-18* (1923). In this work the role of materiel is over-estimated and the human role is underestimated. The theory of "air war" assigned the decisive role in war to the air force. It was considered that victory could be achieved in war simply by winning dominance in the air, after which the air force would neutralize the resistance of the enemy country in a short period of time by extensive offensive operations. Ground forces were given nothing but occupation functions in the country that had been subjected to devastation by aviation.

The military science of fascist Germany was directed primarily to developing the theory of the blitzkrieg, which envisioned a sudden attack and swift advance by tank groupings with aviation support for the purpose of crushing the enemy like "lightning." The plans of German imperialism, which were counted on to gain world dominance, were based on the theory of "total war" developed earlier by the military ideologist of German imperialism E. Ludendorff. He felt that such a war would be lightning-like in nature, but in scope it would encompass the entire territory of the warring states, and to achieve victory it would require the participation in the war of the entire people, not just the armed forces. In French military science the conception of "static warfare" was dominant; defence was considered more effective than attack. Great hopes were placed on the permanent fortification elements of the Maginot Line and the Belgian fortified regions. A continuous front relying on a developed system of fortification was considered to be the basis for waging war. In the United States and Great Britain the theory of "naval power" was most widespread; in accordance with this theory, primary attention was devoted to the navy as the most important armed service.

After the Great October Socialist Revolution, Soviet military science began to take shape. At its foundation lay the principles of Marxism-Leninism concerning war and the army developed by Lenin as applicable to the new conditions of the age of imperialism. He revealed the economic basis of wars and classified them. Lenin pointed out that "there are just and unjust wars, progressive and reactionary wars, wars of the progressive classes and wars of the backward classes, wars serving to consolidate class oppression and wars serving to overthrow it".

From conclusions drawn from the experience of armed proletarian uprisings and wars of the age of imperialism, Lenin developed many points of Marxist military theory, including the decisive role of the popular masses; the economic and moral and political factors in modern warfare; the relationship of military organization and the art of war to the social and state system and the status and development of war matériel; the rules, methods, and forms of military operations; and the unity of political and military leadership in war. He created an integral and harmonious teaching on the new type of army and the defence of the socialist homeland; he pointed out concrete ways to build the Soviet armed forces; and he worked out the principles of training and education for army and navy soldiers, the unity of the army and the people, the unity of the front and rear, the leadership of the Communist Party over the armed forces, centralism, one-man management and collectivism in leadership, effectiveness in troop control, checks on performance, the selection and dis-position of cadres, and conscious military discipline. Lenin taught a creative approach to accomplishing the missions of defending the socialist homeland, and he also taught that the real ratio of friendly forces and the forces of probable enemies, economic and sociopolitical factors, and the state of the armed forces must be taken into account. Working out the theoretical foundations of the building of military strength, Lenin wrote that "without science it is impossible to build a modern army". During the Civil War, Lenin participated directly in guiding military operations. Soviet military science took shape and developed during these years. The works of V. I. Lenin and his practical activity have been invaluable for the development of Soviet military science. The Marxist-Leninist principles of purposefulness, activism, determination, and boldness combined with a high level of skill in carrying out military operations have been enormously significant in all the military vic-tories of the Soviet people.

A large contribution to the development of Soviet military science was made by prominent military figures of the Soviet state, such as M. V. Frunze, M. N. Tukhachevskii, and B. M. Shaposhnikov, as well as N. E. Varfolomeev, V. K. Triandafillov, V. A. Alafuzov, and I. S. Isakov. The progressive Soviet school of military theory gradually took shape. A special role belongs to Frunze's works, including *Uniform Military Doctrine and the Red Army* and *The Front and the Rear in the War of the Future*. Frunze worked out such very important questions of military science as the nature of future warfare, directions for the development of the armed ser-vices and the combat arms, and principles for training and educating personnel of the armed forces. In his three-volume work *The Brain of the Army*, B. M. Shaposhnikov analyzed a large amount of historical material, showed the role and functions of the General Staff, and made valuable proposals on the theory of military strategy, the development of war plans, and strategic leadership. In 1929 the book *The Nature of the Operations of Modern Armies* by V. K. Triandafillov was published. The author made a pro-found scientific analysis of the state and prospects for development of the armies of that time and disclosed the rules for the supply of materiel and their organization. Triandafillov took note of the increased role of tanks and considered them one of the most powerful offensive means in a future war. He investigated the offensive and defensive capabilities of the division, corps, army, and group of armies and studied the questions of the approach of troops to the field of battle, beginning and carrying on battle, and the duration and depth of an operation. In the period 1930-37, M. N. Tukhachevskii published his theoretical military articles on the nature of future warfare and principles of strategy and operational art in both theory and practice. Tukhachevskii proved that new forms of deep battle were being born. He advocated the proposition that there is an inseparable link between the art of war and a country's social system and production base, and he investigated the initial period of a future war.

An outstanding achievement of Soviet military science was the working out of the theory of the deep offensive operation, the foundations of which were outlined in the "Instruction on Waging Deep Battle" (1932). This theory helped develop a way to end the deadlock of static warfare, which had become established during World War I. Soviet military theory received concrete expression in the *Temporary Field Service Regulations of the Workers' and Peasants' Red Army* (1936). The regulations emphasize the decisive nature of the Soviet art of war—establishing superiority over the enemy along the main operational axis, the coordinated action of all combat arms, surprise and speed in operations, and skillful maneuvering. In its recommendations on building the armed forces, Soviet theoretical military thought assumed the probability of war with fascist Germany and its allies. A profound analysis of the state and prospects for development of the armed forces of the probable enemy made it possible for Soviet military science to assume on a sound basis that the war would be intensive and long and would require mobilization of the efforts of all the people, of the country as a whole. The primary type of strategic operations was considered to be the attack, securing the utter defeat of the enemy on his territory. Defence was assigned a subordinate role as a forced and temporary phenomenon ensuring a later transition to the attack.

In its view concerning the initial period of the war, Soviet military science proceeded from the notion that wars in the modern age are not declared and that aggressive states strive to initiate sudden attacks on the enemy. Under these conditions, from the very beginning military action would assume the form of decisive operations and would be primarily mobile in nature. However, static forms of fighting in certain theaters of military action and along various strategic axes were not excluded. Soviet military science assigned an important place to developing the theory of using the air force and large mechanized units in operations and to methods of modern warfare at sea.

The Great Patriotic War (1941-45) showed that the views concerning the nature and methods of military operations developed by Soviet military science were generally correct. From the start of the war it became necessary to further develop such important problems of the theory of the Soviet art of war and practice of conducting operations as leadership of the armed forces in the situation of the initial period of a war, when a general mobilization is being carried out, when groupings of armed forces are being deployed, and when the national economy is being transferred onto a military footing; as the centralization of control over groupings of the armed forces operating in different theaters of military action (axes); and as the coordination of the efforts of the armed forces. The war enriched the Soviet armed forces with an enormous amount of combat experience. During the war there was comprehensive development of the problems of selecting the direction of the main effort considering not only the theoretical principles of the art of war but also the demands of policy and economics; organizing and carrying on a strategic offensive and strategic defence; breaking through the enemy's strategic front; strategic employment of the armed services and the coordination of their efforts for combined accomplishment of important strategic missions; secret formation, use, and restoration of strategic reserves; using the factor of strategic surprise; organizing and conducting operations to encircle and destroy large enemy groupings; directing a partisan movement; and others. The high level of the Soviet art of war manifested itself with particular brilliance in the battles near Moscow, Stalingrad, and Kursk; in the operations in the Right-bank Ukraine and Byelorussia; and in the Iaºi-Kishinev, Vistula-Oder, Berlin, and Manchurian operations.

During World War II the American and British armed forces gained experience in conducting strategic bombing, carrying out large-scale air operations, waging combat action at sea, and conducting operations with field armies and groups of armies in coordination with large-scale aviation forces, primarily where they had an overwhelming superiority over the enemy. Through military science problems were worked out on the conduct of large-scale naval landing operations with participation by ground forces, the navy, aviation, and airborne landing forces; the organization of a strategic coalition for troop leadership; the planning and support of operations; and others.

The postwar development of Soviet military science has relied on conclusions drawn from the experience of World War II and has taken the direction of the further refinement of the theory of the art of war with due regard for the development of armament and combat materiel and the organization of the armed forces. A large contribution to the development of the theoretical principles of military science and to the practice of the art of war during the war years and the postwar period was made by Soviet military leaders, scholars and theoreticians, generals, admirals, and officers of the General Staff, the general staffs of the armed services and the staffs of the combat arms, military educational institutions, military science agencies, and headquarters of army, air force, and navy units.

In the most developed countries the course of military science has been characterized by research on a broad range of problems related to the appearance of nuclear weapons in the 1950's. This new weaponry has brought about a change in the nature of warfare, the forms and means for the conduct of military operations, and new methods for the training and educating of personnel. A greater role has fallen to the psychological preparation of soldiers and officers for war, the development of methods of propaganda and counter-propaganda in "psychological warfare," and other areas.

Military science is not developing identically in all capitalist countries. In the second half of the 20th century it has been most extensively developed in such capitalist powers as the USA, Great Britain, and France. The other capitalist countries borrow a great deal from them.

In the postwar years Soviet military science has developed new theoretical views on the nature of a future war, the role and significance of the armed services and means of armed combat, and methods of waging battles and operations. It has become obvious that a war, if it cannot be prevented, will be waged by essentially new means. A favorable influence has been exerted on the development of Soviet military science by the principles of the Program of the CPSU and the decisions and documents of Party congresses and plenums of the Central Committee of the CPSU. Thorough investigations have been conducted concerning the role and significance of economic, sociopolitical, and psychological and morale factors in achieving victory in modern war. Soviet military science has disclosed and substantiated the nature of a possible future world war and created the theoretical basis for shaping a modern military doctrine of the state.

The aggressive policy of the imperialist states, their preparation for a new war against the countries of socialism, and the unrestrained arms race demand that Soviet military science continue to develop effective ways to ensure high readiness in the Soviet armed forces to crush any aggressor.

INDIAN INTELLIGENCE AND THE KARGIL CRISIS

During the summer of 1999, India and Pakistan fought a 10-week limited war in kargil, a remote area of kashmir. Fighting broke out in May, when Indian troops discovered that a number of armed men had crossed the Line of Control (LoC) and entrenched themselves on the Indian side. Over the following weeks, the Indian army learned that these gunmen were not Islamist guerillas, as it had first assumed, but Pakistani soldiers in mufti. A security crisis erupted, with allegations of 'failure' being thrown at the Indian intelligence agencies.

Initially, critics of the intelligence community believed that it had failed to predict the Pakistani offensive. They assumed that forewarning would have prompted new Delhi to discontinue its then-ongoing rapprochement with Islamabad. However, an official commission of enquiry (set up after the crisis) cast doubt on this view. The enquiry established that the intelligence community had been sceptical about the rapprochement policy and had conveyed as much to the political leadership. The surprise at kargil did not stem from what happened, but rather, an incorrect forecast of *how* it would happen.

Intelligence analysts had predicted a surge in cross-border infiltration by Pakistani and afghan 'mercenaries' (a term which has since been replaced with '*jihadists*'). Their assessment implied that, despite the peace talks, bilateral tensions would escalate. It did not anticipate that the Pakistani military itself would attack across the LoC. such a move was judged to be 'irrational' and was discounted as a possibility by both intelligence analysts and Indian military commanders. Instead, threats from Pakistan were conceptualised in familiar terms, and perceived to unfold in linear progression.

Following the publication of the official enquiry's findings, criticism of the intelligence agencies was recast from strategic to tactical levels. The agencies were now blamed for not correctly identifying the kargil intruders as being Pakistani soldiers. Their warnings of mercenary infiltration supposedly led the Indian army to underestimate the seriousness of the intrusion. Yet, this critique did not explain why intelligence analysts should have predicted the same scenario which had previously appeared irrational to their consumers in the military. Instead, all that it did was use hindsight as a basis for evaluating foresight.

This chapter challenges the still-dominant view that the kargil crisis represented an "intelligence failure". It suggests that the Indian intelligence agencies accurately assessed Pakistani intentions prior to the kargil crisis. Where they went wrong was in predicting the specific form in which these would be enacted. For their part, Indian military officials created an analytical paradigm (or 'model') that reinforced this incorrect prediction. The model assumed that Pakistani risk assessments would be based on an objective reading of politico-military factors. It did not consider the possibility of Pakistani miscalculation. In this regard, the kargil crisis was similar to other cases of warning failure, such as the 1941 Japanese attack on Pearl harbour and the 1962 Cuban missile crisis.

Backgrounder

Kargil is an administrative district in the Indian portion of kashmir, adjacent to the LoC with Pakistan. It is dominated by steep, barren mountains, whose heights vary between eight and eighteen thousand feet. Indian and Pakistani border posts are situated along the outer ridgeline of these mountains. The posts are poorly served by logistics and are subject to the vagaries of extreme weather during winter. Snowfall and the attendant risk of avalanches make forward patrolling along the LoC risky for both sides. Until 1999, there was an unofficial policy of mutual withdrawal during winter months, when the most isolated outposts would be vacated. They would be reoccupied once the summer thaw set in.

Over 70 percent of the kargil population is shia Muslim. This makes the district unique in Indian-administered Kashmir: it is the only Muslim-majority area which has not been affected by separatist violence. Since kashmiri rebels and their Pakistani patrons are overwhelmingly sunni, the shias of kargil have remained apathetic to them. (such aloofness stems from sectarian tension, which has been worsening in Pakistan since the 1980s.) The district is sparsely populated, with 81,000 inhabitants spread over approximately 14,000 sq km. It has very little vegetation and no forest cover. Unlike the nearby kashmir valley, therefore, kargil is demographically and topographically unsuited for guerrilla warfare. Responsibility for local defence rests with the Indian army's 121 Infantry Brigade, which is headquartered in the district's largest town (also called kargil). The brigade reports to the 3 Infantry Division, which is based in a larger adjoining area known as Leh. Connecting Leh and kargil is a road called national highway 1a. This road is a logistical lifeline for troops deployed in the mountaintops, and is one of only two supply routes that goes on to connect Leh with the rest of India. It runs roughly parallel to the LoC at distances of between six and twelve miles and is, therefore, vulnerable to Pakistani artillery fire. since the highway at kargil is snowed in between september and June every year, uninterrupted use of it is vital to stockpiling of military rations and munitions during summer. The other supply route to Leh, though outside the range of hostile artillery, is longer and is also closed during winter. Accurate and well-timed bombardment of the kargil-Leh road would paralyse Indian fighting capacity at the local level.

The proximate origins of the kargil crisis can be traced to the nuclearisation of South Asia in May 1998. India began the process by conducting five nuclear tests; Pakistan swiftly reciprocated. Both countries were subjected to international sanctions. Both, however, grew more self-confident, convinced that their nuclear arsenals would henceforth protect them from external threats. On the Pakistani side, key thinkers came to believe that with foreign governments concerned about the possibility of nuclear war, Islamabad could ratchet up support to the kashmiri separatist movement. Any risk of Indian military retaliation stood nullified by the likelihood of third-party intervention, should war seem imminent.

In mid-November 1998, four Pakistani Generals, among them the new army Chief Pervez Musharraf, drew up plans for an incursion into Indian-administered kashmir, codenamed Operation Badr. The primary objective of the operation was to interdict vehicular movement along the kargil-Leh road. a secondary aim was to relieve pressure on the kashmiri separatist rebellion, which had recently suffered significant reversals vis-a-vis the Indian state. In order to sustain operations, many insurgent groups had already been compelled to recruit foreign-born mercenaries on two-year contracts. According to an Indian estimate, by 1998, these mercenaries (most from Pakistan and Afghanistan) accounted for 70 percent of all insurgent movement across the LoC. reconnaissance for Operation Badr began in November 1998. Pakistani troops probed Indian defences along the LoC, looking for gaps through which large groups of men could infiltrate. Due to the extremely rugged terrain at kargil, they found several such gaps. Unmanned aerial vehicles were used to verify the laxity of Indian border security. Actual movement of troops into

Indian territory, however, did not begin until at least late February 1999. While it was underway, a significant shift was occurring in Indo-Pakistani relations.

Under pressure from the international community, new Delhi and Islamabad initiated a 'peace process' in early 1999. Secret talks culminated in a much-publicised prime ministerial summit, held on 20 February at Lahore in Pakistan. A tentative roadmap towards resolving bilateral disputes was developed, and both governments received accolades for attempting to normalise relations. Despite lack of substantive progress, an illusion of cordiality had been introduced into Indo-Pakistani relations. It was only shattered when the Indian forces discovered the intrusion at kargil, in early May 1999.

By that time, approximately 1,700 Pakistani soldiers had crossed the LoC and occupied seven prominent hilltops overlooking the kargil-Leh highway. They were supported by four times as many logistical troops, who ferried supplies from base camps in Pakistan Occupied kashmir (Pok). The intruders wore civilian clothing, but carried their full complement of military hardware, including assault rifles, machineguns, landmines, mortars and man-portable surface-to-air missiles. They were scattered along 130 defensive positions, located at depths of between three and eight kilometres into Indian territory. Each position was manned by 10 to 20 soldiers. There were also 130 artillery pieces deployed on the Pakistani side of the LoC, ready to provide the intruding forces with covering fire once Indian troops began their anticipated counter-attack.

The kargil intrusion was a historical discontinuity event in two ways. First, never before had Pakistan launched a military offensive against India without a prior build-up of diplomatic tensions. That it would carry out an offensive even as peace talks were underway appeared unthinkable. Second, never in the ten-year history of the kashmir insurgency had Pakistani troops crossed the LoC with the intention of occupying territory on the Indian side. either they skirmished with Indian troops on the LoC itself, or crossed over in mufti to operate as guerrilla fighters in rear areas. Predicting the Kargil intrusion would have required explaining why these two trends in Pakistani strategic behaviour were about to be broken. having outlined the geographic and historical setting of the kargil crisis, this chapter shall now describe the charges that were subsequently levelled against the Indian intelligence agencies.

Intelligence Failures and Intelligence Gaps

Discourse on Indian intelligence has long tended to be consumer-driven, which means that it is shaped by the institutional biases of executive agencies such as the police and military. Such biases often fail to differentiate between strategic and tactical intelligence, presuming instead that all activities loosely labelled 'intelligence' fall under the purview of full-time spy bureaucracies. Meanwhile, lack of communication from the professional intelligence community, in the form of declassified reports, perpetuates this conceptual misunderstanding.

What results is conflation of 'intelligence failures' with 'intelligence gaps'. Public and political debates assume that lack of any information, no matter how specific, amounts to an intelligence failure. They ignore narrower academic definitions, which are more rigorous and can be tested against historical evidence. One example is the definition coined by Abram Shulsky and Gary schmitt, an intelligence failure is essentially a misunderstanding of the situation that leads a government (or its military forces) to take actions that are inappropriate and counter-productive to its own interests. Whether it is subjectively surprised by what happens is less important than the fact that the government or the military is doing or continues to do the wrong thing.

This definition suggests that mere occurrence of an unforeseen event does not automatically qualify as an intelligence failure. Provided decision-makers have been accurately warned about the dangers of the strategic environment within which they have to operate, even a short-term or tactical surprise can do little damage to national security. This is because such surprises are the inevitable result of gaps in intelligence coverage – a hazard faced by intelligence agencies the world over. Even within the most professional and well-resourced intelligence agencies, trade-offs have to be made whenever intelligence resources are allocated to monitor threats. Coverage tends to be optimised to focus on the most likely, as well as the most severe, threats. In the process, a threat scenario that is neither very likely nor very harmful to national security is bound to get lower priority.

Following kargil, the debate on intelligence performance swiftly took on an accusatory and counter-accusatory character. There were four main agencies relevant to this debate. Foremost was the research and analysis wing (r&aw – India's foreign intelligence agency). It was primarily focused on monitoring Pakistan and China. Most of its personnel were police officials, with a handful recruited from other government departments. Military representation existed mainly in the form of an analysis cell headed by a two-star Genera roughly 25 percent of the agency's output dealt with military intelligence, the remainder being dedicated to political and economic intelligence, next in line was the Intelligence Bureau (IB) – described by some as the oldest intelligence agency in the world.

Set up in 1887 to track dissident activity, it evolved into a highly efficient counter-intelligence machine. This agency had the lead role in combating terrorist and insurgent threats to India, irrespective of whether these threats were indigenous or foreign-sponsored. Although theoretically barred from operating overseas, IB operatives posted along India's western borders routinely collected intelligence on Pakistan, owing to Pakistani involvement with several Indian rebel groups.

Third, there was the Joint Intelligence Committee (JIC), an apex body set up to prepare intelligence estimates. It was attended by representatives of all leading intelligence agencies, including the intelligence directorates of the Indian armed forces. Despite its high position in protocol terms, the JIC had been undermined by turf wars. The committee merged with the secretariat of the national security Council secretariat (nsCs) in 1998, only to be reconstituted in 2006 as a separate entity. For the sake of simplicity, this chapter will treat the 1999 nsCs as synonymous with the JIC.

Lastly, there was army intelligence. This term collectively encompassed all Indian army personnel engaged in intelligence work. It included battalion-level intelligence staff, through to the Directorate-General of Military Intelligence (DGMI), which was headquartered in New Delhi. 'Army intelligence' was less an organisation than a system, whereby information flows were streamlined to ensure that time-sensitive data reached local commanders, who needed it most.

Unlike the JIC, IB and r&aw, it did not have a discernible hierarchy, but its exclusively military nature marked it out as distinct in the intelligence process.

Between them, r&aw, IB and army intelligence produced 43 reports during the period June 1998-May 1999, which were later found to have a bearing on Pakistani intentions at kargil. another two reports were generated by Indian border guards stationed in the area. Thus, a total of 45 indications (or 'signals') of Operation Badr existed in the Indian intelligence system by May 1999. Of these, 11 reached the JIC. They were hidden among 8,400 other reports ('noise') sent to the committee, which were completely irrelevant to the looming crisis. An analysis of the origins and destinations of the 45 relevant reports is revealing:

l army intelligence produced 22 reports, none of which were shared with any civilian agencies, including the JIC. Data exchanges were confined to local commanders at the brigade and division level, and only three reports were even passed up the chain of command to DGMI Headquarters in Delhi. Later, the Army justified this practice by arguing that intelligence only needs to flow one-way, in the direction of the end-user.

R&AW generated 11 reports, of which seven were widely disseminated and four were shared only with the army. IB produced 10 reports, of which three were distributed widely, five went exclusively to the Army, and two were sent to the Ministry of Defence.

Only two reports, one each from IB and r&aw, were copied to the Prime Minister. The remainder were disseminated through inter-service liaison channels. Any information of tactical importance was shared directly with 121 Infantry Brigade.

The official *Kargil Review Committee Report*, published in 2000, makes it clear that Indian intelligence agencies possessed less information than the army on Pakistani military activities. Whatever information they did have was shared with the army, at levels deemed appropriate to the nature of the information. The army, on the other hand, being both a producer and a consumer of intelligence, did not share information with anyone outside its uniformed chain of command. Despite this, many commentators feel that the IB and r&aw bear the bulk of the blame for not sharing information with the JIC.

The intelligence agencies had predicted heightened Indo-Pakistani tensions in 1999. These tensions were, however, forecast to originate from mercenary infiltration across the LoC, not a localised invasion by Pakistani troops. Building on this point, in 2006, a former Indian army chief explained that the failure to correctly identify the intruders when they were first detected, slowed the Indian military response. The army initially viewed reports of the intrusion without alarm. Only once its casualties began building up did suspicions arise as to the nature of events at kargil.

Differing implications of the terms *infiltration* and *invasion* lie at the centre of criticism made against intelligence warnings about the kargil crisis. All commentators agree that the Indian intelligence agencies did not predict a cross-border offensive by regular Pakistani troops, aimed at seizing territory. Where they disagree is on whether the Indian army can use this to excuse its own laxity in patrolling the LoC, despite warnings of infiltration. Is it reasonable to expect intelligence operatives to deliver a superlative performance when Indian soldiers are themselves complacent about the threat environment? The answer to this question requires examining: just what did the intelligence agencies predict in 1998-99, why did they do so, and what were the consequences of these predictions?

INDIAN INTELLIGENCE AND THE PROSTITUTES OF INDIAN MEDIA

This is one of the finest articles that has come out of the amazing B. Raman himself (by far my favourite commentator). Here he describes the details of two amazing stories in the Indian intelligence history-one a failure and one an outstanding success... and the frivolous and downright idiotic media that is in India. You just have to listen to the news to know how nonsensical the Indian media news coverage is. Journalists in India are no more than prostitutes. I have had personal experience with them during my stint while starting my company's Corporate Communications department and I don't have any more opinion of them. That is why thankfully there is blogging. Where, hopefully, you can read or listen to some sane and intelligent voices like Atanu Dey etc.

Read B. Raman's latest book "The Kaoboys of R&AW-Down the memory lane".

I wrote the first article on this subject for The Hindu in 1996, after the detection of the penetration of the Intelligence Bureau by the Central Intelligence Agency at a high level. Since then, I must have written at least 20 articles on this subject One of the past cases mentioned by me in the book is the penetration of the Prime Minister's Office by the French intelligence in the early 1980s. I was surprised by the kind of excitement or scepticism this evoked among the anchors of our TV channels and journalists from our media.

'Prime Minister's Office penetrated by French Intelligence, says an ex-R&AW spy', screamed the headlines. 'A claim without corroboration,' commented an anchor of NDTV. A commentator of the same channel sarcastically compared my reference to this to Jaswant Singh's claim of a mole in P V Narasimha Rao's office.

'Is he trying to embarrass the prime minister?' asked the Jumping Jack anchor of another channel. 'Has he violated the Official Secrets Act?' wondered another. My dear friends in the world of journalism, this sensational case of penetration — considered one of the most sensational anywhere in the world — was detected in 1985 shortly after Rajiv Gandhi had taken over as the prime minister. The penetration had taken place when Indira Gandhi was the prime minister and was detected after Rajiv Gandhi succeeded her.

The whole world was shocked by the ease with which two French intelligence officers, assisted by their Polish counterparts, had penetrated the PMO and removed tonnes and tonnes of documents. It was alleged that they were so sure that nothing would happen to them that they used to go to the office of the PMO on Sundays and other holidays, go through all the files and papers, take out what was of interest to them and took out photocopies using the photocopying machine of the PMO using the photocopying paper of the PMO.

It was a scandal of unbelievable proportions. It was found that these people had not only penetrated the PMO, but also the office of President Zail Singh and other sensitive ministries of the Government of India. The scandal and the speculation about it created such a furore in the Lok Sabha that Rajiv Gandhi had to make a statement on the subject on the floor of the house and Dr P C Alexander, who was Principal Secretary to Indira Gandhi and Rajiv Gandhi, had to resign. He did not accept responsibility for the shocking state of negligence in his office, but attributed his resignation to high moral principles.

The investigation brought out that the French and other collaborating intelligence agencies operated through Yogesh T Maneklal, then managing director of Maneklal Industries Limited of Mumbai, who had extensive contacts at the lower levels of the PMO, the President's office and other ministries and persuaded many government servants to work for the French intelligence. He was sentenced to 14 years rigorous imprisonment on July 18, 2002.

The spy ring consisted of S Sankaran, then senior PA in the President's Secretariat; Jagdish Chandra Arora, then PA to the then Secretary, Defence Production; Jagdish Mittar Tiwari, then senior PA to then Additional Secretary, Ministry of Defence; Amrik Lal, then senior PA to erstwhile Joint Secretary (Supply) MoD; V K Palaniswamy of the Ministry of Shipping and Transport, H N Chaturvedi, then Assistant, Ministry of Commerce; T N Kher, then PS to Dr P C Alexander; P Gopalan, then senior PA and K K Malhotra, then PA to Dr Alexander; Swaminath Ram, UDC in the office of Dr Alexander; K C Sharma, then PA in the Planning Commission, and S L Chandra (official position not known). All of them were sentenced to 10 years RI each.

The court found all of them guilty of the charge that 'they had entered into a criminal conspiracy with foreign agents, including Lt Col Mexi Morvan and Lt Col A Bain Bioley of the French embassy and some officials of the Polish embassy and the embassy of the then German Democratic Republic here and collected, obtained and communicated secret official codes, secret and classified documents and information pertaining to defence, shipping, transport, finance, planning, Research and Analysis Wing and Intelligence Bureau reports, official codes and other classified top secret and confidential information and passed the same to foreign agents.'

They had communicated to the French intelligence not only copies of a large number of classified documents, but also the code books used by the Government of India. All these details are available in the records of the Lok Sabha and the court of the additional sessions judge, R K Gauba, before whom they were tried. One is surprised and disturbed that within 25 years of this disgraceful betrayal, most of our national security managers and so-called strategic analysts have forgotten about it. When I draw attention to this, some in the media accuse me of disseminating claims without corroboration, others ridicule me by comparing me with Jaswant Singh, and some others attribute motives to me. This is why we face national security disasters again and again and again. A nation, which has no memory for the past, is bound to repeat its mistakes in the future.

The other comment, which has amazed me, relates to my mention of an alert received from a mole of the R&AW in Yahya Khan's office regarding a pre-emptive air strike planned by the Pakistan Air Force on the forward air bases in the Western sector. An anchor of NDTV said this air strike was meant to divert attention from the fighting in the Eastern Sector. Manoj Joshi, the journalist, pooh-poohed my statement and said when the Indian Army entered East Pakistan it was expected that the PAF would make a diversionary air strike in the West. According to him, a general alert was, therefore, sounded. He implied that the R&AW was trying to take credit for this.

Well Mr. Anchor, well Mr. Joshi, you apparently do not remember or know how the 1971 war started. In 1967, the Israeli Air Force had launched pre-emptive air strikes on the Egyptian Air Force planes parked in its Air Force bases and destroyed them on the ground. Then, the Israeli Army went into action. The Egyptian Army had to fight without air cover. It surrendered.

The Pakistanis studied what the Israeli Air Force had done and decided to emulate it. Their calculation was that if they destroyed a large number of IAF planes on the ground, it could affect the operations of the Indian Army in the East by damaging the air cover available to it. The R&AW got advance intimation of this plan and the IAF was alerted. The intended pre-emptive air strike failed. Indira Gandhi, who was then in West Bengal, flew back to Delhi and in a midnight broadcast declared war on Pakistan. She let the world know that the war was started by Pakistan through its failed pre-emptive air strike and not by India. Mr. Joshi asked: If it is true that the R&AW had a mole as claimed by me, why the mole did not give information about Pakistani plans in the Jammu area? Mr.Joshi, a mole can give only that information to which he has access. This is a basic principle of the craft of intelligence — no access, no information.

The information that the R&AW got advance intelligence about the planned pre-emptive strike was known for over 30 years and acknowledged by Indira Gandhi herself. I had referred to this in my past writings too. All I have done in the book is to identify for the first time the R&AW officer who raised this source and got the information through him so that there is public knowledge of the role played by him.

MUMBAI BOMB BLASTS – INTELLIGENCE AND COUNTER-INTELLIGENCE

While addressing to a press conference on Saturday, Mumbai Police Commissioner A.N. Roy accused the ISI of masterminding the Mumbai train bomb explosions on 11th July this year resulted in killing 200 people. The commissioner provided the details of the plot with names, locations and whereabouts of the people involved in the attacks. He also provided information about the explosives which were kept as RDX packed in the pressure cookers. The commissioner told the newsmen about the interrogation procedure 'narco-analysis', through which the suspects are questioned under the influence of drugs to get the correct answers. He said, ISI agents began planning the attacks in March, and later provided funding and training for the bombers in Bahawalpur to plan that professional, precise and well-planned operation. He added that police had found no evidence of the involvement of Al Qaeda in the attacks.

On the other hand Pakistan Foreign Office spokeswoman Tasnim Aslam completely rejected Indian claim by calling it baseless, irresponsible and (done) out of habit. In his statement Mr. Tariq Azim Khan, the Minister of State for Information said that India had always chosen the path of pointing fingers at Pakistan without evidence. The allegation has appeared at a sensitive time to enhance the stress of President Musharraf who had already spent the previous days of a lengthy overseas trip persuading against Afghan and British implications that the members of his security apparatus were secretly supporting the Taleban revolt intensifying in the Southern Afghanistan. Moreover, it was only two weeks before when Musharraf managed to get India resuming a peace process, which had frozen after the Mumbai blasts.

In the era of a neo-globalisation with multiple actors on the stage to shaping up the future image of the global village, this becomes very important for the regional actors like India and Pakistan to immediately agree on an agenda of regional cooperation for progress, prosperity and better facilities for the people of the two nations. ISI which had been a much stronger power in the past is currently engaged in its revitalisation process with much of its energy being consumed in keeping the fine balance maintained between its modernist and conventional parts. In these difficult times it simply can't afford the sooper adventures like this. If we compare the capabilities of the Regional Analysis Wing (RAW) and the Inter Services Intelligence (ISI) both are complexly rooted in their targeted segments of the respective countries. If one agency has the advantage of entrenching profoundly into the socio-national structure of the targeted country, the other one has the advantage of being deeply ingrained into the religio-sectarian segment of the targeted country. In this complex situation there is always a chance of entry of a third international player to reshape the geo-political structure of the area into its own favour.

The story of making and remaking of the regional map starts from the late seventies when the CIA drafted a map of defeating the USSR in Afghanistan with the help of ISI. The then Pakistani President Gen Zia knew only about the half part of the plan while knowing nothing about the second half of the agenda. Only very few officers within ISI like Brig Irshad Tirmazi could notify the presence of strange phenomena within the Mujahideen's camps in Afghanistan in form of Arab nexus. These were the operative groups mainly belonging to the Middle East, the European countries and the countries like Indonesia. The main features of the nexuses were; having massive 'foreign currency', their daily march towards Russia and the areas bordering China-with their passionate concentration in training of the religious elements for the sectarian (Shia-Sunni) violence.

During the Zia regime the tension between India and Pakistan remained alive especially on the issues of Kashmir and the Eastern Punjab. Well before successfully implementing his type of regional agenda, Gen Zia passed away in a mysterious plane crash and right after his death there started the second half of the international agenda for regional reshaping. It was a time when the unseen hands brought India and Isreal closer for defense and intelligence cooperation after a no relationship history of more than 40 years. Although Israel provided India with the devastating artillery weapon, 160 mm mortars and modern ammunition during 1971 war against Pakistan yet the deal remained secret as a condition by Mossad. Even after the 71's war the defense relations had not been adequately established between the two countries.

It was in 1992 when the formal diplomatic relations established between India and Israel with the visit of the Deputy Director of Israel Foreign Ministry Moshie Yaeger. Following the establishment of formal diplomatic relations in 1992, India and Israel had signed a number of agreements on economic, scientific, agricultural and cultural cooperation. In December 96 Israeli President Weizman visited India that became the first ever visit by any Israeli President to India with a 24-member business delegation.

Although the relations between India and Israel kept on developing after 1992 with strong ties on defense and economics yet 1998 can really be considered as the revolutionary year in the history of the Indian intelligence. In this year the Mossad transferred to India the most sophisticated intelligence techniques to penetrate deep into religious/separatist groups. Before that point the ISI clearly superceded the RAW in terms of making networking within socio-political systems while after acquiring the newer techniques the RAW not only got the capability of breaking the networks but also to exert the counter-intelligence through religious grouping. During this year Indian Home Minister L. K. Advani visited Israel with his delegation comprising the heads of Indian intelligence agencies like RAW, IB, and central police organizations for their training on the latest intelligence techniques. Followed by these developments the Israeli intelligence agencies opened offices in New Delhi on the lines of United States FBI.

It was the time when the international plan was simply ready to be implemented to shape up the new world diagram. Maulvi Masood Azhar a 30-year old Sunni cleric from Bahawalpur was in BSF custody at 'Papa II' interrogation center in India. Here he meets Omar Sheikh with a history of being infiltrated into India and participated in some acts of terrorism. He was arrested and jailed by the Indian authorities to meet Maulvi Maood Azhar and to plan the drama of hijacking the Indian plane. Omar Sheikh belonged to the Arab-European Nexus of 200 UK Muslim citizens with natively linking to Pakistan, hired by some agency in the UK and sent to Pakistan to get training in the camps of Harkat Ul Ansaar (HUA) and joined the HUA's contingent in Bosnia with full complicity of the British and American intelligence agencies. These intelligence agencies had masterminded the Arab Nexus, a large corps of jihadi personal of Arab origin to mix up with Afghan Mujahideen in their war against the Soviet troops.

Maulvi Masood Azhar met there a number of 'jehadi' persons some belonging to Jamiat Ulma E Hind (JUH) and some to Arab Nexus where they planned the Hijack of Indian plane and made their future agenda to be implemented in Pakistan. On 24th December 1999, an Indian aircraft flight IC 814 carrying 174 passengers and 18 crew (Kathmandu-Delhi) was hijacked on its way to New Delhi at about 1730 Hours IST. It landed at Amritsar and was refused fuel and ultimately landed at the Kabul airport. Three arrested jehadi persons Masood Azhar, Omar Sheikh and Mushtaq Ahmed Zargar had been handed over to the Taliban militia at Kandahar. The five hijackers had left the aircraft and had been taken to an undisclosed location by the Taliban.

On 11th September 2001, the tragic incidence of the World Trade Center took place followed by the announcement of President Bush to start a long-term global war against terror to bring the perpetrators to justice. It was the time for India to inform the US about the involvement of Pakistan in the attack. It is said that Prime Minister Vajpai personally presented a copy of the cheque to President Bush which was given by the then ISI chief Gen Mehmud to one of the terrorists of the 9/11 attack. In this way, India played a key role in providing the US authorities the HOT information about Pakistan as the funding source for the September 11 attacks. The Times of India first reported on October 10, 2001 that India told the US that some $100,000 had been wired to the leader of the hijackers, Mahmud Atta, by British-born terrorist Omar Sheikh.

John S Pistole, deputy assistant director of the FBI's counter-terrorism division confirmed about the information, however, did not specify how those accounts in Pakistan were funded, how those found their way to Omar Sheikh and how the copy of the cheque reached to the Indian Prime Minister. Nobody knows about the secrets behind that deal but everybody knows about the immediate acceptance by the Pakistani government of the 7 point US agenda to role back Islamism, Talibanism and terrorism from Pakistan and Afghanistan.

Indian authorities also told the US that the trail led back from Omar Sheikh to the then Chief of ISI, Lt Gen Mahmud Ahmad who was subsequently forced to retire by Pakistan resident Pervez Musharraf. The Indian authorities provided the FBI with the details, including Omar Sheikh's mobile numbers.

Later the same Omer Sheikh was found guilty in the murder of the Wall Street Journal reporter Daniel Pearl. The case was highlighted around the globe and once again became the cause of embarrassment for Pakistan around the globe. Maulvi Masood Azhar established Jaish E Mohammad (JEM) and remained involved in the activities of sectarian and religious terrorism. Another example of 'international intelligence cooperation' is the information of the suicidal attack against Gen Pervez Musharraf. Very recently, the former Indian Defense Minister George Fernandes has said that India was aware of an assassination attempt on Pakistani President three years ago. He said that he had warned Islamabad two days before the attack in December 2003. The above-mentioned examples simply highlight the capabilities of the Indian intelligence agencies in masterminding intelligence and counter intelligence operations.

We are living in the post cold war era when the super power has nothing to do with the Pakistani abilities of running or winning a war. Knowingly or unknowingly, Pakistan can be pushed back to the post 9/11position by the 'international cooperation of intelligence'. It is for the broader interests of the 2 countries in specific and the South Asian Region in general to establish the long-term socio-economical relations and peace treaties between the regional players to ensure better living conditions, better education and medical facilities for the inhabitants of the region. Otherwise the intelligence and the counter intelligence adventures between the two countries will give the international players the opportunities to implement their global agenda which is nothing but the 'Bandar Bant'.

8

Chinese Security and Military Strategy

China's primary national goal is to become a strong, unified, and wealthy nation that is respected as a great power in the world and as the preeminent power in Asia. The Chinese see their country as a developing power whose nuclear forces and seat on the UN Security Council already bestow some of the attributes of a great power.

They look forward, however, to achieving a status of parity in economic, political, and military strength with the world's leading powers by the middle of the next century.

China's grand strategy for achieving this national goal is to promote rapid and sustained economic growth; raise the per capita income of its people to the global norm for advanced nations; improve the social quality of life for its people including health and education on a par with the leading nations of the world; raise technological levels in sciences and industry; maintain the political unity and stability of the nation; protect national sovereignty and territorial integrity; secure China's access to global resources; and promote China's role as one of the five or six major poles in a new multipolar world.

Although China continues to promote the notion of national self-sufficiency and independence, its strategy also encompasses greater integration into global affairs. This involves adjusting commercial policies in order to gain maximum benefits from foreign trade and investment, which have served as the twin engines of China's economic development. Politically, there is a greater willingness to participate in multinational fora and a public relations effort to foster a benign image of a China interested in peaceful development and progressing toward meeting international norms. China does not seek hegemony in Asia or elsewhere, although its leaders hope to achieve a position where Asian countries and those with interests in Asia take no actions which conflict with China's interests.

This strategy also encompasses a domestic political component, namely the continued governance of China by the Chinese Communist Party (CCP). China's strategic vision is that of the CCP and its leaders remain firmly committed to its realization. The CCP has ruled China for nearly half a century and, during that period, its leaders have exhibited no inclination to share their monopoly of power. China's leaders, however, are beset by a host of internal problems—some the result of the country's economic success, others the legacy of the planned economy they are gradually dismantling—which could threaten the stability and longevity of the regime if unresolved over time. Large-scale unemployment (likely to grow as reform of state-owned enterprises proceeds), separatist and human rights agitation, worker migration from rural to urban areas, an ever growing population, environmental and ecological concerns, and widespread corruption within both state and Party entities are contributing to popular discontent and disillusionment over the future of both China and its Communist Party.

China's security strategy strives to enhance the military, political, and economic components of national power. Beijing places top priority on continued economic growth and industrial sector development. China's National Defence Law identifies six military tasks that underlie this objective:

(1) Modernize the People's Liberation Army (PLA);

(2) Defend China's territorial sovereignty;

(3) Deter and resist aggression by global and regional hegemons;

(4) Support the Party's reunification policies;

(5) Ensure domestic security and stability;

(6) Support the national economic modernization program.

China seeks to take advantage of the current relatively benign international environment, in which there are no major external threats to China's security, by selectively modernizing its military forces in a measured and fiscally responsible manner. Beijing assesses that, barring a declaration of independence by Taiwan, the chance of a large-scale unavoidable conflict is almost negligible over the next decade and a half.

Military Strategy

Since the early 1990s, the focus of Chinese military strategy has been on preparing for potential military contingencies along China's southeastern flank, especially in the Taiwan Strait and South China Sea. Thus China's goal is to field forces capable of rapidly deploying to fight and win a future regional war under high-technology conditions along China's periphery. The Persian Gulf War underscored for Beijing the need to improve the PLA's ability to fight against an adversary which possesses advanced information technologies and long-range, precision-guided weapons. Chinese perceptions of an emerging military-technological revolution have increased the urgency of gaining capability to fight a high-technology war.

To realize this goal, the PLA has undertaken a long-term military modernization program which currently is focused on reducing overall size of the force by some 500,000 personnel; equipping it with more modern weapons, either acquired from abroad or produced domestically; and, developing a better educated and technologically skilled force, both in officer and enlisted ranks, to support and sustain these forces, China is trying to establish a more effective national mobilization system for shifting the military, government, and industry from peacetime to war footing.

If war were to become inevitable, China's military strategy would be to contain and limit the conflict, and to fight with sufficient force and tactics to win as quickly as possible, achieving a military solution before outside powers could intervene and before vital trade and investment were disrupted.

NUCLEAR MATERIAL SECURITY

Nuclear material security is a concern for all states in the context of a terrorist threat. Physical security has long been considered a subset of international safeguards, but it has never been a prerequisite for placing nuclear material under international safeguards. It can be a requirement of bilateral nuclear trade, however, and the United States requires physical security measures on some of the nuclear material it exports, mostly in conjunction with military programs. Often, physical security measures are implemented as a matter of course in implementing safeguards, since states have to account for missing material in their physical inventories. India and Pakistan may provide particularly attractive targets because they have weapons-grade material on their soil, but terrorists' interest in a radiological dispersal device may make any or all radioactive sources potentially attractive to steal. India and Pakistan became parties to the Convention on the Physical Protection of Nuclear Material in 2002 and 2000, respectively. This Convention, which entered into force in 1987, was designed to protect nuclear material in transit between countries. The CPPNM defines a range of nuclear terrorist activities and requires parties to criminalize those activities. It does not cover physical protection of domestic nuclear material in storage or use, nor does it cover byproduct material. The United States and other members of the Convention have been working for several years to expand the scope of the agreement, and agreed in September 2002 to extend physical protection to domestic use and storage. The IAEA has circulated proposed amendments to the convention, which may be considered in 2005. Both India and Pakistan have been active in discussions on expanding the Convention.

Since 1995, the International Atomic Energy Agency has conducted (although mostly outside of the regular budget) physical protection assessment programs, called International Physical Protection Advisory Service missions. States must request assistance, and then an international team conducts a confidential vulnerability assessment and recommends measures to address physical protection shortfalls. Neither India nor Pakistan has requested such a mission, and in the opinion of some observers, they are unlikely to do so because of the sensitivity of their facilities. However, in May 2002, the IAEA conducted a joint safety and security workshop in Islamabad. While Pakistan has participated in IAEA technical cooperation programs, India has not participated since the 1980s. In 2002, India requested a regional workshop on physical protection focused on security awareness and culture. India was among several states in which the IAEA conducted physical protection-related seminars in 2003.

Nuclear Weapons Security

Since the 1998 nuclear tests, India and Pakistan appear to have accelerated nuclear weapons development and, possibly, deployments. Most observers still believe that neither Pakistan nor India has deployed warheads mated with delivery systems. Fissile material components (pits) are thought to be kept separately from the rest of the warhead. Such a physical separation helps deter unauthorized use and complicates theft. In the early years of the U.S. nuclear weapons program, fissile material components of warheads were physically separated; in the earliest bombs, the two were mated in the bomb-bay of the aircraft. When nuclear missiles entered the U.S. inventory, the warheads were physically separated from the missiles. In addition to physical separation, however, there need to be rules and procedures for authorized use; it is not clear what those are for India or Pakistan. India and Pakistan have been moving towards more structured nuclear command and control authority, organization, and strategic planning. However, there is no information on whether they have implemented two-man rules (a requirement for the concurrent involvement of at least two people to be able to fire a weapon) or other procedures for ensuring no unauthorized use.

There is no reliable information on where fissile material is shaped or machined into components for weapons, or where fissile cores are kept if they are separated from other weapon components and delivery systems for India and Pakistan. Some observers believe that nuclear weapons parts are "probably distributed in a number of tightly secured facilities at different locations throughout Pakistan." Physical security in the case of Pakistan is provided by the military. India has kept strong civilian oversight of the weapons program, with the military kept predominantly at arm's length. However, the details of security in both cases are unknown. In April 2000, the Indian government ended independent safety oversight at BARC, the "nerve centre" of the Indian nuclear weapons program. Some analysts have interpreted this change as an indication of accelerated nuclear weapons work at BARC. On October 2, 2001, Pakistan's Foreign Ministry issued a statement that "Our nuclear assets are 100% secure, under multiple custody." Media reported that Pakistan had moved nuclear weapons components to several undisclosed locations. Subsequently, President Musharraf reorganized elements of the Pakistan Atomic Energy Commission (PAEC) and investigated several nuclear weapons scientists who reportedly had ties to Islamic extremists.

Personnel Security

In terms of personnel security, concerns have focused mostly on Pakistan, and most recently, on the activities of Pakistani nuclear freelancer Dr. A.Q. Khan. At the end of 2003, evidence from Libya revealed that Khan had sold a variety of nuclear materials, technology, equipment, and even a bomb design, to Libya, Iran, and North Korea over two decades. Although there were reports that President Musharraf knew of improprieties regarding Khan in 1999, Musharraf took no steps to rein in Khan until 2001. At that time, Khan was "forced" to retire as director of Khan Research Laboratories and given a job as special advisor to President Musharraf.

Before that, however, he had amassed millions of dollars in selling nuclear technology to rogue states. Pakistani officials claimed that they tightened controls on their nuclear weapons program with the creation of the National Command Authority (NCA) in February 2000. One of the features of those controls is the screening of key people in the Pakistani nuclear weapons program every two years by the Inter Services Intelligence Agency, Military Intelligence, the Intelligence Bureau, and the Strategic Plan Division of the NCA.

However, "top-level people (including scientists) are controlled by their organizations and not psychologically screened." Much less is known about Indian personnel security. Although India set up a Nuclear Command Authority similar to Pakistan's in January 2003, there is little information on whether associated personnel screening measures have been implemented.

Nuclear Material Safeguards: IAEA Safeguards

Most of the material and facilities in India and Pakistan is not subject to international safeguards. In India, there are safeguards on 6 reactors (Tarapur 1 & 2, LEU-fuelled power reactors; Rajasthan RAPS-1 and -2, which use natural uranium; and Koodankulam-1 and -2, LEU-fuelled power reactors). In addition, the Tarapur plutonium reprocessing facility (Prefre) is safeguarded when safeguarded fuel is used in the facility and the Tarapur MOX fuel fabrication plant has safeguards when it runs safeguarded material through it. The Hyderabad fuel fabrication plant has partial safeguards.

Key nuclear weapons-related facilities in India that are not subject to IAEA inspections include the Bhabha Atomic Research Centre (BARC) in Trombay, which houses the Cirus and Dhruva research reactors for plutonium production, plutonium reprocessing plants and a pilot-scale uranium enrichment plant. These sites, as well as storage sites for weapons-grade material or for weapons themselves could be highly attractive to terrorists because they may contain weapons-usable nuclear material.

Pakistan has IAEA safeguards on a few facilities. The KANUPP power reactor, which uses natural uranium, Chasma-1, LEU-fuelled power reactor, and two research reactors at Rawalpindi that have used HEU in the past are under international safeguards. The following facilities are not under safeguards: the Khan Research Laboratories at Kahuta, which include a uranium enrichment plant and facilities for fabricating HEU into weapons; centrifuge enrichment plants at Sihala, Golra and Wah/Gadwal, the Chasma reprocessing plant, and PINSTECH and SPINSTECH facilities related to reprocessing at Rawalpindi.15 These nuclear material production sites, as well as weaponization, storage and assembly sites (if separate facilities exist), could be high-value targets for terrorists.

CHINA'S DEFENCE FORCES

Chinese military modernization encompasses all the defence services. The ground army, the Peoples Liberation Army (PLA), which was previously had been the centre of gravity of the Chinese Armed Forces, remains the largest service and provides the bulk of senior leadership for the military, but it has felt the impact of force reductions as the emphasis has shifted, a result of maritime security needs.

The PLA primary responsibility is defending China from external threats. Its secondary mission is domestic security in accordance with the law; that is, when requested by local authorities and approved by the central leadership. The ultimate command authority for the PLA is the Central Military

Commission. The command chain runs through four general headquarters departments, in Beijing, to the forces deployed in seven military regions throughout the country. All three support national economic development with labour and service projects. It can mobilize to provide rescue and relief support in the event of floods, earthquakes, and other natural disasters.

The PLA's modernization program includes the complex and difficult task of: reduction in force size; changes in force structure; reform of the structure and missions of the reserves and militia; changes in the personnel system; influx of new equipment; doctrinal revision to prepare the PLA to fight and win "Local Wars Under Modern High-Technology Conditions" or "Local Wars Under Informationalization Conditions"; improvements in the frequency, content, and methods of military training with emphasis on joint operations; transformation of the PLA logistics system; enhancement of all soldiers' standard of living, pay, and lifestyle; modification of the professional military education system.

Defence Modernization

Defence modernization is not new. For decades prior to 1990, China acquired or built a range of sophisticated weapons. Between 1984 and 1986 the United States sold to China naval antisubmarine weapons, antiaircraft missiles, and antitank weapons, as well as half a billion dollars worth of radar, navigation, and computer equipment, to upgrade interceptor aircrafts in China's possession. But Chinese purchase of Western hardware and technology suddenly stopped due to Tiananmen Square events in 1989, and the reemergence of Sino-Russian cooperation in Defence. The reawakening of Chinese tradition in research and development, and the reverse engineering of obtained hardware spearheaded China to become a manufacturer of sophisticated weaponry. It became one of the significant global suppliers of arms.

Since the 1990s Russia impacted the PLA modernization but under different historical conditions. It also enabled the PLA's first manned spaceflight to perform military reconnaissance in 2003, and enabled future PLA radar surveillance and reconnaissance satellites for all-weather strike capability.

Also, Russian technology and assistance facilitated the PLA Navy (PLAN) to launch its first second-generation nuclear powered and conventional submarines. It assisted the PLA in building three new classes of stealth warships. The strategic relationship helped modernize PLA Army main battle tanks, armoured personnel carriers, amphibious tanks, airborne tanks and anti-tank missiles. Between both nations, there is an increasing emphasis on broader technological development cooperation, whereby China seeks to attract Russian technological investment, and China also invests in high technology in Russia. In 1993, there were 300 Russian scientists in China on long-term Defence-related programs. In 2000 there were 1,500. In fact, high technology development contracts between both nations jumped to approximately seventy contracts between 2001 and 2002, in shipbuilding, nuclear energy, aerospace and Defence industry companies.

In the past few years, however, it has become quite obvious that Defence industry cooperation between Russia and China is on the decline. In the 1990s, China was the main importer of Russian weapons, accounting for up to half of Russian arms exports in 2004-2005. By 2007 that figure had shrunk to just 25 per cent. The projection for 2008-2010 is a mere 12-17 per cent. China has almost stopped buying complete weapons platforms from Russia. It is now interested only in components, subsystems, engines, and technical expertise. Other than Russia, it is believed that Ukraine sold approximately $1-2 billion in military products to the PLA in the 1990s, benefiting from Russian and Ukrainian military competitive relations. This consisted of supplying space and missile technologies, conducting training for PLA astronauts, and possibly selling advanced liquid fuel rocket engines, as well as being the principle source for air-to-air missiles. It is also reported that Ukrainian companies developed new naval radars which are part of air-Defence destroyers.

Another source of supplies was Israel. During the 1970s and 1980s, technology was transferred for tank weapons, anti-tank missiles, surface-to-air missiles, cruise missiles, military electronics and aircraft design – all of U.S. origin. Most of this came to a stop after the 1989 Tiananmen events due to U.S. bipartisan pressures. Some collaboration with Israel continues. In late 2000, a U.S-Israeli committee was reportedly created to review Israel's sale of such technologies. Nevertheless, such sales have surfaced. In 2002, it was reported that Israel sold a large number of its Harpy anti-radar drone to the PLA. A December 2003 report notes that Israel may be trying to revive some military-technical commercial ties that may focus primarily on counter-terrorism.

In 2004 Europe was ready to end its 1989 arms embargo against the PRC. After the mid-1990s, Britain, France, Spain and Italy modified their interpretations of the sanctions to allow increasing "dual use" technology. Europeans have sold Defence electronics and helicopter technology to the PLA. By 2002-2003, stronger China-EU links were being developed.

In fact, Britain sold microsatellite technology used in anti-satellite capabilities and Rolls Royce turbofan engine technology used on fighter-bombers. The French and Italian contributed to the PLA's first modern attack helicopter. The Germans and the French sold marine engines for PLA submarines, and combat ships. There is also EU-China cooperation in "space science, earth observation, environmental monitoring, meteorology, telecommunications and satellite navigation, microgravity research for biology and medicine, and human resource development and training."

Analysts suggest that in order to reach a high level of Defence modernization, China will likely try to form new alliances with European arms makers as quickly as possible, thereby, creating anxiety in the Asian region, the U.S, and Moscow. But to remain competitive with Europe, it is possible that Russia may become more eager to sell whatever it has that is new and more deadly. For example, the fear of European competition may drive Russia to allow the PLA to co-produce up to 20 of its most modern and effective conventional submarines.

It can also be expected that many European Defence companies that now cooperate with U.S. defence companies will seek cooperative alliances with PLA-controlled companies. Such moves should be viewed with concern in Washington.

Defence Spending Statistics

Today, global military expenditure stands at over $1.6 trillion in annual expenditure at current prices for 2010, and has been rising in recent years. This represents a 13 per cent increase in real terms since 2009 and a 50 per cent increase since 2001. Out of these figures, the USA is responsible for 43 % ($698 bn) of the world total, distantly followed by China with 7.3% ($119 bn), UK (3.7%), France (3.6%), and Russia (3.6%). Recently, a report by the Stockholm International Peace Research Institute (SIPRI) found that of the top 100 arms-producing companies, 78 are based in the West, with 45 in the United States and 33 in Western Europe. Regardless of the global financial and economic crisis, military spending has increased, with only a few exceptions. The contributing factors are: foreign policy objectives, real or perceived threats, armed conflicts, contributions to multilateral peacekeeping operations, and availability of economic resources. The last point refers to rapidly developing nations like China and India that have seen their economies boom in the last decades. Among larger economies, both developing and developed: 16 of the 19 states in the G20 saw real-term increases in military spending in 2009. As stated above, defence is big business. It is also a reflection of a global trend of military modernization. In essence it is also the forever present pursue military superiority and strategy of power projection - a clear strategy of the West.

China's Defence Tradition

Defence, being an expensive acquisition, is also an expensive endeavour requiring management of operations, maintenance and repair, and upgrading of high value, complex assets for ground, sea, air and space. Therefore, an integrated logistic and technological modernization is a must to facilitate the functionality of the enterprise on hand. This approach guarantees organizational leadership, management of manpower and supply, agility and flexibility, and to maintain reduce and sustain costs. This is the essence of military modernization. Yet, this modernization goes hand-in-hand with ancient tradition. The defensive orientation was evident since the early imperial period. Historically, China has feared invasions from its northern neighbours; hence, the Great Wall for the purpose of keeping the "barbarian" armies out.

The ancient philosopher most readily identified as a defensive strategist, as well as conflict negotiator and defensive tactics adviser, is Mo Zi (Mo Tzu). He deplored war because strong states invade weaker states. This philosopher-engineer devised defensive war-fighting techniques in the event that peaceful avenues of conflict resolution failed. Mo Zi followed a victory-denial strategy, a vital component of Mao's strategic doctrine which holds that should deterrence fail, then defensive war fighting capabilities in the form of a protracted war of resistance should be put in place.

Another sage, Sun Tzu, stated in the oldest book on strategy, The Art of War, "War is a matter of vital importance to the state; a matter of life or death, the road either to survival or to ruin".

Therefore, a defensive stance is the most suitable stance, and in keeping with the wisdom of the sage, and the decision of Chinese leadership was not to participate in an arms race during the Cold War. This is a position that the current, and possible future leaders of China will uphold.

Mo Zi is not alone in providing a philosophical antecedent to contemporary victory-denial strategy. Where Mao's strategic thinking differs from Mo Zi, but agrees with Sun Tzu, is in the interpretation of defensive strategy. He stated that "invincibility lies in defence; the possibility of victory in the attack". In other words, while maintaining the pre-eminence of defence, there should nevertheless be no let up in offensive capabilities.

Analysis

Today, China's defence modernization is balanced within the parameters of historical events, relations with its neighbours, territorial and border issues, resource and energy needs, secure shipping lanes for trade, the global trend of military modernization, and the United States as the sole global power – all which are linked and vital for a sustained economic development. Historically, the Great Game of the 19th Century pitted the British and Russian empires against each other for domination of Central Asia. Likewise, the implosion of the Soviet Union in the 20th Century will ignite new contests for power in this region under the label of the New Great Game. A region full of energy resources and of great importance for China as a result of what has been labelled the New Silk Road – an artery of natural gas and oil pipelines linking it with China's north-western borders, and the dilemma that the Straits of Malacca, as a choke-point, that it represents for China.

Again, the fact that good neighbours don't make good friends is a reality for China. There are pending continental border territorial and maritime claims/disputes that have not been resolved, as well as the issue of Taiwan.

Since the Open Door policy, China's trade and development has expanded to the four corners of the globe, linking it to the world economy and vice versa via sea shipping lanes. Therefore, the responsibility of safeguarding China's vital interest from piracy and other threats is a duty. China, as any sovereign nation, cannot rely nor depend on foreign defence forces. Many analysts argue that the studies of modern Chinese history focused on China's 'response to the West' concentrate overwhelmingly on subordinating the equally. In other words, China views that its territorial integrity that must be protected by two walls – significant and longer-lasting overland links with Russia and Central Asia that can be defended by modernized land forces, and the maritime contacts with Western Europeans, Americans, and Japanese, which require a modernized maritime defence force.

Some analysts claim that Beijing assesses that Washington is trying to sustain a "unipolar" balance of power by strengthening its security alliance with Tokyo and by expanding NATO's reach beyond Western Europe, along with of course the access of India to US nuclear capabilities in clear violation of the Nuclear Non-Proliferation Treaty. Therefore, China will most likely continue to promote what has been referred to as a "strategic partnership" with Russia marked by cooperation over border issues, trade and investment, and military sales, as well as continued close relations with other regional powers, like Pakistan and Iran.

There are also those that believe that the PLA's modernization goals are more manageable because, unlike the U.S. Army, the PLA does not seek to project force across oceans, and it limits its scope of operations to what it considers as the protection of Chinese sovereignty, including Taiwan and much of the South China Sea. The PLA does not have foreign bases or a web of defence commitments throughout the world. Moreover, unlike the U.S. Army, the PLA remains a party-army bonded by loyalty to the Chinese Communist Party.

Today, China ranks as number two as a global military power. In fact, the U.S. remains and will continue to remain the undisputed leader, showcasing the world's largest navy, continuing to increase its defence budget, and its engagement in military activities in hotspots; on the other hand, China has slowly edged out Russia but only by the slimmest of margins in available manpower and financial capital. The most interesting aspect of the defence modernization of China is the following. Even more importantly than buying individual Russian-made weapons, China has been able to acquire and license a wide range of Russian military technology, and to make use of Russian military expertise to design some new weapons - indeed, sometimes entire new weapons systems - of its own.

In the 1990s and the early part of this decade, many if not most of the Russian military design bureaus and research facilities worked for the Chinese, who had become their main customer. As a result, though many of the latest Chinese weapons systems developed over the past decade bear the hallmarks of Russian sources – but more and more hardware and technology will have Chinese characteristics.

Unity and territorial integrity remain a constant priority for China. The reality of today's international and interconnectedness is complex and dynamic. Hence, the critical need for defence modernization to keep up with a sustained level of growth under a national strategy of development. China's land and maritime borders are mined with many pending issues and claims that have the potential to spark conflicts, as they did in the past. Within this historical reality, China's leadership, from Mao to the present, understands the critical importance of maintaining a defence structure that would guarantee the consolidation of historical milestones, the continuity of its civilization, and the path to modernization. This can only be achieved by embracing the necessary means, as was laid down by Deng Xiaoping through under the Four Modernizations, to continue on the path to a modern China with a momentum that is embraced by the leaders and the population.

Analysts point at the forward leaps that China has taken regarding its defence modernization. Having acquired hardware and technology from different sources, it would only be naïve not to assume that China would not employ its long tradition of research and development for its own military hardware, weapons systems, strategies, and know-how with Chinese characteristics.

SECOND ARTILLERY'S PLACE IN CHINA'S STRATEGY

As the CMC drastically reduces personnel strength while continuously increasing the military budget, is it possible for an outsider to perceive any implications for the role of nuclear weapons in the grand strategy? The answer to this question would be found in the repository of Chinese nuclear weapons, the PLA's Second Artillery Corps (Second Artillery), also known as the Strategic Missile Force. Second Artillery operates China's land-based and tactical ballistic missiles, strategic nuclear weapons and conventionally armed SRBMs. It is composed of 100,000 officers, NCOs and conscripts and is the smallest of the various branches and services in the PLA's order of battle. Its nuclear inventory is approximately 400 warheads—280 strategic and 120 tactical.

It should be noted that being the smallest branch of the PLA, Second Artillery actually increased in numbers despite the troop reductions cited above. Second Artillery controls its own budget. Additionally, the budget for its nuclear weapons has reportedly been constantly maintained at five percent of the overall defence expenditure, which is a not a paltry sum considering that the defence spending was estimated to be between $50-80 billion this year.

What do these well-funded forces contribute to China's defence? According to the *White Paper,* "Second Artillery Force organizes and commands its own troops in case of launching nuclear counterattacks with strategic missiles and conducting operations with conventional missiles. Under it are missile and training bases, and... support troops."

Evan S. Medeiros noted in *Evolving Nuclear Doctrine*: "Indeed, the nuclear counterstrike campaign is the only nuclear contingency that the PLA leaders has identified for the Second Artillery." China's entire nuclear arsenal is estimated at approximately 400 warheads. Presently, it is assumed that virtually all operational and deployable warheads in their nuclear arsenal are in Second Artillery's hands. Why?

The airborne leg of their proto-triad is composed of 100 B6 BADGER (1965 vintage) and 30 A-5 FANTAN (1970 vintage) aircraft. It is unclear if these platforms are still assigned to strategic strike missions.

Additionally, the problem-plagued, 1980s-vintage, XIA-class, (Type 092) SSBN (nuclear-powered ballistic missile submarine) never successfully performed one patrol and, therefore, still does not pose a credible threat. However, the *White Paper* stated that the "Navy aims at gradual extension of the strategic depth for offshore defensive operations and enhancing its capabilities in integrated maritime operations and nuclear counterattacks." Supporting the *White Paper,* Lt. Gen Mi Zhenyu, senior strategist at China's Academy of Military Science wrote: "China's political and economic focus lies on the coastal areas [and] for the present and a fairly long period to come, strategic focus will be in the direction of the sea." In 2006, the PLAN launched two new JIN-class (Type 094) SSBNs that are expected to be deployment-ready by the end of the decade.

"IMPROVE THE SURVIVABILITY OF THE STRATEGIC NUCLEAR WEAPONS"

There are other dramatic changes occurring within the Chinese nuclear forces, changes that have been on-going for decades at a modest pace. Have the Chinese told outsiders what their strategy would be regarding the upgrade of their forces? In 1989, then-deputy commander of the Second Artillery, Major General Yang Huan, published a paper on the Defence Industry of China informing the world of China's intentions:

... we should improve current weapons to raise the quality and the comprehensive fighting capability. Science and technology should be our guideposts... strengthening the study of single-item high technology weapons. We should work hard on the survival, fast reaction, accuracy, and break-through and high-command technologies for weapons systems. These should be the direction for the development of our strategic nuclear weapons.

- Improve the survivability of the strategic nuclear weapons... We should strengthen research on small, solid fuel and highly automated mobile missiles and on the technology of invisibility, for reinforcing defence work against nuclear or nonnuclear strike; and improve the survivability of missiles before launch and in flight...
- Improve the striking ability of strategic nuclear weapons...
- Improve the penetration technology of strategic weapons.

There is seemingly no deception intended in General Yang Huan's words. In fact, he actually provided a litany of items on Second Artillery's things to do list. Since his article appeared 18 years ago, China has been able to introduce road-mobile, strategic, nuclear-tipped ICBMs, the DF-31 and the extended-range DF-31A, which may target of most the world, including the continental United States.

These missiles are solid-propellant—a major improvement over the previous liquid-fuelled missiles. Another significance of that upgrade is that China's ICBMs are no longer confined to silos. Additionally, launch times have been reduced from several hours to minutes, since there is no requirement to fuel the missiles immediately prior to launch with highly-corrosive, liquid rocket fuel.

It is obvious that making nuclear ICBMs solid fuelled and road-mobile tremendously increased their survivability. Another open source document in the Liberation Army Daily from 30 May 2001 praised the then-new Russian road-mobile ICBM calling it an assassin's mace weapon: '"... that could ensure "the most reliable" nuclear retaliation."'

The sea-based leg of their triad has also been upgraded with the addition of the JIN-class SSBNs, which will carry the naval version of the DF-31—the JL-2 SLBM. The XIA SSBN was designed to carry 12 JL-1 SLBMs and the JIN was designed to carry 16 JL-2 missiles. The addition of the nuclear-powered JINs armed with nuclear-tipped SLBMs will provide the CMC with an additional, survivable nuclear option in its grand strategy.

A review of the items on General Yang Huan's, that many of those items have been acquired: they have improved current weapons to raise the quality and the comprehensive fighting capability, they have improved the survivability of strategic nuclear weapons, and they have obtained small, solid fuel and highly automated mobile missiles. One hears on TV commercials: Yang Huan also called for improving the striking ability of strategic nuclear weapons as well as improving the penetration technology of strategic weapons. In this case, the Chinese are waiting to see how effective the U.S. national missile defence (NMD) system will be. The Chinese will not be able to design countermeasures for the NMD system until they (and the United States as well) know if it will really work. According to Saunders: Chinese responses to BMD could consist of three categories of programs: expansion of China's current BM forces, technical countermeasures to penetrate and defeat U.S. BMD system, and the possible use of asymmetric measures such as the development of ASAT weapons to attack key components of the U.S. system.

The Chinese have proven themselves to be capable of creating and deploying military technology without the advanced knowledge of foreign intelligence services. For example, Bill Gertz wrote about China's Yuan-class submarine that was built secretly and completely underground.

China also fired a warning shot across the bow of countries possessing space-based intelligence satellites by successfully destroying an old Chinese weather satellite with an ASAT. If the Chinese can successfully hide the construction of a submarine, successfully launch its ASAT, and deploy road-mobile ICBMs with miniaturized warheads, can they develop other assassin's mace weapons without their adversaries' knowledge? An affirmative answer would suggest that hedging will also continue on all sides, since no side can be certain of what the other side is doing and, therefore, cannot base its security on the belief that it knows everything that the other side might do to improve its relative position.

The Inferior Defeats the Superior

Chinese leaders know that they cannot defeat the United States in a face-to-face encounter. They have studied the results of the Gulf Wars. They also know that the United States, whose forces would confront theirs in a face off over Taiwan, would somehow have to be neutralized in a short-term conflict to achieve the desired results, or face defeat in a long-term conflict. The CMC knows that the U.S supply lines are long, that U.S. forces require enormous amounts of fuel and ammunition, and that they require intricate communications paths—both terrestrial and space-borne. This issue received detailed attention in *The Science of Military Strategy*:

In regard to information systems, we should firmly destroy their surface facilities, jam and cut the enemy's information feedback transmission circuits first, and then try our best to knock off his awareness platforms and damage his information flow which can form capabilities, so as to achieve the effect of "decapitation."

Chinese military planners would have to devise a means of interrupting U.S. supplies and communications for just as long as it would take for them to seize and occupy Taiwan. The Chinese do not want a protracted war, but would like a *fait accompli*. According to *Military Power,* in order to successfully accomplish their military strategy:

China's leaders have placed a near-term emphasis on asymmetric programs and systems to leverage China's advantages while exploiting the perceived vulnerabilities of potential opponents—so-called Assassin's Mace (*sha shou jian*) programs.

The Chinese have adapted Sun Tzu's ancient stratagems to today's strategic requirements. In this particular case, the doctrine is called "The Inferior Defeats the Superior." Michael Pillsbury has culled Chinese open source writings and described the process by which the Chinese will implement this assassin's mace program.

In order to be successful at the doctrine of "The Inferior Defeats the Superior," China assumes it can initially lull the opponent into complacency, or deceive him to take steps that will help China win. The premises here are quite elaborate... These concepts of how "The Inferior Defeats the Superior" are claimed to be unique to China, and to have [sic] developed by Chinese strategists over thousands of years. For this reason, PLA authors employ extensive examples from Chinese ancient military campaigns which they claim are the heart of Mao's military doctrines. Westerners are presumed to be ignorant of these Chinese "lessons learned" about Assassin's Mace employment concepts and the doctrines of "The Inferior Can Defeat the Superior."

Pillsbury further explains why the Chinese shroud assassin's mace programs in a veil of secrecy:

... some of the doctrines are considered to be highly classified in China, especially as they are taught in classified courses in military operations in the senior PLA schools. Available open sources thus only hint at the full set of concepts of the Inferior Defeats the Superior. Nor do open sources necessarily provide a full set of Assassin's Mace Weapons, either. After all, the need to surprise and even paralyze the opponent is an explicit goal of both these weapons and this doctrine. It is hardly to be expected that they would be fully described for the opponent to read and study in advance.

Having gained awareness of one of China's assassin's mace concepts and how the Chinese leadership has intentionally shrouded it in secrecy, one can better understand that Chinese military developments, as seen by Western observers, may indeed only be what the Chinese want outside observers to see. The Chinese do not try to hide the fact that they have been downsizing the PLA's end strength.

The most recent troop reductions brought the PLA down to 2.3 million personnel. That figure is almost identical to that of the U.S. Armed Forces. It is interesting to note that a country of over 1.3 billion people has the same number of soldiers as the United States with a population of only 300 million.

There are other sweeping changes occurring in China's military. The PLA, PLAN (navy) and PLAAF (air force) are undergoing a Chinese version of Goldwaters-Nicols in order to function more along the lines of U.S. joint operations. Additionally, the Chinese have coined a term: "informationalization" or what the United States calls "command, computers, control, communications, intelligence, reconnaissance and surveillance (C 4ISR)." The white paper stresses satellite and airborne sensors, unmanned aerial vehicles and information warfare. The Chinese have been funding these changes by increasing its military budget at a rate of 10 percent for the past 20 years. This year's defence budget's increase is 18 percent over last year's. There is more money for technology while there are fewer troops in the field.

9

National Security System and Defence Planning

The system of national security is the aggregate of concepts, strategies, policies, means, regulations and administrative structures of a state, as well as of public/social institutions of the Republic of Moldova whose role is to implement, protect and promote the national interests of the Republic of Moldova. At the same time, the national security system of the Republic of Moldova is a mechanism in which its components interact, a mechanism that is based on the national interests and values of the Moldovan society, used for the implementation of the strategic objectives of the country, in compliance with the national security policy guidelines. The state will implement functional and efficient standards in building a national security system.

NATIONAL SECURITY STRATEGIC POLICY FRAMEWORK

The purpose of the National Security Strategic Policy Framework is to provide strategic planning and guidance for Commonwealth departments and agencies so their work on national security is properly coordinated, priorities are clear, resources are allocated effectively and performance can be evaluated appropriately. Implementation of this framework has started and is expected to reach maturity by 2011-2012.

Priority Setting

Each year, the most important step in this framework is the determination by Ministers in the NSC of the national security priorities and NIPs. To assist Ministers in developing these priorities, ONA coordinates, on behalf of the NICC and with the support of ASIO, the Australian Crime Commission and natural hazards agencies, an annual all-hazards National Assessment on

Australia's national security challenges. It identifies changes in the strategic environment that might affect Australia's national security over the following three to five years.

The National Assessment provides the foundation for the development by the Office of National Security in PM&C of the draft national security priorities and NIPs. Once the NIPs have been set by the NSC, they are translated by the NICC's *National Intelligence Collection Management Committee (NICMC)* into more detailed Collection Requirement Papers to guide intelligence collection. ONA has lead responsibly for developing papers on 70% of the NIPs, with the Australian Security Intelligence Organisation responsible for 10% and other agencies the remainder.

Evaluation

The NSA evaluates the performance of agencies with national security responsibilities each year, providing feedback to the Prime Minister and the national security community. Performance is assessed against the national security priorities and tasking which has arisen during the year. The evaluation does not look at individual agencies but at achievements, shortfalls and areas of concern or risk across the national security community as a whole.

The NSA also produces an annual memorandum for Ministers on the performance of the AIC. Separately, ONA, under its own Act, is responsible for evaluating Australia's foreign intelligence activities. ONA prepares an annual Foreign Intelligence Evaluation Report for the Prime Minister which considers the performance of AIC agencies over the previous year and considers future needs. In doing this, it draws on the Collection Evaluation Reports prepared regularly in the NICMC to evaluate the collection efforts of agencies (domestic and foreign) against each of the NIPs.

ONA's Foreign Intelligence Evaluation Report and ASIO's Current Priorities and Work Environment statement feed into the NSA's AIC performance evaluation report.

Resourcing

The NSA provides a consolidated national security budget memorandum to government, prioritising all national security budget proposals. This assists Ministers to consider proposals in the context of the national security priorities, the overall strategic environment and the annual performance evaluations. As part of this process, and in accordance with his statutory responsibilities, the Director-General of ONA advises the NSA and relevant departments on the adequacy of resources available for foreign intelligence activities and any improvements or changes that should be made to remedy inadequacies.

THE NATIONAL SECURITY SECTOR

The Republic of Moldova understands the need for a national security system based on a clearly defined by a relevant normative documents institutional frame and highly qualified personnel that will operate in compliance with the law. This institutional frame constitutes the national security sector of the Republic of Moldova. The national security sector of the Republic of Moldova includes state force institutions (*operational level)* with a duty to protect the citizens and the state and state civil institutions (*administrative level)* with a duty to govern, plan, control and supervise the national security system. The national security sector is responsible for the implementation of the national security aim.

Given the multidimensional character of the security, the functioning of the national security sector is influenced by factors that determine the security environment and by the activity of authorities from the sectors of vital importance to the state. Reformation of the national security sector of the Republic of Moldova is a complex process with spillover effects on state and non-state institutions from outside the definition of the national security sector of the Republic of Moldova, as stipulated by the present Concept.

This process includes the following components: political, military and defence, foreign policy, intelligence and counterintelligence, constitutional order, justice, economic, financial, energetic, industrial, communications and infrastructure, social protection and environment - all of which are interdependent.

The process of national security sector reformation is based on the need of the Republic of Moldova to achieve an adequate security and stability level that would allow it to develop as a state and reach steady economic development, which will bring along sustainable security and stability. The national security sector reform is implemented with the participation of the civil society, mass-media, human rights organizations and relevant international institutions.

The process of reforming the national security sector particularly includes, but not limit itself to: improvement of the national security sector efficiency in line with the needs, guidelines and aim of the national security; consolidation of the national security sector's react capabilities to changes in the domestic and international security environment; assurance of functional civil control over the national security sector; strengthening the civil governance of the national security sector; consolidation of the national security sector's legitimacy; quality and quantity rescaling of the national security sector in a way that will allow conducting of the necessary planning activities and resource allocation in conformity with the priorities of the Moldovan society; effective prevention of conflicts, crises and emergency situations; reintegration of the country.

The Institutions of the National Security Sector

State force institutions and state civil institutions which form the national security sector are: the National Army of the Republic of Moldova; Border Guard Service; Carabineer Troops, Security and Intelligence Service; Police bodies and Emergency Department of the Ministry of Interior; Custom Service; Penitentiary Department of the Ministry of Justice; State Protection and Guard Service; the Centre for Combating the Economic Crimes and Corruption; the permanent Parliamentary Committees on Defence, Security and Public Order as well as the parliamentary Committee on Foreign Policy and European Integration; the Ministry of Defence; Ministry of Interior; Ministry of Foreign Affairs and European Integration; Ministry of Reintegration; Ministry of Finance; Ministry of Justice; the Prosecutor General Office.

The good functioning of the national security sector is indispensable with the activities of the institutions with the competences on multiple dimensions of security.

This refers to the activity of the Ministry of Economy and Trade; Ministry of Industry and Infrastructure; Ministry of Ecology and Natural Resources; Ministry of Informational Development; Ministry of Health Care; Ministry of Social Protection; Ministry of Transportation and Roads; Ministry of Education and Youth; Ministry of Local Public Administration; Ministry of Agriculture and Food Processing; Academy of Science of Moldova; Standardization and Metrology Service; Bureau for Interethnic Relations and Judicial System.

The administrative competences in the national security system defined by the Constitution of the Republic of Moldova and the country's legislation in force are exercised by the President of the Republic of Moldova, the Parliament and the Government. The general coordination and adoption during peace time of the recommendations for decision making regarding the national security and the national security sector are carried out by the National Security Council.

The Civil Dimension of the National Security Sector

The National Security Council is the structure meant to carry out the general coordination of the national security sector's institutions and activities of the other institutions exercised on different dimensions of the national security as well to adopt the recommendations for decision making on national security. During peace time the National Security Council exercises its attributions of the consultative body. In case of an emergency, siege or war the

Council will serve as a body with deliberative functions. On a basis of the provisions of the article 77 of the Moldovan Constitution, the President of the Republic of Moldova chairs the National Security Council.

The proper functioning of the Council is ensured by its Secretary, who is a civil person of the administration of the Republic of Moldova's President.

The permanent members of the National Security Council are: the President of the Republic of Moldova, the Speaker of the Parliament, the Prime Minister of the Republic of Moldova, the chairmen of the permanent Parliamentary Committees on National Security, Defence and Public Order, as well as for Foreign Policy and European Integration, the Minister of Foreign Affairs and European Integration, the Minister of Defence, the Minister of Interior, the Minister of Reintegration, the Minister of Finance, the SIS Director, the President's advisors on Domestic as well as on Foreign policy, the Secretary of the National Security Council.

While drafting its Rule and Regulations, the National Security Council will decide on establishing the positions of the permanent advisors and non-permanent members of the Council.

The positions of the permanent advisors will be covered by the senior level officials from the state force institutions (*operational level*). The decision to invite the permanent advisors of the Council or its non-permanent members will be taken in accordance with the issue examine in the Council's session.

The functions of the National Security Council:

- Integrated analysis of the security situation. Caring out this function allows the comprehensive evaluation of the security situation which serves as a basis for elaboration/adjusting of the national security policy and adoption of adequate decisions. The main element of this task is the assessment of the multiple treats to the national security of the Republic of Moldova. The method for the threat assessment is the exchange of information and unification of efforts in the process of gathering information concerning threats. To fulfill this duty decisions are needed to create sufficient capabilities for the National Security Council.
- Adopting the recommendations on allocation of necessary resources in order to cope with the threats to the national security. Fulfilling this task allows balancing security allocations with other allotments of major importance for the country, as well as tackling thoroughly the national security concerns.
- Monitoring, controlling and supervising in the national security system. Caring out this task guarantees the efficient use of the allocated resources

with the aim at consolidating security; analyzing the efficiency of the security plans or relevant structures; maintaining the ability of the different institutions to activate in crisis or emergency situations; supervising the process of expenditures, administration and implementation of the policies by the state force institutions; promoting political control and trust building between the institutions within the national security sector.

- Identifying the national security priorities. Caring out this duty allows structuring the national security priorities and planning the stages for accomplishing these priorities.
- Coordinating the activities in case of urgency or crisis. In case of crisis the Council will act as a body with deliberative tasks.
- Administering and monitoring the reformation process of the national security sector.

The National Security Council uses the capacities and expertise of the Interdepartmental Committees to manage the developments in the national security sector, like the National Committee on Implementing the Individual Partnership Action Plan, the State Committee on Strategic Defence Review etc. The Council may decide to set up new inter-institutional structures. The National Security Strategy of the Republic of Moldova and the Rules and Regulations of the National Security Council approved by a Decree of the President of the Republic of Moldova will refer in details on sub-divisions in the Council's structure, other structures associated with it and its functioning mechanism.

The Military security and the Armed Forces

Armed Forces of the Republic of Moldova are responsible for ensuring the national security state of affair by military methods. The Armed Forces' main task is to ensure the Republic of Moldova's defence in any circumstances. The Armed Forces offer necessary support to the relevant public institutions in case of civil emergency, natural calamities, technological accidents or disasters. The Armed Forces participate in the international peace operations, humanitarian and combating international terrorism missions.

The cooperation with the North Atlantic Treaty Organization and the objective of reaching by the Republic of Moldova's Armed Forces the maximum level of inter-operability will offer a basis for building and developing a viable, credible, efficient, operational and modern defence system for the country. This process envisages setting up and institutionalizing the system of defence planning through adopting necessary regulations. The reformation tasks of the armed forces of the Republic of Moldova are:

Achieving sufficient defensive capabilities, through the setting up and permanently maintaining forces that are credible, quantitatively sufficient and trained according to the modern standards, able to adequately react to the existent and potential risks and threats;

Restructuring and modernizing the military force, through:

- Re-dimensioning the armed forces and establishing their new structure, professionalizing military personnel, modernizing and standardizing the training for performing military missions;
- Maintaining functional capacity of the armament and existent equipment and increasing its quality both through modernizing it and through acquiring new modern equipment.

In the same context, it will be taken into consideration the need for adequate staff social protection, efficient management of the equipment, armament and excess infrastructure etc. With the aim at building and developing its defence system, the Republic of Moldova will develop a comprehensive Strategic Defence Review (SDR). National Military Strategy will reflect the priorities and objectives of the Republic of Moldova's defence system development. The respective documents will take into consideration the Republic of Moldova's international commitments.

Consolidation of the Domestic Security

The domestic security and public order is an important component of the national security along with military security and other dimensions of the security of the Republic of Moldova. The main tasks of the institutions meant to ensure domestic security refer to guaranteeing stability in the Republic of Moldova, combating criminal phenomenon, protecting people and property rights.

The Activity of the Security and Intelligence Service

The goal of the Security and Intelligence Service (SIS) of the Republic of Moldova is to ensure the domestic security and maintain constitutional order through preventive and special means of non-military nature. In order to achieve this goal and the general aim of the national security, the SIS collects and process the information on the ground of what the fundamental thesis of the national security policy are formulated. The Security and Intelligence Service collects, verifies, assesses, keeps and develops the necessary information for acknowledging, prevention and counter any actions that bring or might bring threats to sovereignty, independence, safety, constitutional order and territorial integrity of the Republic of Moldova.

The SIS gathers information about evolution and events occurring outside the country, which allow formulating defence, economic and foreign policies of the Republic of Moldova. The SIS functions are: recognition, prevention and countering espionage and subversive activities against the Republic of Moldova, actions with impact on the democratic institutions of state and other actions that are threatening the state's security; providing counterintelligence information for the Armed Forces of the Republic of Moldova; assuring the security of the Moldovan institutions overseas and of the forces participating to a peace missions; prevention and countering of the terrorism, of the financing and supporting terrorism and extremists movements activities; setting up and maintaining the secure functioning of the of the government communications; protection of the classified information; conducting of other activities envisaged by legislation.

Obtaining pertinent information in reasonable time limits on developments that may threaten the national security is crucial for maintaining the constitutional order and domestic security of the Republic of Moldova. In order to efficiently counter the security threats, the ISS also develops an international cooperation and an inter-agency cooperation within the country. The international cooperation the SIS participates is important for obtaining the information on regional crisis, combating terrorism, preventing the proliferation of weapons of mass destruction, illegal arms, drugs and human being traffic. The SIS in cooperation with the law enforcement bodies acts to prevent the infiltration of the organized crime in politics and public administration.

The Activity of the Law Enforcement Agencies

The activity of the law enforcement agencies aims at maintaining public order. The phenomenon of organized cross-border crime is the biggest threat to the public order and security of the Republic of Moldova. The fight against organized cross-border crime is conducted in cooperation with the subdivisions of the Ministry of Interior, Border Guard Service, Centre for Combating Economic Crimes and Corruption and Prosecutor General Office and the Penitentiary Department of the Ministry of Justice. The fight against organized crime is aimed at curbing and preventing criminal activities on accumulation of illegal profits on a big scale.

An increased attention shall be drawn to benefiting from the opportunities offered by the Interpol and Europol as well as by the cooperation with the law enforcement agencies in the neighbouring states. There is a need for setting up a witness protecting system in order to participate to the relevant international programs.

Border Management and Illegal Migration

The efficient management of the state border that includes supervision and qualified control is essential for ensuring the national security of the

Republic of Moldova. The border security system is shall be adjusted to the relevant requirements applied in the European Union. Modernization of the state border management of the Republic of Moldova should be conducted in a way that offers opportunities for open cooperation with neighbours and does not imply new barriers. The process of adjusting of the national legislation to the acquis communitaire in that field will be regarded as a priority.

The Border Guard Service in cooperation with other competent authorities acts to prevent illegal border crossing and to ensure the efficient procedures to the state border crossing points, being responsible for maintaining high standards of the border control. Setting up border integrated management system is essential for guaranteeing the border security, increasing the efficiency of the fight against illegal migration, organized crime, terrorism and other forms of criminal cross-border activity. The cooperation between the Border Guard Service, the Ministry of Interior, the Ministry of Foreign Affairs and European Integration, SIS and other competent agencies dealing with illegal migration issues will follow the objective to build an integrated control system of the migration flow and to ensure the efficiency of the measures already adopted to counter the existing risks.

Crisis Management Services

The goal of ensuring domestic security entails adequate capability and proper training in order to promptly react to the emergency civil situation, natural disasters and ecologic catastrophes. In an emergency situation it is necessary to guarantee the functioning of the sectors of vital importance to the state, to protect the infrastructure and secure the public information. In order to ensure the functionality of the institutions of vital importance to the state in emergency situations it is necessary to reorganize the system of strategic reserves and to adapt it to the nation's needs. The sufficient equipment and proper training of the staff of the MoI's Department on Emergency Situations, law-enforcement bodies, institutions of the energetic, transportation, communication, and ecologic, health care and social protection systems are crucial. The consolidation of the economic, energetic, intellectual property, social and ecologic security of the Republic of Moldova. Regional development.

Consolidating Economic Security

The rapid, balanced and durable economic growth is vital for achieving the goals of the security policy of the Republic of Moldova. It is in the national interest of the Republic of Moldova to promote the diversification of the foreign economic relations. In that respect it is important to maintain a stable economic environment, which, along with other factors, will ensure the attractiveness of the Republic of Moldova for foreign investments. The Republic of Moldova ensures the credibility of its financial system. In order to settle the international crisis and their economic consequences, it is necessary to ensure a long lasting stability and a fund reserve in the financial system of the country.

The goal of the economic policy is to achieve a durable economic and social development. Taking into consideration that a stable macroeconomic environment is an important precondition for growth, its preservation becomes an essential task of the economic policy of the Government. In this respect, the long-term priorities of the Republic of Moldova are the following: creating favourable conditions for economy functioning, stimulating setting up the efficient and competitive industrial structures, as well as reducing disproportions and economic risks. Apart from these tasks, it is important to improve the national taxation policy, paying considerable attention to tax collection.

To ensure economic security, it is necessary to diversify the economy with the orientation to the goods and services with the high added value. During the process of diversification of the national economy it is necessary to increase the significance of the promising industries that were underdeveloped up to date, meanwhile maximally using the advantages offered by the current industries. The Republic of Moldova will promote a development policy oriented to innovation, setting up and functioning of the innovational system. Enhancing competitiveness and reaching out to new foreign markets will be encouraged. Creating necessary conditions for the economic development, it is important to create a favourable environment for business promotion, to develop a state policy on goal-oriented assistance, to improve the fiscal system and its management, as well as to set up a system for training and business consultancy.

A competitive industry considerably influences the economic development and the security of the country. The volume increase of the competitive products with the high added value and their export may diminish the deficit of the foreign trade. Thus, the attraction of investments in the industrial sector will enhance. According to the international standards, the Republic of Moldova increases its security measures in the field of transport. The country's economic development is also related to the ability to maintain and enhance the transit loads flow. The main tasks in developing the transportation services are ensuring the services' competitiveness, building oil and oil products pipelines, modernizing the road network, the East-West rail road corridor and the connected infrastructure. The Republic of Moldova pays increased attention to developing transportation infrastructure and to the integration process in the European and global transportation network. The Republic of Moldova is firmly decisive to continue its active participation in expending the trans-european transportation network, benefiting at large from its geographic position as a bridge between the EU and countries from the CIS zone.

Consolidating Energetic Security

Regulation of the energy market and the development of an adequate infrastructure have to ensure sufficient electric power supply for consumers, as well as an appropriate exercise of the essential state functions. On the gas market, the activities of gas suppliers must be carefully monitored. It is essential to identify opportunities for a diversification of gas supply sources for the country. On the thermal agents market, proper conditions will be created in order to provide heating to the population even in cases when the supply with the basic fuel is interrupted. On the bunker oil market, a minimum quantity of fuel will be stored to match at least the EU quantitative standards and to ensure its efficient use in cases when a regular supply with bunker oil is interrupted. There is a need to foresee a possibility for storing a certain quantity of bunker oil outside of the country. The situation in the energy sector could have a serious impact over the economic security and over the country's further development. It is necessary to create oil reserves in the country. With the liberalization of the energy industry market, which implies joining a common European energy and oil market, ensuring security of the supplies system should be one of the major requirements. The use of local energy resources and an increase of their efficiency, creation of new energy capacities built on advanced technologies are regarded as priority goals aimed at reducing the country's dependency on the imported resources.

A successful implementation of the Energy Strategy should contribute to the settlement of some conceptual problems as it is an important component in a multidimensional approach towards the energy sector. Gradual integration of the Republic of Moldova's energy system in the South-east European Energy Community will increase, primarily, integration in the Pan-European energy system while contributing simultaneously to reducing the country's unilateral energy dependency as energy issue is being examined on the regional level. In the context of the National Gasification Program, it is viewed as of primary importance to develop the main gas pipelines, branches and local network infrastructure. With the launch of the Giurgiulesti Terminal it is expected that the country's energy dependency will decrease.

Consolidating Social Security

To strengthen the citizens' social security, it is essential to solve the problems related to the employment market, to establish a durable system of social security that will cover the vulnerable groups and to educate and train a highly qualified work force able to ensure the continuity of the economic growth. In public health-related emergency situations an increased number of people might need medical assistance due to the outbreak of contagious disease, mass intoxication or exposure to radiation. The Republic of Moldova develops its national system to cope with public health emergencies according to the European standards. It is important in that respect to build on the accumulated experience in the PfP.

Combating contagious diseases, including spreading the HIV/AIDS and tuberculosis, is the state's responsibility. In the Republic of Moldova the measures on preventing the expansion of the very dangerous contagious diseases are implemented according to the international medical regulations. National programs are put into practice to reduce drug addiction, to limit the spread of HIV/AIDS and tuberculosis. The capacity and durable development of the social security system, which protects the citizens in case of social risk and offers handicapped people means to support their lives, play an important role in preventing social tensions and ensure the welfare of the society.

The main tasks of the social security system are to provide the social insurance and assistance. The system of state social insurance precedes the state pension insurance, maternity and sickness, unemployment insurance, as well as the cases of industrial accidents or professional diseases.

The category of ensured people will be extended, the pension age will be gradually increased, a support system of those unemployed will be developed (including payment of allowances) which will facilitate the return of unemployed citizens on the work market. The state social insurance services cover three main fields: medical assistance (allowances), social care and social rehabilitation. The provision of these services as well as the number of categories of people who will benefit from alternative social services will grow. The management of the social assistance and financial system will be improved. The education of the society regarding the social care and rehabilitation issues, citizen's rights and obligations will be further promoted. The functioning of social assistance is assigned to the state and local public administration.

Public Health Care

The public health is an important indicator of the social unity and equality, welfare and poverty as well as of the environment factors and cultural standards. In order to rapidly improve the people's health in the Republic of Moldova, it is necessary to increase the efficiency of the medical practice of the society on the ground of certain scientific measures meant to improve the health, to prevent diseases and to increase life duration. To fulfill this task it is necessary to consider the public health's risk factors as well as the environment protection, consumer security, health insurance and labour security.

The aim of the health care is to ensure the medical service quality available for the population while improving the structure of the assigned services, to strengthen and increase the quality of the routine health services, to guarantee the cost efficiency and rational approach to the patients, as well as to create the ground for a system of integrated departmental medical services to act in the emergency situation both on the local and national level. In other terms, the goal is to reach high quality, easily accessible health care for the population and a system of first medical assistance on low costs, equitable, qualitative and rapid for all citizens of the Republic of Moldova.

The Unitary Character of the Society

The consolidation of a balanced and democratic society in the Republic of Moldova occurs through implementing its policies on social integrity. The whole society plays an important role in the development of the country and in ensuring the social security. Thus, the civil society is built with the aim at involving all population groups in the country's development. The integration process entails political integration, social and regional integration of the society, as well as the language and culture integration. In order to ensure an efficient functionality of the Republic of Moldova as a unitary state, which protects the multiethnic and multi-linguistic essence of its people, it is vital to implement a demographic policy targeting to stop the demographic decline and the overall ageing of the Moldovan society, as well as reaching in future of a positive rate of population growth.

The Republic of Moldova guarantees the rights of the persons belonging to the ethnic minorities or different social groups and helps them to integrate in the society. The Republic of Moldova will continue to support the public information on political processes, on the country's history and culture, opportunities and rights to participate in these processes, thus stimulating civic spirit and involvement. Along with naturalization of foreign citizens, their involvement in the social and political life will be promoted. Improving the organization of work force, reducing (preventing) the unemployment, consolidating the links between the education and employment market as well as preventing unfavorable regional differences are able to diminish to the minimum the risk of social rejection.

In the process of integrating the society in the education area, the most significant target groups are youth and children. The state's education and cultural policy system will guarantee acquiring and inheriting both the general human values specifically promoted by the Republic of Moldova and the opportunities for preserving the intercultural education and cultural identity of the ethnic minorities. The educational system will continue to promote learning the state language of the Republic of Moldova, thus facilitating the integration of the society. The national cultural policy anticipates the state and municipal responsibilities in further preserving and developing all nationalities that live in the Republic of Moldova, their cultural inheritance and involvement in the contemporary life.

STRUCTURE OF INDIAN INTELLIGENCE SYSTEM

National Security Council (NSC)

1. Strategic Policy Group,
2. National Security Advisory Board
3. Secretariat represented by the Joint Intelligence Committee (JIC).

A: The Intelligence Bureau.

B: Research and Analysis Wing.

National Security Council (NSC) of India is the apex agency looking into the political, economic, energy and strategic security concerns of India. It was established by the A B Vajpayee government on November 19, 1998, with Brijesh Mishra as the first National Security Advisor (NSA).

Prior to the formation of the NSC, these activities were overseen by the Principal Secretary to the Prime Minister.

Organization

The three-tiered organization of the NSC comprises

1. The Strategic Policy Group,
2. The National Security Advisory Board
3. Secretariat represented by the Joint Intelligence Committee (JIC).

The Strategic Policy Group is the first level of the three tier organization of the National Security Council (NSC) of India. It forms the nucleus of the decision making apparatus of the NSC.

This group consists of the following members:

Military

* Chiefs of Staff of the Army, Navy and Air Force.

Civilian

* Cabinet Secretary
* Foreign Secretary
* Home Secretary
* Defence Secretary
* Finance Secretary

* Secretary (Defence Production)
* Secretary (Revenue)
* Governor of the Reserve Bank of India (RBI)
* Director of the Intelligence Bureau
* Secretary of the Research and Analysis Wing (RAW) of the Cabinet Secretariat
* Secretary of the Department of Atomic Energy
* Scientific Advisor to the Defence Minister
* Secretary of the Department of Space
* Chairman of the Joint Intelligence Committee (JIC).

Other invitees will be brought in as and when required.

The Strategic Policy Group undertakes the Strategic Defence Review, a blueprint of short and long term security threats, as well as possible policy options on a priority basis.

The National Security Advisory Board forms the third element of the National Security Council (NSC) set up in India. It consists of persons of eminence outside the Government with expertise in external security, strategic analysis, foreign affairs, defence, the armed forces, internal security, science and technology and economics.

The board meets at least once a month, and more frequently as required. It provides a long-term prognosis and analysis to the NSC, and recommends solutions and address policy issues referred to it.

The Joint Intelligence Committee (JIC) of the Government of India analyzes intelligence data from * the Intelligence Bureau, * RAW and the Directorates of Military, Naval and Air Intelligence. The JIC has its own Secretariat that works under the Cabinet Secretariat.

It is the third tier of the National Security Council (NSC) setup. The Intelligence Bureau is India's internal intelligence agency.

Origins

It was recast as the Central Intelligence Bureau in 1947 under the Ministry of Home Affairs. The reason for the perception may be because in 1885, Major General Sir Charles Metcalfe MacGregor was appointed Quartermaster General and head of the Intelligence Department for the British Indian Army at Shimla. The objective then was to monitor Russian troop deployments in Afghanistan, fearing a Russian invasion of British India through the North-West during the late 19th century.

In 1921, a new state-run surveillance and monitoring agency — Indian Political Intelligence (IPI) — was established, in reaction the development of

Indian anarchist activities in England. IPI was run jointly by the India Office and the Government of India and reported jointly to the Secretary of the Public and Judicial Department of the India Office, and the Director of Intelligence Bureau (DI in India, and maintained close contact with Scotland Yard and MI5.

Responsibilities

Shrouded in secrecy, the IB is used to garner intelligence from within India and also execute counter-intelligence and counter-terrorism tasks. The intelligence bureau is comprised of employees from law enforcement agencies mostly Indian Police Service officers as well as from the military.

The current chief of the IB is Mr. Narsimhan who replaced Mr. Ajit Kumar Doval. In addition to domestic intelligence responsibilities, the IB is particularly tasked with intelligence collection in border areas, following the 1951 recommendations of the Himmatsinhji Committee (also known as the North and North-East Border Committee), a task entrusted to military intelligence organizations prior to independence in 1947. The IB was also tasked with other external intelligence responsibilities as of 1951

Activities

Understanding of the arcane workings of the IB is largely speculative. One known task of the IB is to clear licenses to amateur radio enthusiasts. The IB also passes on intelligence between other Indian intelligence agencies and the police. The IB also grants the necessary security clearances to Indian diplomats and judges before they take the oath. On rare occasions, IB officers interact with the media during crises. The IB is also rumoured to intercept and open around 6,000 letters daily.

The Bureau is also authorised to conduct wiretapping without a warrant. This clause is mostly misused by ruling governments to spy on their political opponents, sometimes indicting them on false criminal charges. The IB also has numerous authors who write letters to various newspapers and magazines to support the government's perspective. According to a recent report the government is trying to bring in a restriction on wiretapping without a warrant.

Lapses

The IB was India's external and internal intelligence agency. Due to lapses on the part of the intelligence agencies to predict the Sino-Indian War of 1962, the IB was split up and entrusted with the task of internal intelligence. The external intelligence branch was handed to the newly created Research and Analysis Wing.

Research and Analysis Wing

Indian Intelligence Agency

The Cabinet Secretariat's Research and Analysis Wing (R&AW) is India's premier external intelligence body. It was created as an independent unit in September 1968 from the Intelligence Bureau which at that time handled both internal and external intelligence. Its headquarters are on Lodhi Road in New Delhi. The current director of the organization is P K Hormese Tharakan, who was with R&AW from 1989 to 2001, and is an IPS officer.

PROFILE, STRUCTURE AND FUNDING

Most available information about the R&AW is largely speculative. Relative to other intelligence agencies of comparable size, the R&AW maintains a very low media profile and is largely ignored by Indian writers, filmmakers and the general public. It reports directly to the Prime Minister's Office (PMO) and its operations and structure are not revealed to Parliament. The R&AW's budget and funding are not discussed in public forums. According to some reports, part of its funding comes from "discretionary grants" provided to various government bodies, especially Indian embassies and representatives abroad. Estimates of its annual budget vary wildly among experts-from $16 million to $145 million. One consequence of such a low profile is that it is very difficult to judge R&AW's effectiveness and performance. Reports cover the entire range of judgements from "highly effective and professional" to "inadequate and riddled with internal politics".

The cadre for R&AW is drawn by deputation from state police forces and other intelligence agencies. The Research Analysis Service instituted during the times of Indira Gandhi is the All India Level Service of R&AW.

Founded in 1968, RAW focused largely on Pakistan. Its formation was initially motivated by reports of Pakistan supplying weapons to Sikh militants, and providing shelter and training to guerrillas in Pakistan.

Numerous missions were assigned to RAW upon its creation. These included monitoring political and military developments in neighboring countries that affects Indian national security. In the 1980s RAW played a large role in creating the LTTE in Sri Lanka. Consequently, considerable attention is paid by RAW to Pakistan and China, countries that are traditional rivals of India.

CHANGING THE INDIAN INTELLIGENCE CULTURE

In his R.N.Kao Memorial lecture delivered at the headquarters of the Research & Analysis Wing (R&AW) on January 19, 2010, Vice-President Hamid

Ansari has done well in raising in public issues such as accountability and parliamentary oversight to which the Indian intelligence community is still a stranger.

The concept of an accountable and competent intelligence community, which uses the need for secrecy only for protecting its operations and not for covering up its inadequacies and irregularities, has been accepted and implemented by the intelligence agencies of many democracies— — parliamentary as well as Presidential types— of the world during the last three decades. Nobody in those countries has since argued that these concepts have come in the way of the effectiveness of the intelligence process and hence should be re-considered. The overall consensus is that these changes have proved beneficial and hence should be continued and, if necessary, further refined. In India too, these issues have been raised from time to time since the State of Emergency imposed by Indira Gandhi in 1975-77, but follow-up action has been avoided either because of resistance from sections of the intelligence community or because of the reluctance of the political leadership to introduce any changes which might dilute the scope for political misuse of the intelligence machinery for partisan purposes or both.

Accountability of intelligence agencies demands, firstly, that they should have a legal existence and, secondly, that they should have a formal charter of their functions and responsibilities. Forty-two years after its formation in 1968, the R&AW still does not have a legal existence. It was set up by a brief executive order issued on behalf of Indira Gandhi in September 1968. Till today, this order has not been accorded parliamentary sanctity by having necessary legislation authorising its creation passed by the Parliament. No Government, which has held office since 1968, has considered it necessary to have an Act passed by the Parliament providing legal legitimacy to the R&AW. No one has raised the question as to how the various Governments have been incurring expenditure on the R&AW year after year without having its creation approved by the Parliament. In the 1980s, when Indira Gandhi was the Prime Minister, a law was enacted by the Parliament banning strikes in the intelligence agencies. To my knowledge, that is the only Act of the Indian Parliament in which there is a reference to the R&AW by name. When that law was passed, nobody in the Parliament thought it fit to ask: What is this R&AW about? When was it created? Who created it? Has its creation been approved by the Parliament? It goes to the credit of A.K.Verma, who headed the R&AW from 1987 to 90. that he took the initiative in drawing the attention of the Governments of Rajiv Gandhi and V.P.Singh to the fact that the R&AW had been functioning without a legal cover and a formal charter. He wanted the Government of the day to do something about it, but nothing was done.

The fact that the Intelligence Bureau, which was created by the British before 1947, and the Central Bureau of Investigation (CBI), which came into existence after 1947, had been functioning without formal charters of their functions and responsibilities, was highlighted by the L.P.Singh Committee, which was set up by the Morarji Desai Government to enquire into the functioning of these two organisations during the State of Emergency. It not only stressed the need for formal charters to prevent their future misuse, but also prepared for the consideration of the Government detailed model charters for adoption. No action was taken on its recommendations by the Indira Gandhi Government which came back to power in 1980 or its successors. The report was consigned to the Archives—seen, but not read and implemented.

Shri Atal Behari Vajpayee and Shri Lal Krishna Advani were among those who were in the forefront of those who criticised—— during the election campaign of 1977—— the alleged misuse of the intelligence agencies by the Indira Gandhi Government during the Emergency. When Shri Vajpayee became the Prime Minister and Shri Advani the Home Minister in 1998, one naturally expected them to take the initiative in taking the L.P.Singh Committee report out of the Archives and implement it. The expectations were belied. The Task Force for the revamping of the intelligence apparatus set up by the Vajpayee Government in 2000, which was headed by Shri G.C. Saxena, former head of the R&AW, recommended the acceptance by the Government of the principle of formal charters for the intelligence agencies. To give greater meat to its recommendations, it wanted to have a look at the detailed charters for the IB and the CBI proposed by the L.P.Singh Committee. The Home Ministry, then headed by Shri Advani, avoided making available to the Task Force the entire report of the L.P.Singh Committee. However, the Task Force's recommendation for formal charters was accepted and implemented by the Vajpayee Government. One does not know whether the recommendations of the L.P.Singh Committee were taken into consideration while drafting the charters.

The credit for first raising the idea of a parliamentary oversight on the intelligence community should go to Shri Jaswant Singh, who was the Chairman of the Estimates Committee of the Rajya Sabha when Shri V.P.Singh was the Prime Minister. Shri V.P.Singh saw merit in the idea and wanted it to be examined. There was no opposition to the idea from the intelligence professionals then in service including this writer, but when Shri V.P.Singh developed differences with the BJP, he did not pursue it.

Since then, none of the political parties has shown interest in making the intelligence agencies accountable for their performance and integrity and in making their professional performance subject to an independent assessment.

Secrecy is an important operational principle for an intelligence agency. Unless an intelligence agency is able to ensure the secrecy of its operations, no source or agent will stick his neck out to work for it. Its capability for collecting technical intelligence will also be affected.

But secrecy should not be allowed to be used as an excuse for covering inefficiencies in performance and irregularities in functioning and financial management. Irregularities do occur in matters such as the personnel policy and diversion of the resources sanctioned by the Government for operational objectives for non-operational purposes. The public and the Parliament have a right to know to what extent the agencies have been producing results and what are the areas of their non-performance. The Parliament has a right to know what kind of financial controls are in place, who exercises those controls and to what extent they are effective. The Parliament has similarly a right to check whether the principle of secrecy in recruitment is being misused to pack the organisations with unsuitable persons, taken not for their qualifications, but for their connections.

It is possible to introduce some of these checks and balances in the functioning of our intelligence community without damaging their operational secrecy. There is reluctance from the political class because it sees the agencies as instruments for partisan exploitation and not for defending national interests. There is reluctance from sections of the intelligence officers themselves because they think that unchecked secrecy gives them an aura of power and influence which they do not want to lose. Ansaris may come and Ansaris may go, but the intelligence agencies will go on functioning in the same manner with the complicity of the political class unless there is sustained public pressure on the political class and the agencies to change the culture of our agencies. I am not very optimistic because I do not see on the horizon any political leader who is genuinely convinced of the need for a change.

Every country gets the intelligence community it deserves. We will continue to have the community which we have deserved unless Shri Ansari's call is followed up.

LAWS AND REGULATIONS

India is a longstanding parliamentary democracy with a bicameral parliament. A parliament sits for 5 years unless dissolved earlier for new elections, except under constitutionally defined emergency situations.

State governments are elected at regular intervals except in states under President's Rule, i.e., rule by the central Government. On the advice of the Prime Minister, the President may proclaim a state of emergency in any part of the national territory in the event of war, external aggression, or armed rebellion. Similarly, President's Rule may be declared in the event of a collapse of a state's constitutional machinery. The Supreme Court in May 1995 upheld the Government's authority to suspend fundamental rights during an emergency. Although the 25 state governments have primary responsibility for maintaining law and order, the central Government provides guidance and support through use of paramilitary forces throughout the country.

Serious abuses have included extrajudicial executions and other political killings and excessive use of force by security forces combating active insurgencies in Jammu and Kashmir and several northeastern states; torture and rape by police and other agents of government, and deaths of suspects in police custody throughout the country; poor prison conditions; arbitrary arrest and incommunicado detention in Jammu and Kashmir and the Northeast; continued detention throughout the country of thousands arrested under special security legislation; lengthy pretrial detention; and prolonged detention while under trial. The organization and responsibilities of intelligence and security agencies do not appear to be established or regulated by legislative acts of the Parliament of India.

Official Secrets Act (OSA)

Under the Official Secrets Act (OSA), the Government may restrict publication of sensitive stories, but the Government sometimes interprets this broadly to suppress criticism of its policies. Human rights activists state that government pressure caused one national, English-language daily to suppress some stories and transfer a staff reporter.

Newspapers Incitements to Offenses Act

The 1971 Newspapers Incitements to Offenses Act remains in effect in Jammu and Kashmir. Under the act, a district magistrate may prohibit the press from publishing material resulting in "incitement to murder" or "any act of violence." As punishment the act stipulates that the authorities may seize newspapers and printing presses. Despite these restrictions, newspapers in Srinagar regularly publish militant press releases attacking the Government and report in detail on alleged human rights abuses. The authorities allowed foreign journalists to travel freely in Jammu and Kashmir, where they regularly spoke with militant leaders, and filed reports on government abuses.

Special Protection Group Act

The Special Protection Group Act, which received the assent of the President on the 2nd June 1988 provides for the constitution and regulation of an armed force of the Union for providing proximate security to the Prime Minister of India and the members of his immediate family and for matters connected therewith. The SPG Act had an extremely significant fallout with far reaching implications. It legally circumscribed the parameters restricting SPG protection exclusively to the Prime Minister and his immediate family members. This became a controversial issue when the question of providing protection to Rajiv Gandhi was debated after he had ceased to be the Prime Minister of India in December 1989.

Criminal Procedure Code

The Criminal Procedure Code provides for an open trial in most cases, but it allows exceptions in proceedings involving official secrets, trials in which statements prejudicial to the safety of the State might be made, or under provisions of special security legislation. Sentences must be announced in public.

The police must obtain warrants for searches and seizures. In a criminal investigation, the police may conduct searches without warrants to avoid undue delay, but they must justify the searches in writing to the nearest magistrate with jurisdiction over the offense.

The authorities in Jammu and Kashmir, Punjab, and Assam have special powers to search and arrest without a warrant. The authorities sometimes require permits and notification prior to holding parades or demonstrations, but local governments ordinarily respect the right to protest peacefully.

At times of civil tension, the authorities may ban public assemblies or impose a curfew under the Criminal Procedure Code. There are three classes of prison facilities. Prisoners are not classified by the nature of their crimes, but by their standing in society. Class "C" prisoners are those who cannot prove they are college graduates or income taxpayers. Their cells are overcrowded, often have dirt floors, no furnishings, and poor quality food. The use of handcuffs and fetters is common. Class "B" prisoners—college graduates and taxpayers—are held under markedly better conditions. Class "A" prisoners are prominent persons, as designated by the Government, and are accorded private rooms, visits, and adequate food, which may be supplemented by their families. Class "A" prisoners are usually held in government guest houses.

Indian Telegraph Act

The Indian Telegraph Act authorizes the surveillance of communications, including monitoring telephone conversations and intercepting personal mail, in case of public emergency or "in the interest of the public safety or tranquillity." These powers have been used by every state government. The Union Government also uses the powers of the Indian Telegraph Act to tap phones and open mail.

Armed Forces Special Powers Act of 1958

The Armed Forces Special Powers Act of 1958 remains in effect in several states, i.e., in Jammu and Kashmir, Nagaland, Manipur, Assam and parts of Tripura.

Armed Forces (Jammu and Kashmir) Special Powers Act

Under the Armed Forces (Jammu and Kashmir) Special Powers Act passed in July 1990, security forces personnel have extraordinary powers, including authority to shoot suspected lawbreakers and those disturbing the peace, and to destroy structures suspected of harboring militants or arms.

Disturbed Areas Act

The Disturbed Areas Act has been in force in a number of districts in Andhra Pradesh for more than a year. The Disturbed Areas Act remains in effect in several states, i.e., in Jammu and Kashmir, Nagaland, Manipur, Assam and parts of Tripura. It gives police extraordinary powers of arrest and detention. Human rights groups allege that security forces have been able to operate with virtual impunity in parts of Andhra Pradesh under the act.

Jammu and Kashmir Disturbed Areas Act

Under the Jammu and Kashmir Disturbed Areas Act passed in July 1990, security forces personnel have extraordinary powers, including authority to shoot suspected lawbreakers and those disturbing the peace, and to destroy structures suspected of harboring militants or arms.

Public Safety Act

The Jammu and Kashmir Public Safety Act (PSA) of 1978 covers corresponding procedures for that state. Over half of the detainees in Jammu and Kashmir are held under the PSA. The Government acknowledges that, as of August 1997, it held about 1,600 persons in connection with the insurgency in 5 detention centers in Jammu and Kashmir, compared with 2,070 persons acknowledged held in 1995. Of these 1,298 were held under the Public Safety Act

National Security Act (NSA)

The National Security Act (NSA) of 1980 permits detention of persons considered security risks; police anywhere in the country (except Jammu and Kashmir) may detain suspects under NSA provisions. Under these provisions the authorities may detain a suspect without charge or trial as long as 1 year on loosely defined security grounds. The state government must confirm the detention order, which is reviewed by an advisory board of three high court judges within 7 weeks of arrest. NSA detainees are permitted visits by family members and lawyers and must be informed of the grounds for detention within 5 days (10 to 15 days in exceptional circumstances).

At the end of 1997 approximately 500 persons continue to be detained under the NSA. The NSA does not define "security risk." Human rights groups allege that preventive detention can be ordered and extended under the act purely on the opinion of the detaining authority. Such a subjective decision cannot be overturned by any court.

Terrorist and Disruptive Activities Act (TADA)

Although the law that had been subject to the most extensive abuse—the Terrorist and Disruptive Practices (Prevention) Act (TADA)—lapsed in May 1995, 3,785 persons previously arrested under the act continued to be held in a number of states at year's end, and a small number of arrests under TADA continued for crimes allegedly committed before the law lapsed.

Criminal cases are proceeding against most of those still held under TADA, with more than 3,000 charged under other laws in addition to TADA. In March, the Government asserted that all TADA cases would be reviewed. In February 1996, the Supreme Court eased bail guidelines for persons accused under TADA, taking into account the large backlog of cases in special TADA courts. In reply to a question in the Jammu and Kashmir state assembly in May 1997, the Government reported that 15,826 people were detained under TADA in the state between 1990 and 1995.

The Government acknowledges that, as of August 1997, it held 772 persons under the TADA in Jammu and Kashmir. TADA courts use abridged procedures. For example, defense counsel is not permitted to see witnesses for the prosecution, who are kept behind screens while testifying in court. Also, confessions extracted under duress are permitted in evidence.

NATIONAL SECURITY FRAMEWORK

In his National Security Statement of December 2008, the Prime Minister outlined the national security challenges facing Australia. He defined national security as "Freedom from attack or the threat of attack; the maintenance of our territorial integrity; the maintenance of our political sovereignty; the preservation of our hard won freedoms; and the maintenance of our fundamental capacity to advance economic prosperity for all Australians". To improve the leadership and coordination of the organisations and agencies most directly responsible for national security, the Prime Minister announced a new coordination structure and a new priority-setting, resource allocation and evaluation framework.

made to initiate domestic weapons production by the Ministry of Defence when Mr. Krishna Menon was the Defence Minister. The Sino-Indian conflict in 1962 aroused a new defence consciousness in the country. After taking care of immediate postwar requirements, systematic defence planning started in 1964. Defence requirements were assessed on a five-year basis and the First Five Year Defence Plan (1964-69) was drawn up. This plan took into account the resources available and assistance which could be expected from friendly foreign countries. The plan was primarily based on an expansion and modernisation programme considered necessary by each Service in the light of the respective threat perception assessed. It also proposed a defence production base that would gradually reduce the country's external dependence, provide for improvements in border roads and communications, and a modest expansion of DRDO. The Government recognised the imperative need to synergise 'defence' and 'development' instead of planning each on a separate and unrelated level. The MoD emphasised the "inevitable need to harness all resources of the country for the country's defence and for the defence effort to derive full sustenance from the country's economic development plans".

Thereafter, the National Development Council authorised the Chairman of the Planning Commission to review the needs of both development and defence. A Planning Cell was established in 1965 in the Ministry of Defence 'to deal with the wider aspects of defence planning'. The new system was intended to facilitate medium and long-term defence planning and to maintain constant liaison with the Planning Commission and other ministries. It was expected that the MoD would derive maximum advantage from the development effort by being able to place its priorities for consideration along with the overall economic and industrial plans drawn up by the Planning Commission. The experience of the First Five Year Defence Plan showed that the development of weapons and equipment was a long drawn out process. The Government realised that there could be no forward movement in attaining self-sufficiency in weapons and equipment unless these requirements were planned over a reasonably long period, long enough to cover the span of development and production of new weapons systems and other fighting tools.

The inadequacy of foreign exchange reserves was another hindrance in planning and implementation. In order to mitigate some of these drawbacks, the Second Five Year Defence Plan (1969-74) was instituted on a "roll-on" basis. After a year, an additional year was added so that the Defence Services would have before them a revised and updated five-year plan. In this context, the MoD commented: "Opportunity is taken by this annual exercise to take note of and reflect the change in priorities, the shifts in emphasis and the latest concepts and programmes to reorient the plan within the scheme of resources so that the aims and means are most effectively balanced." This system was expected to facilitate the planning of projects that took five years or more and to revise or eliminate projects, depending on the prevailing foreign exchange situation and availability of domestic resources.

For a period of five years, firm assurances were to be given on the availability of resources. This, unfortunately, never happened. In 1971, it was impossible to adhere to the discipline and the pattern of the roll-on plan. Instead of roll-on annual revisions, immediate requirements dominated the Government's attention that pre-empted plan efforts. In its 1971-72 Annual Report, the MoD acknowledged that having a Planning Cell in the ministry was an insufficient and unsatisfactory method of meeting a crisis.

The Planning Cell was not taken seriously in the crucial stages of economic planning and the argument that defence needs would be adjusted in the overall allocation of resources was proved wrong. In 1974, an Apex Group headed by the Union Minister for Planning again suggested that steady long-term defence programmes would be more cost effective and economical rather than fluctuating allocations due to periodic economic and security crises. In order to integrate defence planning with the overall economic planning effort, defence and economic development plans were made co-terminus.

Planning Machinery

Most of the defence planning machinery and planning methodology was developed in the decade 1964-74. The Joint Intelligence Committee (JIC) was established in the Cabinet Secretariat to provide external and internal threat assessments. Inputs for this purpose were to be provided by all Intelligence agencies of the Government. The Service Chiefs were to assess the broad military aims and a strategy, coordinated in the Chiefs of Staff Committee, was to be approved by the Defence Minister. However, this was seldom done. Each Service ended up planning its own force level, choice of weapons and equipment, and build-up of infrastructure. In 1977, the Government formed a Committee for Defence Planning (CDP) to "undertake regular assessments relevant to defence planning in the light of all factors having a bearing on national security and defence". However, this committee could not function smoothly nor meet the desired goals.

Planning units were also established in the Department of Defence Production and DRDO. A Planning and Coordination Cell was created in the MoD to coordinate and compile various plans into a 'Defence Plan' for Cabinet approval. As the bureaucrats in the ministry had no professional knowledge or background, this cell could only compile different requirements without any analysis. In Army Headquarters, the Deputy Chief of Army Staff was made responsible for preparing the Army plan. A Perspective Planning Directorate was established in the late 1970s. Naval and Air plans were prepared in the respective Planning Directorates. Financial considerations, nonexistent at this level earlier, were introduced through Finance Planning Sections attached to these Directorates. In 1986, the Directorate General of Defence Planning Staff (DGDPS), comprising officers from the three Services, DRDO, and Ministries of Defence and External Affairs, was established under the Chiefs of Staff Committee (COSC) to coordinate and harmonise defence planning. Civilian officers from the Ministries probably did not find the job professionally satisfying and were gradually withdrawn, thus leaving the DGDPS a tri-Service set up.

All these measures enabled each Service headquarters to prepare defence plans in a more rational manner. But due to lack of clear political direction and each Service primarily planning for itself, joint planning, coordination between Services and other departmental plans of the MoD, were largely ignored. After the Kargil conflict in 1999, the Group of Ministers (GoM) and later the Cabinet Committee on Security (CCS) approved several reforms. An Integrated Defence Headquarters (IDH) was established and the DGDPS was merged with it. The creation of the post of Chief of Defence Staff (CDS), whose tasks would include ensuring intra and inter-Services prioritisation of defence plans and improvement in joint functioning of the Defence Services, was recommended. The reforms also included establishment of a Defence Intelligence Agency and creation of Defence Equipment Production, Research and Planning councils in the IDH and MoD, respectively. Unfortunately, the CDS, who would be the cornerstone of integrated operational planning for defence, has not been appointed.

Analysis of the System

Despite several years of planning efforts, defence planning in India is characterised by seesaw bouts of frenzied activity followed by long periods of relative inaction. Five-year defence plans have rarely been formally approved before commencement. The Tenth Defence Plan, now in its third year, is yet to be accorded formal government approval. Adhocism is the order of the day, leading to knee-jerk responses and haphazard planning, making India a reactive rather than proactive nation in matters pertaining to national security. Whenever India's major adversaries plan a big defence purchase, there is an outcry for similar acquisitions, resulting in piecemeal decisions regardless of long-term impact and overall requirements. The Defence Forces are forced to follow "a case-by-case" approach to modernisation and procurement of arms, ammunition and equipment to replace obsolescent items, in many cases long after their life cycle is over and they cannot be maintained in a cost effective manner. The Army's Vijayanta tanks, MiG-21s of the IAF, and IL-38 maritime reconnaissance aircraft of the Navy are some examples. Weapons development, procurement and absorption are complex processes. A lead-time of 15-20 years is required to plan and execute major projects. Despite this, for several years, a large amount of the capital acquisition budget has been surrendered. In the prevailing era of strategic uncertainty, the changing nature of warfare demands a judicious mix of threat and capabilities-based forces that can operate efficiently as combined arms, joint Services teams and components of multinational coalition forces.

DEFENCE PLANNING AND POLICY

As regards the planning process, the Government has taken a number of measures to improve the structure, process and procedure relating to defence planning based on the recommendations of Group of Ministers on 'Reforming the National Security System'. The preparation of Long Term Plans, Five Year Defence Plans and Annual Budgetary proposals have been brought under the newly established Integrated Defence Staff (IDS) to bring about greater inter-service coordination in planning. The IDS also interacts closely with Defence (Finance) in the formulation of Plans and Budgets.

The Government has set up a Defence Acquisition Council headed by the Raksha Mantri and consisting of Raksha Rajya Mantri (s), the three Service Chiefs and Defence Secretary, Secretary (Defence Finance), and Secretary (Defence Production) to assist the Raksha Mantri in taking decisions in the totality of the new planning process, including capital acquisitions and major modernisation projects. The Government has also set up a dedicated institutional structure for defence procurement, the Defence procurement Board, headed by the Defence Secretary for acquisitions on the capital account. Planning processes have been further tightened under budgetary pressures and the need to establish greater synergy and jointness amongst the Armed Forces. This has also necessitated greater coordination in planning and procurement among the three services.

The Ministry in its written note submitted on the current status of the implementation of the 10th Plan has inter alia stated that: "The projections of the Ministry of Defence for the Tenth Defence Plan were reviewed thrice between March 2003 and July 2004 bearing in mind the needs of defence modernization and the likely constraints to the availability of funds for defence in the Tenth Plan. The Ministry of Finance have now agreed in principle to the latest projection made by the Ministry of Defence of Rs. 4,18,101 crore. However, a firm indication of annual outlays for the remaining year of the 10th Plan has not yet been given by the Ministry of Finance.

Meanwhile, in the absence of a formal approval of the allocation for defence in the Tenth Plan, defence planning has been harmonised with the allotments for defence in the annual budgets of the Government. Actual expenditures in 2002-2003 and 2003-2004 were Rs. 55,620 crores and Rs. 60,300 crores respectively. An allocation of Rs. 77,200 crores has been made in the Budget Estimate for 2004-2005 against a projection of Rs. 90,928 crores. About, Rs. 11,000 crores additional funds have been allocated beyond the Budget Estimate for the capital head.

The projected expenditure in 2005-2006 and 2006-2007 are Rs. 1,00,960 crores and Rs. 1,10,251 crores respectively. However, an amount of Rs. 83,000 crores only has been allocated in the Budget Estimate (B.E.) for the current financial year 2005-2006.

While some compromises are inevitable in the absence of a formally approved Plan, every effort has been made to ensure that the annual budgets have been utilized in accordance with the Plan projections of the Ministry of Defence and that any negative impact on ongoing modernization, infrastructure development and procurements of equipment is minimized. Ongoing projects and commitments have been reviewed and prioritized so that the main objective of the Tenth Defence Plan to carry forward the process of modernization of the Armed Forces is not adversely affected. A modest outlay of over Rs. 950 crores has been made for new schemes for the Army. (No increase is being sought)".

In response to a query regarding the existence of a core plan the Ministry though a written reply has inter alia stated that : "There is no formal draft core plan to make up for the delay in the finalization of the Tenth Defence Plan. Meanwhile, in the absence of a formal approval of the allocation for defence in the Tenth Plan, defence planning has been harmonised with the allotments for defence in the annual budgets of the Government. While, indigenous production/Research and Development is being made in accordance with the decisions flowing from the Defence Acquisition Council, defence procurement is being made in accordance with annual acquisition plans for the three services as approved by the Defence Procurement Board. Adequate measures have been taken to minimise any adverse effect on ongoing modernisation schemes. On-going projects and contractual commitments have been reviewed and prioritised to minimise the effect of any shortfall in actual allocation vis-à-vis projections, both in respect of modernisation plans and in essential procurement. Keeping in view, the rising competing demands on limited resources, the budgetary framework has been fine-turned in such a manner to ensure most effective utilisation of Government resources".

While presenting a detailed picture on the entire planning exercise that has been undertaken in the recent past, the representative of Ministry has stated as under:

"In the year 2001-02, projections for the 10th Plan were examined in the Ministry of Defence. These projections were made by the different Services and the Departments. They added up to Rs. 4.97 lakh crore. In January, 2002 the Ministry of Finance indicated the likely availability of Rs. 4.21 lakh crore. So, there was a gap of about Rs. 75,000 crore. Therefore, the Chief of Integrated Defence Staff and Chief of Staff were requested for giving their views. They recommended slightly reduced allocation of Rs. 4.61 lakh crore. In February 2003, in consonance with the recommendations, it was done. The matter was again taken up with the Finance Ministry in March 2003. But we did not have received any response from them thereafter.

We had to carry out a review of our projections. This was because if some scheme was supposed to be sanctioned in the first year of the Plan, it will involve expenditure in the first, second, third years and leading up to the fifth year. If, for the first two years, projected allocations are not utilized, there is no way the original amount, which was projected for the entire five years could be spent in the last three years. It is because in defence acquisition, we are not really buying things off the shelf and paying out for the whole thing. So, if you take a case of some scheme or project costing Rs. 5,000 crore in five years with simplistic allocation of expenditure of Rs. 1,000 crore each year, and if in the first two years, it is not sanctioned and in the third year it is sanctioned, we are not going to have anything in the first two years, but the expenditure will be Rs.3,000 crore in the remaining three years and not Rs. 5,000 crore. When we received the projects, we reviewed what would be and what would not be sanctioned. Then the revised figures came to something like Rs. 4,18,000 crore as indicated. But they did not give us any annual allocations, not capacity utilization, etc".

On the lessons learnt and the measures that are being implemented to overcome the nagging delays of Defence Planning, the Defence Secretary deposed that : "Presentation of the fourth year Budget is made to the Parliament. As has already been mentioned, there is the Ministry of Defence and there is the Ministry of Finance which are the players in this exercise. The exercise for preparing the plan is undertaken by us well in time, much before the start of the year in which the next Five Year Plan is going to start. For example, for the 11th Plan, to answer your question, we have already started the exercise. For doing that planning as to what would be needed, considering the gaps that is there in the Tenth Plan – if any exercise of this nature is to be undertaken – we might have a wish list; it might represent a large figure. But we still have to have some kind of an indicative figure from the Ministry of Finance saying that we have asked for this much amount, which may not be available, but we can have so much amount at the outer limit, beyond which we cannot go. This kind of an indication is no forthcoming. This is what happened in this current year. If you contrast it with the situation of the Ninth Plan, as the Chairman was enquiring, the Ninth Plan was approved on 1st January, 1998.

Therefore, it was approved in the first year. It was a very major achievement and they indicated a total allocation of Rs. 2,20,000 crore. The Annual Budget, as it took place during those five years if you total up those they came to Rs. 2,43,000 crore. That means the annual allocation was more than the indicative figure of the Plan. That was a situation which was quite in contrast to what is prevalent just now where, firstly, the figure itself was not known to us till December – finally what we wanted and how much they can give. This went till December of 2004. If we were to juxtapose the Tenth Plan indicative figure of Rs. 4,18,000 crore divided by four years, which are known, it is nowhere. There was no relation. Therefore, this figure becomes an academic figure. That is the point that we have been discussing, that is the outlays have to be finalized at the beginning of the plan and secondly Annual Allocation should be conforming to the overall outlay".

Adding further on the issue, the Defence Secretary has also stated that : "As has been mentioned earlier, how initial projections of Rs. 4,97,000 crore was done at the beginning of the Tenth Plan (2001-02).This was also communicated to the Finance Ministry with the break up. They needed it in a particular format. It was given in that format. Subsequently, they had indicated Rs. 4,97,000 crore is too much and we may plan within Rs. 4,21,000 crore. There was a gap of about Rs. 75,724 between the projection and what they had indicated. By that time certain time had elapsed. We were involved in an internal exercise of readjusting. In December 2004 they indicated Rs. 4,18,000 crore, which was what we had projected earlier".

Explaining the details of the ongoing measures to formulate the Eleventh Defence Plan and how these initiatives have a bearing on the implementation of annual plan programmes, the Defence Secretary has briefed the Committee : "As I just said, we have started our exercise of preparing the Eleventh Plan which means that the Integrated Defence Staff which gets inputs from all the three Headquarters puts together the long-term perspective plan requirements of each service and makes them into one composite plan called the Defence Plan. It sees whether there is any overlapping of capabilities or whether there is any repetition or commonalties. So, it does such modifications and vetting and then it is projecting that requirement to the Ministry where we see whether it is all right or whether it needs any change or not.. Accordingly, we pass it on to the Ministry of Finance for approval. Of course, we have discussions with the Ministry of Finance because they might also like to understand the details. So, that dialogue is there. Our request is, if the Ministry of Finance were to give its indications well before the start of the first year of the Eleventh Plan, then that would help everybody to know what is going to be the situation during the five years of the Eleventh Plan. Secondly, we do need some kind of a figure to show that this is the total figure and whatever amount it might be would be divided in the five years in this fashion in the Annual Budget so that the Annual programmes can then be fine tuned to adjust to the availability. Otherwise, there is likely to be a mismatch between what we might project and the money availability".

When asked whether the Ministry of Finance had intimated the details of the 10th Plan allocations in time, the Defence Secretary has stated that : "It was towards the end of the third year. This was one part of the problem. The second part, as I said, is annual allocations are nowhere matching even this figure. Therefore, how do we do the Planning? We do not know what will be the figure for the fifth plan. Budget has been submitted for the fourth year. It totals up to Rs. 2 lakh something".

The Ministry of Defence in its written Action Taken Reply on the recommendation of the Committee on long term planning of three Services contained in the First Report on Demands for Grants of the Ministry of Defence for the year 2004-05, has stated as under : "A draft Long-Term Integrated Perspective Plan (LTIPP) covering the 15-year period from the Tenth to the Twelfth Plan (2002-2017) was formulated in June 2004 in consultation with the three Services. Since more than two years of the current Tenth Plan period have already elapsed, a new approach paper has been made formulating a Long Term Integrated Perspective Plan (LTIPP) covering the period from 2007-2022. This Plan is expected to be finalised by the Integrated Defence Staff by the last quarter of 2005."

The Committee are unhappy to note that the Ministry of Finance has failed to finalise the 10th Defence plan even after three years of the plan have passed. Non-finalisation of the 10th Defence Plan at its beginning by the Ministry of Finance has created a great deal of uncertainty about the availability of adequate finance for the acquisition of the vital equipment, modernization, etc. The Ministry of Defence had projected a demand of Rs. 4,97,000 crore in 2001 for the Tenth Plan. However, the Ministry of Finance has given indicative figure of Rs.4, 18,000 crore in December 2004,without any firm commitment. The total allocations in the first four years of Tenth Defence Plan just come to about Rs.2, 76,300 crore which is nowhere near their requirements. This gap between the demand and allocations, has adversely affected the defence planning and our preparedness. The Committee take a serious note of this and want the Government to finalise the Tenth Plan immediately and take steps to utilise the committed amount in full. The Committee would like to be apprised of the fmalisation of the Plan as well as the follow-up steps being taken to utilise the total allocation of the Tenth Plan.

The Committee also observe that due to non-finalisation of the Tenth Plan in time, the long term perspective plan of the Forces has got affected and is presently at the fmalisation stage with a revised plan schedule spanning from 2007-2022. The Committee, while expressing their displeasure over the present situation, recommend that the Ministry of Defence should reorient the plans and strive to adhere to the schedules envisaged. As regard the 11th Plan, the Committee desire that it should be finalised at least an year before the plan period starts. It is high time that the Government prepared a road map for self-reliance. The Committee strongly feels that India should not be taken as a weapons/arms market by the global suppliers and action in this direction should be visible by the end of Tenth Defence Plan and 11th Plan should entirely be devoted to self-reliance.

The Committee has also observed that the surveillance capabilities of our forces are in adequate. This is primarily due to non-availability of low-level radar systems with the three services. The Committee feel that all round effort should be undertaken by the Government to ensure that the entire country is covered. The Committee feel that the Ministry should explore all possibilities of acquiring the required radar systems in adequate numbers without any delay.

Bibliography

Ajey Lele: *Strategic Technologies for the Military : Breaking New Frontiers*, Sage, Delhi, 2009.

Alfred Rolington. *Strategic Intelligence for the 21st Century: The Mosaic Method*. Oxford University Press, 2013.

Allen Carlson, *Unifying China, Integrating with the World: Securing Chinese Sovereignty in the Reform Era,* Stanford: Stanford University Press, 2005.

Allison, Graham: *Nuclear Terrorism: The Ultimate Preventable Catastrophe*, New York: Times Books, 2004.

Alperovitz, Gar. *The Decision to Use the Atomic Bomb*. New York: Vintage Books, 1996.

Amitabh Sikdar: *India and China : Strategic Energy Management and Security*, Manas, Delhi, 2009.

Anderson, J.: *Transnational Democracy: Political Spaces and Border Crossings*, Routledge: London and New York, 2002.

Anil, K.C.: *Military and Democracy in India: Challenges, Politics and Power*, Sumit Enterprises, Delhi, 2009.

Arend, A.: *International Law and the Use of Force*, London, Routledge, 1993.

Benjamin, Joseph : *China-Pak Relations : Prospect and Retrospect*, Reference Press, Delhi, 2004.

Berger, Peter, *Pyramids of Sacrifice*. New York: Basic Books. 1974.

Bhaskara Rao: *Military Conversion : Impact on Science and Technology*, Discovery, Delhi, 2003.

Bhat, T.P. : *India and China : Trade Complementarities and Competitiveness*, Bookwell, Delhi, 2008.

Bookman, Milia Zarkovic, *The Political Economy of Discontinuous Development*. New York: Praeger. 1991.

Brautigam, Deborah, *Governance and Economy: A Review*. World Bank Policy Research Paper. December. 1991.

Bryner, Gary C. : *Blue skies, green politics : the Clean Air Act of 1990 and its implementation*, Washington, D.C., CQ Press, 1995

Budge I: *The New Challenge of Direct Democracy*, Oxford, Polity Press, 1996.

Cassius Dio, *Dio's Roman History*. Translated by Earnest Cary. New York: G.P. Putnam's Sons, 1916.

Chakravarty, B C Dr.: *Indian Armed Forces - Official History of the 1965 Indo-Pak War.* Ministry of Defence.

Charles H. Harris & Louis R. Sadler. *The Border and the Revolution: Clandestine Activities of the Mexican Revolution 1910-1920.* HighLonesome Books, 1988.

Cheek, Timothy: *Mao Zedong and China's Revolutions: A Brief History with Documents.* Boston: Bedford/St. Martin's, 2002.

Chitkara, M.G. : *Indo-Pak Relations Challenges Before New Millennium*, APH, Delhi, 2001.

Debray, Regis. *Revolution in the Revolution.* New York: Grove Press, Inc., 1993.

Deepak, B R : *India and China : 1904-2004 : A Century of Peace and Conflict*, Manak, Delhi, 2005.

Dhanalaxmi, Ravuri. *British Attitude to Nepal's Relations with Tibet and China, 1814-1914.* Chandigarh, India: Bahri, 1981.

Dixit, A.K. : *Military Wars and Rescue Techniques*, Cyber Tech Pub, Delhi, 2010.

Dixit, Prabla: *Communalism: A Struggle for Power*, New Delhi, Orient Longman, 1981.

Durkheim, Emile, *The Division of Labor in Society*. Houndmills, Basingstoke, Hampshire, England: MacMillan. 1984.

Enloe, Cynthia, *Ethnic Soldiers: State Security in Divided Societies*. Athens: University of Georgia Press. 1980.

Evelyn Goh, *Meeting the China Challenge: The U.S. in Southeast Asian Regional Security Strategies*, DC: East-West Center, 2005.

Fatima, T. : *Islamic Law and Judiciary*, Deep & Deep Publications, New Delhi, 2001.

Fletcher, Arnold: *Afghanistan, Highway of Conquest*, Ithaca, New York, Cornell University, 1965.

Francis Dvornik, *Origins of Intelligence Services*. New Brunswick, NJ: Rutgers University Press, 1974.

Friedman, G.: *The Future of War of Cyber Crimes*, N.Y., Random House, 1996.

Gao, Mobo: *The Battle for China's Past: Mao and the Cultural Revolution*, London, Pluto Press, 2008.

Gaur, Mahendra : *Indian Policy of Neighbour*, Delhi, Kalpaz Pub., 2006.

Gautam, P.K. : *Environmental Security : New Challenges and Role of Military*, Shipra, Delhi, 2010.

Ghose, S.K.: *Politics of Violence: Dawn of a Dangerous Era*, Springfield, Nataraj, 1992.

Ghosh, Ajoy : *China-Pak Conflict : Threat to South Asian Security*, Reference Press, Delhi, 2003.

Gupta, S.: *Disrupted Borders: An Intervention in Definitions of Boundaries*, London: River Oram Press, 1993.

Gupta, SC: *History of the Indian Air Force 1933-45*, Pubications Division, Ministry of Defence, Delhi, 1961.

Gurr, Ted R., *Minorities at Risk*. Washington, D.C.: U.S. Institute of Peace Press, 1993.

Hays, Peter L. and others: *Countering the Proliferation and Use of Weapons of Mass Destruction*, New York, NY: McGraw-Hill, 1998.

Heimanson, Rudolph: *Dictionary of Military*, N.Y.: Oceana Publications, 1967.

Henry Landau, *The Enemy Within: The Inside Story of German Sabotage in America*. G.P. Putnam Sons, 1937.

Hoffman, Bruce, *Inside Terrorism*, New York: Columbia University Press, 1998.

Holsti, K.: *The State, War, and the State of War*, Cambridge, Cambridge Univ. Press, 1996.

Horowitz, Donald, *Ethnic Groups in Conflict*. Berkeley and Los Angeles: University of California Press. 1985.

Hout, Wil, *Capitalism, and the Third World: Development, Dependence and the World System*. Hants, Aldershot, England: E. Elgar. 1993.

Huntington, P. : *The Soldier and the State : The Theory and Politics of Civil-Military Relations*, Natraj Pub, Delhi, 2005.

Huntington, S.P.: *The China Modernisation Military and the State*, N.Y., Vintage Books, 1964.

Ian Sayer & Douglas Botting. *America's Secret Army, The Untold Story of the Counter Intelligence Corps*. Franklin Watts Publishers, 1989.

Ishmael Jones, *The Human Factor: Inside the CIA's Dysfunctional Intelligence Culture*, New York: Encounter Books, 2010.

Jagannath P. Panda: *China's Path to Power : Party, Military and the Politics of State Transition*, Pentagon, Delhi, 2010.

James E. : *Tibetan Treasury of Aphoristic Jewels*, Bloomington, IN: Indiana University Press, 1968.

John Keegan, *Intelligence in War*. New York: Knopf, 2003.

John M. Seidl: *Politics American Style: Race, Environment and Central Cities*, New York, Prentice-Hall, 1972.

Keane J.: *Democracy and Civil Liberty*, London, Verso, 1988.

Kumar, Raj : *Weapons and Military Technology*, Sumit Enterprises, Delhi, 2009.

Kunju, N. : *Indo-Pak : Nuclear Cold War*, Reliance, Delhi, 2002.

Kuznets, Simon, *Economic Growth of Nations: Total Output and Production Structure*. Cambridge, Mass.: Belkap Press of Harvard University Press. 1971.

Laquer, Walter, *The New Terrorism: Fanaticism and the Arms of Mass Destruction*, Oxford: Oxford University Press, 1999.

Marie Lecomte : *Hindu Kingship, Ethnic Revival, and Maoist Rebellion in Nepal*, Oxford University Press, Delhi, 2009.

Martin H. Greenberg: *Studies in Nuclear Terrorism*, Boston: G.K. Hall & Co., 1979.

Mary, W.: *Asian Power and Politics: the Cultural Dimensions of Authority*, Cambridge, Belknap Press, 1985.

Mellor, John W., *The New Economics of Growth: A Strategy for India and the Developing World*. Ithica, New York: Cornell University Press. 1976.

Morris, W.H.: *The Government and Politics of India*, London, Hutchinson, 1971.

Nayyar, K K : *National Security : Military Aspects*, Rupa, Delhi, 2003.

Nelson, Joan M., *Economic Crisis and Policy Choice: The Politics of Adjustment in the Third World*. Princeton, New Jersey: Princeton University Press. 1990.

Pemble, John. *The Invasion of Nepal: John Company at War*. Oxford: Oxford University Press, 1971.

Peter G. Tsouras: *Dictionary of Military Quotations*, Manas, Delhi, 2006.

Posen, B.R.: *The Sources of Indian Military Doctrine*, Ithaca, 1984, Cornell Univ. Press.

Radhakrishna: *Handbook of Military and Defence Services*, Sumit Enterprises, Delhi, 2009.

Raj Kumar: *Weapons and Military Technology*, Sumit Enterprises, Delhi, 2009.

Richard A. Gabriel and Karen S. Metz, *From Sumer to Rome; The Military Capabilities of Ancient Armies*. New York: Greenwood Press, 1991.

Roopinder Singh: *Marshal of the Air Force Arjan Singh - Rupa Charitravalli series* , Rupa Publications, Delhi, 2002.

Rosen, P.: *Societies and Military Power: India and its Armies*, Ithaca, Cornell University Press, 1996.

Rostow, Walt W., *The Stages of Economic Growth: A Non Communist Manifesto*. Cambridge, England: Cambridge University Press, 1971.

Rudolph, Heimanson: *Dictionary of Military*, N.Y.: Oceana Publications, 1967.

Sachs, Jeffrey, *Developing Country Debt and the World Economy*. Chicago: University of Chicago Press. 1990.

Samir Chopra: *The India-Pakistan Air War of 1965*, Manohar, New Delhi, 2005.

Samuel P. Huntington: *The Soldier and the State : The Theory and Politics of Civil-Military Relations*, Natraj Pub, Delhi, 2005.

Seth, Vijay: *The Flying Machines - Indian Air Force 1933-99*. Seth Communications, Delhi, 2000.

Sidney Fox: *Klaus Dose, Molecular Evolution and The Origin of Life*, New York: Marcel Dekker, 1977.

Singh Jadoan: *Military Geography of South East Asia*, Anmol, Delhi, 2001.

Singh, R.S.N. : *Asian Strategic and Military Perspective*, Lancer, Delhi, 2005.

Singhal, D. P.: *India and Afghanistan: 1876-1907. A Study in Diplomatic Relations*, St. Lucia, University of Queensland, 1963.

Strange, Susan: *The Retreat of the State: The Diffusion of Power in the World Economy*, Cambridge: Cambridge University, 1996.

Suresh Goel: *International Encyclopaedia of Military, Security and Intelligence Agencies*, MD Publications, Delhi, 2009.

Sutton, J., *Technology and Defence Market Structure*, MIT Press, Delhi, 1998.

Tanham, George K.: *The Indian Air Force: Trends & prospects*. Rand, Santa Monica, Delhi, 1995.

Thapa, Deepak : *Understanding the Maoist Movement of Nepal*, Centre for Social Research and Development, Delhi, 2003.

Tilly, Charles *From Mobilization to Revolution*. Reading, Mass.: Addison-Wesley. 1978,

Tse-tung Mao: *Mao and the Nepali Revolution*. London: Oxford University Press, 1965.

Tufail, Kaiser: *Great Air Battles of the PAF*. Ferozesons, Karachi 2004.

Van Der Veer: *Patterns of Middle Class Consumption in India and China*, Sage, Delhi, 2008.

Vijaya Lakshmi Sharma : *Technology Tools and Appliances*, Shilpi Publications, Allahabad, 1997

Index

❑❑❑